ORGANIZATIONAL PSYCHOLOGY

ORGANIZATIONAL PSYCHOLOGY

H.L. KAILA

Formerly Professor and Head

Department of Psychology

SNDT Women's University

Mumbai

ISBN: 978-93-89307-94-8

Edition: 2019

Printed at: Rekha Printers

Dedicated to

This book is dedicated to one and all concerned with the Behavioural Science applications in organizations towards improving work environments for better employee performance and well-being.

Foreword

The recent advances in the field of Industry and Business due to political and economic variability have provided great challenges to the academicians and the practitioners of organizational psychology. Professor Kaila is famous for meeting these demands by providing the most appropriate, researched and documented reading material for all.

The improvements in workplace have a lot bearing on the applications of psychology. The inputs of psychological concepts (such as counselling, testing, training, work-life balance, stress management, behavioural safety and so on) to the workplace are definable and measureable. Hence, organizations look forward to psychological interventions for integrating them into the business environment by involving employees at various levels and making them responsible towards organizational excellence and growth for economic development.

In his book, Dr Kaila has included the theoretical concepts, researches, case studies and applications of Organizational Psychology which are of much interest and use to not only the students who would study this subject matter in much depth but also to the practising managers in organizations. The contents coverage is quite wider than the books available currently.

The best about this book is 'the research cases based on Indian organizations included in every chapter of this book.

I feel happy to recommend this book as a text as well as a reference book to the students, teachers and practitioners. In the galaxy of scholars Professor Kaila deserves great commendation for his commitment and productivity.

Professor Jitendra Mohan
President: International Society of Mental Training for Excellence
President: Asia Pacific Association of Psychology
Editor-in-Chief: Indian Journal of Psychology
Professor Emeritus of Psychology Panjab University, Chandigarh, India

Preface

Selecting, developing and retaining (high performing) employees is a great challenge for employers as well as HR managers. These functions can only be managed through strong base of human resource concepts, policies and strategies in organizations. Towards this objective, this manuscript makes an attempt to put forth comprehensive literature, interviews, case studies from Indian researches and review questions on a variety of topics of Organizational Psychology. Topics like human resource planning, employee recruitment and selection, training and development, employee engagement and organizational commitment, organizational culture, motivation and job satisfaction, work-life balance, leadership and group dynamics, performance management, employee counselling have been provided with the main focus on students to develop insights for improving the workplaces to become psychologically meaningful and satisfying for the workforce.

An introduction to industrial/organizational psychology - the first chapter provides an important foundational prologue for this book for students to make an informed beginning in this field.

Research methods and statistical techniques are essential parts of any Organizational Psychology studies. These two topics are special additions of this volume so as to support students in understanding the quantification of organizational behaviours for practical applications and measureable outcomes.

H.L. Kaila

Acknowledgements

I would like to generously thank Dr C. Manohar, Executive Director & Dean, IBMR International Business School, Bengaluru; Kamlesh Vaishnav HR & Administration, Aventis Pharma Limited, Ankleshwar; Reena Kumar AGM; (HRD) Durgapur Steel Plant, Ranchi, Raghunath B. Mane, Suzlon Energy Limited, D.K. Kashyap HR Department, UltraTech Cement Limited, Chandrapur; Ajit Desai QHSE Department, Bayer CropScience Ltd. Thane, Dr Hari Haran DGM (Academic) Management Training Institute, SAIL, Durgapur; S.P. Damle TUV India Pvt. Ltd. Mumbai; A. A. Raichur HPCL, Mumbai; Someshwar Kale, Manubhai Panchal, Bilag Industries, Vapi; N. K. Bansal, Indian Oil Institute of Petroleum Management; Delhi, Suresh K. Singh, IOCL, Mumbai; Prof. Usha Nayar, TISS; and Prof. Ravishankar, Mumbai, who have directly and indirectly contributed to the preparation of this book.

I would like to extend my gratitude to Prof. Vipin Chilana – IBPS; U.K. Deshmukh, ONGC, Uran; K.K. Kanchan, Bharat Forge Limited, Pune; Vijay Bukkawar, Mumbai, Director General, National Safety Council, Mumbai, Director General, Central Labour Institute, Mumbai; Dr Abhijit Gangopadhyay, Somasekhara Rao Kottakki, HPCL; Dr K. K. Jayan, Learning Centre, BPCL-Kochi Refinery; S.P. Garg, General Manager, Noida; Pawan Sharma, Usar; S. V. Reddy, Manager (F&S), Rajahmundry (AP), GAIL (India) Limited, S Raghavendran. MMH IC – HR, Larsen & Toubro, Chennai; K. S. Rao. Sr Manager-HSE; (O&D) HPCL; Dr Jatin Pancholi, Professor of Psychology, London; P. Satyanarayana, Aditya Birla Group; G. Majumder, Dy General Manager (HR&A), WBPDCL, Kolkata; and the Industrial Psychology Students of SNDT Women's University, Mumbai for their valuable suggestions for this book.

I am personally thankful to Prof. Jitendra Mohan for writing the Foreword for this book. I am deeply grateful to Indrani Dutta, Hemant Jha, and Amit Kumar for their efficient support and feedback on this manuscript.

Last but not least; I express my thanks to my dear wife Anjana and daughters Sunayna and Sunanda for their incessant presence.

H.L. Kaila

The Author

Dr Harbans Lal Kaila, earned his Masters' degree in Psychology from Guru Nanak Dev University, Doctorate from Tata Institute of Social Sciences, and is a Professor of Psychology. He has 30 years of professional experience in the field of Industrial/ Organizational Psychology, Women at Work, Counselling/School Psychology, has published books/articles and participated in national/international conferences. He pioneered Behaviour Based Safety (BBS) training in India and is a member of expert panel for National Safety Council. He has served at the Central Labour Institute, Ministry of Labour for 10 years and at the SNDT Women's University, Mumbai for 18 years. He is an Emeritus Professor at JJT University, Rajasthan, and BBS project director at GAIL India.

Dr Kaila has been a resource person for organizations such as ITC, ESSAR, Reliance Industries, Colourtex, Reliance Energy, Ultratech, Chambal Fertilizers, Sandoz, Tata Motors, M&M, Billimoria, BPCL, ONGC, Suzlon, TUV, Bajaj Auto, Bayer CropScience, Serum, SMC, NPC, SAIL, GE, IOCL, HPCL, GAIL, HCC, Vedanta, L&T, RCF, Ampacet and has conducted more than 100 organizational surveys at various locations in India.

Dr. Kaila has represented India at the International Conferences at New York, Berlin, Muscat, Rome, New Zealand, London and Sydney. He is an Editor of *Journal of Psychosocial Research.*

Contents

1

An Introduction to Industrial/ Organizational Psychology

Learning Objectives

This chapter would help the readers:

- to understand the fundamental concepts of organizational psychology and its approaches;
- to acquaint with the models and historical evolution of organizational psychology;
- to be familiar with the challenges and careers in organizational psychology.

An Opening Story: Challenge of an Organizational Psychologist

The use of psychometric test is one of the very popular applications of organizational psychology. In an organization, a battery of aptitude tests was used to select new employees. The two major characteristics of any psychological tests are the reliability and validity which in short means that the psychological test-selected employees would be high performers. Surprisingly, in this particular engineering company, these psychological test-selected employees were rated as low performers by their respective supervisors. This posed a serious dilemma for an organizational psychologist as to whether the tests used were wrongly selected. It is also true about 'using psychological test for selection' that it would select those candidates who 'can-do' the job, meaning they would have high potential to perform on the job but whether they 'will-do' the job would depend upon an environment in which they are placed. It was found in further analysis that these psychological test-selected employees did not perform well because they lacked the support and encouragement from their supervisor at the workplace. The high performers would expect their work environment to be conducive and supportive of what they do. These test-selected employees could not perform as they got discouragement from their immediate superior. This experience provides a great learning to the organizational psychologist that scientific selection through the use of psychological tests does not guarantee high performance of employees unless they find their work environment to be encouraging.

1.1 INTRODUCTION

It is realized by companies all over the world that there is a significant difference between the organizational policies/procedures and its implementation, and this difference is visibly reflected in the employee's behaviour. The interventions of organizational psychology help to bridge this gap. Due to increasing emphasis on human resources development and management, subjects like organizational behaviour and organizational psychology have gained much significance across the world.

Industrial/organizational psychology is an important area of study and research and is related to the fields like engineering, medicine, commerce, management, etc. It is the human beings who are behind every aspect of safety, quality, environment, and productivity in an organization. He /she needs to be understood, motivated, directed, guided, and led properly in the growth of every business organization.

Organizational Psychology is indeed an extremely important subject which certainly enhances people's awareness and effectiveness in interpersonal situations, improving their ability in handling conflict and managing change at individual, group, and organizational levels (John W. Newstrom and Keith Davis, 1998).

1.2 WHY ORGANIZATIONAL AND NOT INDUSTRIAL PSYCHOLOGY?

We need to highlight the basic difference between an industry and an organization before we move on to discuss why we today need organizational and not industrial psychology. An industry is a generalized term used to address a particular group of organizations or a type of industry, such as chemical or engineering industry, automobile or petroleum industry, etc. An industry can also be further categorized into small scale or medium or large scale industry depending upon its size and number of employees. An organization is a specific term that refers to an individual company or a firm within each industry. For example, within the chemical industry group, there are many organizations or companies such as Rashtriya Chemical & Fertilizers (RCF), Chambal Fertilizers & Chemicals Limited (CFCL), Aarti Industries, and so on. There can be a hundred or thousand organizations within each industry type in the country. Each organization can be small or big consisting of 50 or 5,000 employees. An organization can be a private or public sector or multinational organization. Every organization is a matter of study in psychology.

For many decades, the universities and colleges all over the world have taught the subject of Industrial Psychology. Even today in India, many of them use the same title. But increasingly the trend is to refer to the term organizational psychology. The difference between the two would be basically about the emphasis and focus on the context, and climate of each organization and be more specific on organizationally relevant issues rather than generalize for industries on the whole. Moreover each organization is different in terms of its leadership styles, motivational strategies, reward systems, organizational hierarchy and structure, and so on. Essentially, employee behaviour needs to be understood in the backdrop of an organizational culture.

Organizational psychology is principally concerned with understanding, prediction, and control of human behaviour at respective work stations. Organizations have different managerial paradigms and perspectives. The organizational climate and management philosophy differ from one group to another group of companies. For example, in India, the Larsen & Toubro company is known for its excellence and professionalism. Reliance group is known for perfection in quality. Hence each company's culture and values differ from the others. Hence there is a need to study each organization's values, culture, and emphasis on quality, environment, safety, and so on. Even within each group of companies, its member organizations would depict varied emphasis on learning, training, and development of employees, and diverse subcultures across its departments/sections.

The organizational psychology researchers across the world are now focusing their attention on a variety of important issues such as human resource planning, talent management, human capital index, assessment centres, employee engagement, employee counselling, competency mapping, training needs analysis, motivation and job satisfaction, work-life balance, attrition and retention, organizational commitment, business etiquette, behaviour-based safety management, delegation in organization, performance management, leadership styles, research methods and statistics and so on. This book has a special chapter or section on each of these above mentioned topics.

1.3 DEFINITION AND MEANING

There are as many on definitions on industrial/organizational psychology as the number of authors on the subject. Three features should be emphasized in any definition.

- Organizational Psychology (OP) is the systematic study of human behavior,
- The study is about behaviours in an organization, and
- Knowledge about human behaviour would be useful in improving an organization's effectiveness.

1.3.1 Three Central Definitions

The definitions below are central to almost all the newer and classic issues, operations, processes, and concerns of the subject of organizational psychology.

According to Keith Davis and John Newstrom (1989), Organizational Psychology is the scientific study and application of knowledge about how people as individuals and as a group act within an organization. It strives to identify ways in which people can act more effectively. Both the individual effectiveness and organizational effectiveness are closely inter-correlated.

Greenberg and Baron (2010) defined Organizational Psychology as the field that seeks knowledge of behaviour in organizational settings by systematically studying individuals, groups, and organizational processes. It means that understanding behaviour at work is a long and continuous process.

According to Stephen Robbins et al., (2010), Organizational Psychology is a field of study that investigates the impact that an individual, group and structure have on the behaviour within an organization for the purpose of applying such knowledge towards improving organizational effectiveness. This would also mean that necessarily all these three phenomena are inter-correlated and together contribute towards how effectively or ineffectively an organization performs.

> **Good to Know**
>
> The study of organizational psychology basically incorporates the study of the following:
>
> (a) Human behaviour
>
> (b) Human behaviour in an organization and
>
> (c) Human behaviour in an organization which is beneficial to the latter.

Both the individual as well as organization impact each other's behaviour and performance. Hence, it is vital to discern the perceptions of employees and how they would experience the different aspects of an organization such as leadership styles, managerial practices, and how the management appraises and rewards its employees, and how an organization selects and promotes its employees for various positions during their career ladder, from time to time.

From the day an employee joins until he/she retires from an organization comes under the scope and subject matter of an Organizational Psychology. For example, as told by an earlier Human Resource Director of the Larsen & Toubro company that *once we recruit a person, we see to it that he/she retires from our company,* which precisely would mean that we look after his/her growth, development, and provide challenges and keep the person motivated so that he remains interested in the organization. That is why we have employees working with us for a long number of years and these are the members of our company who build and sustain the organizational culture and its values.

1.4 HISTORY AND DEVELOPMENT

The history and development of organizational psychology has huge contributions of a great number of authors, scholars and researchers from various institutions/universities all over the world. There are numerous academic developments that led to the evolution from personnel to industrial to organizational psychology due to the changing emphasis that have been laid, just as the thinking on science and technology evolved from time to time. Some historical developments of organizational psychology are given below.

1.4.1 An Emphasis on Scientific Management (1856–1915)

The Industrial Revolution that began with the expansion of large factories in the late 18th century led to great changes in the production of textiles and other products. The factories that evolved posed tremendous challenges to the organization and management of machinery and manpower that had not been confronted before. Managing these new factories with the requirement of large flows of material, people, and information over long distances created the need for innovative methods for dealing with the new management issues.

Frederic Winslow Taylor (1911) was one of the first to attempt to systematically analyse human behaviour at work. He attempted to do something to the complex organizations what engineers had done to machines. Just as machine parts were easily interchangeable, cheap, and passive, so too should the human parts be the same in the machine model of organizations. This involved breaking down each task to its smallest unit and to find the best way to do each job. Then the engineer, after analysing the job should instruct the worker and make sure that the worker does only those motions essential to the task. Taylor looked at the interaction of human characteristics, social environment, task, and physical environment, capacity, speed, durability, and cost.

The productivity under Taylor's model went up dramatically and his concepts gained much popularity across the world. New departments and units evolved, such as industrial engineering, personnel, and quality control. There was also growth in middle management as there was a separation of planning from operations. Rational rules replaced trial and error. The management became formalized and the efficiency increased.

This change did not come about without resistance. First, the old line managers resisted the concept that management was a science to be studied, not something one was born with.

Taylor also studied issues such as physical/mental fatigue and safety. He urged the management to study the relationship between work breaks, and the length of the work day and productivity and convinced many companies that careful introduction of rest pauses and a shorter day could increase productivity. Nevertheless, the industrial engineer with his stop-watch standing over workers measuring each part of the job and one's movements became a group resistance. Thereafter, many workers protested and considered it dehumanization of work.

Good to Know

In order to systematically analyze human behaviour at work, Taylor critically looked at interaction of human characteristics, social environment, task, and physical environment, capacity, speed, durability, and cost.

Even today, one should not think that the core concepts of scientific management have been abandoned. They have merely been modified and updated. While this model proved to be a dramatic improvement for organizations, it was actually a management framework which was based on status, positions, and authority.

1.4.2 The Hawthorne Studies (1923–1933)

The Scientific Management approach was criticized for severe labour/management conflict, apathy, boredom, and wasted human resources. This was followed by the Human Relations Movement. Elton Mayo claimed that this alienation of the workforce cropped up from the breakdown of the rigid social structures caused by industrialization, the factory system (Kyle Bruce, 2006).

The most famous Hawthorne Studies showed how work groups provide mutual support and effective resistance to management schemes to increase output. This study found that workers didn't respond to classical motivational approaches as suggested in the Scientific Management and Taylor's approaches, but rather workers were interested in the rewards and punishments of their own work group.

These studies conducted in the 1920s started as a straightforward attempt to determine the relationship between work environment and productivity. The results of the researches led them to feel that they were dealing with socio-psychological factors that were not explained by classical theories which stressed on formal organization and strict leadership.

Good to Know

Human relations approach developed in the 1930s argues that humans are emotional beings and in order to achieve their potential they need to feel valid and important.

The Human Relations Movement pushed managers toward gaining participative support from lower levels of the organization in solving organizational problems. The movement also fostered a more open and trusting environment and a greater emphasis on groups rather than just individuals. This movement gave way to the more humanized work environment.

The Hawthorne Studies helped to realize that an organization is not merely a formal arrangement of functions but is also a social system.

The following chart shows a contrast between a traditional approach and human relations view:

Traditional approach assumes that:	*Human relations approach assumes that:*
people mainly work to satisfy their economic needs and they largely work to satisfy their individual needs	people are motivated by many needs and not just economic need
people work to make the most of the rewards at work	organizations are socio-technical systems and people's behaviour is influenced by the social context and informal work group; management system is just one influence
there is no conflict between the individual and organizational objectives	job roles are more complex than just job descriptions

1.5 SCOPE AND GOALS OF OP

Organizational Psychology (OP) is important as it is influenced by a complex set of dynamic forces that affect the nature and functioning of an organization. These forces are the people, structure, technology and the environment (Keith Davis and John W. Newstrom 1989), as explained below (Fig. 1.1).

1. People: Practically speaking, the organizations exist with its people. It is through, by, and for the people that organizations attain their objectives. Understanding and retaining people who work in the organization is extremely important. Besides job security, employees believe in greater self-expression, autonomy, participation, fulfilment and growth. In order to retain talented employees, organizations are required to take suitable measures such as:

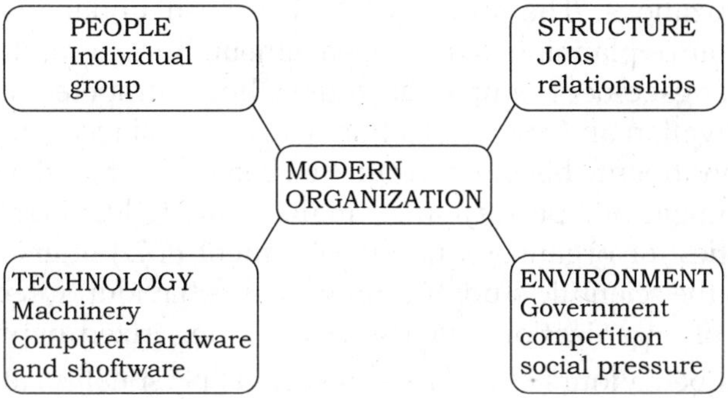

Fig. 1.1 Forces affecting nature and functioning of a modern organization.

- building relationships with employees
- creating an environment of openness and confidence
- demonstrating care and concern for employees
- empowering employees and
- shaping employee's competencies

2. Structure: Structure defines the formal relationships and utilization of people in an organization. These people have to be related in some structural way so that their work can be effectively coordinated. Their relationships create complex problems associated with interpersonal conflicts, negotiation, and decision making.

Many organizational structures have become flatter. Other structures have grown more complex as a result of mergers, acquisitions and new ventures. Finally, many firms have moved from traditional structures to team-based ones.

3. Technology: Technology provides the resources with which people work and it affects the task that they have to perform. The great benefit of technology is that it allows people to do more and better quality work. These technological advancements also place an increased pressure to maintain the delicate balance between technical and social systems.

4. Enviroment: The environmental pressures that affect the performance of an organization include all those elements like government policies and procedures, competition from other organizations within the industry sector/type, political stability, national/international economic market factors, and events that lie outside the boundaries of the organization. Citizens expect organizations to be socially responsible. Competition for new products comes from around the globe. External factors influence the attitude of people, affect the working condition, and provide competition for resources and power.

1.5.1 Scope of OP

Besides understanding the important forces such as the people, structure, technology, and the environment (as described above), OP is the designated field to study human behaviour in organizations. The scope of OP has been understood and executed in terms of human resource planning, talent management, human capital index, assessment centres, employee engagement, employee counselling, competency mapping, training needs analysis, motivation and job satisfaction, work-life balance, attrition and retention, organizational commitment, business etiquette, behaviour-based safety management, delegation in organization, performance management, leadership styles, research methods and statistics for organizational development (OD) interventions. The subject of OP encompasses the scientific study of individual behaviour, interpersonal behaviour and the behaviour of organizations themselves as categorized hereunder.

- Intrapersonal behaviours cover aspects such as personality, attitude, perceptions, learning, motivation, and job satisfaction. These are the individual specific forces which are important factors to study the organizational performance.
- Interpersonal behaviours include group dynamics; intra- and inter-group conflict, leadership, communication, transaction analysis, stress management, and so on. How people come and work together plays a significant role in the organizational effectiveness.
- Study of an organization covers its formation, structures, size, formal and informal, and organizational hierarchy. These factors are crucial to review and revise from time to time in order to face the organizational performance challenges.

The field of OP emphasizes all these levels of analysis on the individual, the group, and the formal organization (H.L. Kaila, 2007).

1.5.2 Goals of OP

Importantly, OP has four major goals or objectives (Sudarshan Kumar Bhatia, 2009). These goals are to describe, understand, predict, and control behaviour of employees for achieving excellence in quality, safety, health, and environmental aspects of an organization (Fig. 1.2).

Describing Behaviour

The first goal of OP is to describe systematically how people behave under a variety of conditions. Achieving this goal allows managers to communicate various aspects of human behaviour in organizations.

Understanding Behaviour

An important goal of OP is to understand and explain the causes of people's behaviour. Organizational Psychology tries to find the reason behind human action. It attempts to understand why people behave as they do.

Predicting Behaviour

Predicting employee behaviour is another goal of OP. It helps managers to identify the productive and unproductive employees. Thus, a manager can take appropriate actions to increase effective behaviour and control ineffective behaviour.

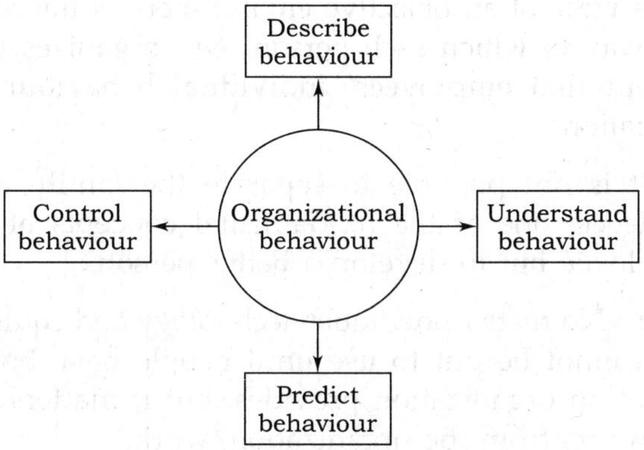

Fig. 1.2 Goals of organizational psychology.

Controlling Behaviour

The final goal of OP is to control or influence behaviour in ways that is beneficial to everyone in the organization. Controlling ineffective/maladaptive behaviours such as poor performance, alcoholic or substance abuse, non-cooperation with team members, absenteeism, health and safety issues, work-life balance problems, difficulty in retaining employees are significant concerns of the managers.

1.6 CONCEPTS OF OP

The fundamental concepts of OP are about the nature of people and the nature of organizations. These concepts serve as the philosophical foundation of OP and guide its development (Anjali Ghanekar, 2001).

The nature of people	*The nature of organizations*
• Individual differences	• Social system
• Perception	• Mutual interest
• A whole person	• Ethics
• Motivated behaviour	
• Desire for involvement	
• Value of the person	

1.6.1 Nature of People

Organizational Psychology has six basic concepts about the nature of people.

Individual Differences: Managing people would have been so easy if all human beings were the same and their behaviour was motivated by the same factors. But this is not the case. People have much in common, but each person is also individually different.

Perception: People's view of an objective environment is filtered by their perception which is the unique way in which each person sees, organizes, and interprets things. Managers must accept that employees' individual behaviours are based on their perception of the situation.

A Whole Person: It is not possible to separate the family life of a person from his/her work life. Hence, one of the fundamental concepts of OP is not merely to develop a better employeé but to develop a better person.

Motivated Behaviour: No matter how much technology and equipment an organization has, these resources cannot be put to use until people have been motivated. It does not matter much what an organization provides, but it matters most to an employee what he/she needs/wants from the organization/work.

Desire for Involvement: Organizations need to provide opportunities for meaningful involvement—a practice which would result in mutual benefits for both the parties.

Values of the Person: People deserve and want to be treated with care, respect, and dignity. They refuse to accept the idea that they are simply economic tools. They want to be valued for their skills and abilities and to be provided with opportunities to develop themselves.

1.6.2 Nature of Organizations

With regard to organizations, three fundamental concepts are:

Social System: Just as psychological needs, people also have needs for social roles and status. Their behaviour is influenced by the group as well as by their individual drives. In fact there are two types of social systems—one is formal (official), and the other is informal.

Mutual Interest: An organization needs people, and people need an organization. If mutuality is lacking, it makes no sense to try to assemble and develop cooperation. Mutual interest can be attained only through the integrated efforts of an individual and its employers.

Ethics: Managers are under constant pressure to perform better and increased profits. This often results in breaking rules. Ethical practice is the fundamental concept that OP strongly advocates.

1.7 CHARACTERISTIC FEATURES OF OP

The growing popularity of OP has been an account of positive uniqueness of the field. The three distinct features of OP (Jerald Greenberg and Robert A. Baron 2010) are:

- It is interdisciplinary in nature.

- It has a firm foundation of research knowledge and conceptual framework.
- Its theory and research has found acceptance among practising managers.

Each of these characteristics of OP is explained below.

1.7.1 OP is Interdisciplinary

The other major sciences that have contributed to OP are psychology, sociology, social psychology, anthropology, and political science. Hence, OP is interdisciplinary in nature. Organizational Psychology implies that it would have a strong conceptual base as well as applications based on various disciplines. People from various sociocultural and educational backgrounds come and work together to run the business organizations, this is how the workplace practically becomes multi-perspective and multidisciplinary in its approach to produce products and services meaningful to the society. It deals with all areas and functions of an organization, be it production, safety, quality, or maintenance. It does not exist in isolation but works closely with all disciplines of the organization for best organizational performance. For example, to know whether any engineering-based technologies or products developed at the workplace such as mobile phone or a particular automobile are being appreciated or disliked by the large mass of end users or whether it requires re-designing is a subject matter of OP surveys. The best technology may fail if it is not found appropriate and comfortable by people.

1.7.2 Conceptual Frameworks

The strength of OP is its research knowledge, applications, and conceptual frameworks which are drawn from various perspectives and disciplines. As such OP is interdisciplinary in nature. The key to its success revolves around the related process of theory, research, and regular managerial practice. Nonetheless, there is always a variation from the conceptual framework when it is put to practice at the workplace due to the dynamic nature of work, operations, and conditions.

The conceptual theory of organizational psychology and its comprehension remain a basic guiding force for clarity of business goals and their achievement. For example, an understanding of different concepts of leadership styles would surely make a positive difference in the application of appropriate leadership for managers in an organization.

1.7.3 Managerial Acceptance

The third strength of OP is the increasing acceptance of theory and research by practising managers. As a result, OP has progressed substantially.

The managerial acceptance of OP takes place only when its concepts are clarified and applied with due regard to its measurable outcomes in improving the managerial practices. For example, work conflicts are real time issues when people work together, but the mature knowledge and application of conflict management styles help employees to resolve and come out of these conflicts much before they start adversely affecting the team members' performance.

1.8 APPROACHES OF OP

The central approaches of OP are: human resources, contingency, result-oriented, and systems that are interwoven and reflect the basic nature, principles, and assumptions of OP (Jerald Greenberg and Robert A. Baron, 2010). All these approaches together have contributed towards the development of OP as a subject as mentioned hereunder.

1.8.1 Human Resources Approach

The first and basic premise of OP has come from the Human Resources Approach that aims at creating a work environment which would provide the employees with opportunities to develop their abilities to the maximum possible extent. It is assumed that the work satisfaction of employees enhances when they make complete use of their abilities. The approach (which is supportive in principle) is concerned with the growth of employees towards a higher point of competency and creativity as they are the vital resource in any organization. The managers do not control the employees, rather they extend dynamic support towards their development. As a result, it improves the effectiveness of an organization when employee abilities are completely utilized.

1.8.2 Contingency Approach

The basic assumption of OP is that different solutions are needed for different contexts. The Contingency Approach also recognizes that each organization in unique and so are its problems. This approach stresses that the managers must carefully analyse each situation, identify important variables in the situation, and select the method that is best suited for the particular situation. This approach believes that there is no single best solution for organizational issues. Hence, Contingency Approach is better than other approaches. This approach emphasizes further on research related to organizational problem areas. Since this approach is more broad-based in nature, different departments and leaders in an organization have freedom of choice to adopt diverse ways to handle their short-term as well as long-term issues concerning their projects.

1.8.3 Result-oriented Approach

Organizational Psychology is beyond just achieving the economic inputs and outputs. This approach necessarily means 'focusing on results' in terms of increasing work efficiency and improving employee job satisfaction of employees. It focuses on creating high customer satisfaction, building sound partnerships with suppliers, training employees, continuously improving operational processes, and developing strong teams. This approach has three main targets – higher economic, human and social outputs which can be archived by continuous upgrading of all organizational methods.

1.8.4 System Approach

Organizational Psychology expects managers to have a system or holistic approach which would support every function in the company. So individual departmental managers need not only focus on issues as their own but also in terms of how do their issues and decisions impact the entire organization as a social system.

Organizational Psychology believes that the company would have various departments for carrying out numerous business functions and these departments are interdependent parts of the larger organization as a whole. Every function of the industrial business – whether production or quality, safety or maintenance – is not only dependent on each other to complete its respective jobs but also complimenting its functions towards the organizational outputs. Hence, an organization consists of a system and subsystem with many variables that affect all others. Each system and subsystem require certain input, has a process and produces an output. So they are interconnected to be seen as a system.

1.9 THEORIES OF OP

Organizational theories are basically the study of formal functioning of organizations' theoretical frameworks. OP provides the fundamental concepts associated with organizational theory and design. No organization would follow a single theory but an amalgamation of theories would prevail into the various organizational sections or departments.

An organization is a gathering of people working together under a defined structure for the purpose of achieving predetermined outcomes through the use of financial, human, and material resources. There are a number of approaches to the structure and management of organizations (L. Daft Richard et al., 2010).

A host of theories are historically developed in OP and these are the classical theory, neoclassical theory, systems theory, learning organization theory, contingency theory, chaos theory, diversification theory and matrix organizations theory. They are also reflected in the various approaches as seen above. However, each of these theories is briefly featured with its fundamental assumptions below.

1.9.1 Classical Theory

The Classical Theory, based on the works of Frederic Winslow Taylor (1911), has evolved into classical organizational theory with the principles of chain and unity of command, span of control, specialization, and the use of vertical levels of authority. This is the oldest theory of management, has a focus on efficiency and production. The organizational design of the classical theory is bureaucratic in nature having the following characteristics:

- Authority and communication flow downward through a rigid chain of commands.
- The vertical growth represents many levels of supervision and indicates a one-boss philosophy (unity of command).

- The number of people supervised is small (span of control).
- Bureaucracy results in a line structure, so called leader–follower relationship.
- This type of structure facilitates large-scale administration by coordinating the work of many personnel.
- Highly structured rules, policies, and procedures.
- People are placed in functional specialty areas with standard pay structures, roles, and responsibilities.

In progressive multinational organizations today, we may not find the Classical Theory much in existence as it is bureaucratic in nature and does not allow much participation or influence from the employees. However, government organizations still follow some aspects of this theory of OP.

1.9.2 Neoclassical or Humanistic Theory

Neoclassical theory (based on Hawthorne Studies, 1923–1933) is a step ahead of the Classical Theory and is humanistic in nature. This theory proposes a less formal structure of an organization, and less control with more participation in decision making. It is the flat structure of an organization developed along horizontal lines with fewer levels of management. It views managers as coaches, not as authority figures, who are concerned with employee motivation, satisfaction, and creativity. It believes that with the humanistic viewpoint, the communication is enhanced, but managers may be overburdened. It seeks to validate human behaviour aspects in organizations through research like the Hawthorne Study.

1.9.3 Systems Theory

The Systems Theory as propounded by Bertalanffy Ludwig Von (1962) is holistic and interconnects different functions of an organization. According to this theory, a system is a set of interrelated parts arranged in a unified whole. Productivity is viewed as a function of the interplay among people, structure, and the environment. The organization is a complex social and technical open system that requires human, financial, and material resources. This theory provides interconnections within the organization, and between the organization and the environment. A major flaw of this theory is that changes in environment directly affect the structure and function of the organization. Its main advantage is that it seeks to explain synergy and interdependence.

1.9.4 Contingency Theory

The contingency theory of OP (developed by F.E. Fiedler, 1971) provides an environmental perspective and is more research based and broad in nature with the assumptions that the organization's structure must be matched to its environment to enhance performance. The optimal form of an organization is contingent on the circumstances faced by that organization. The managers must carefully analyse each situation, identify important variables in the situation, and select the method that is best suited for the particular situation. According to the contingency theory of leadership, a leader's success would depend upon the function of a range of factors such as subordinates, tasks, and group.

1.9.5 Learning Organization Theory

The Learning Organization Theory speaks of an environment where employees are exposed to more learning arrangements as a progressive outlook of an organization. This organizational design (Carla Curado, 2006) is a systems model based on the rapid sharing of information through computer technology. It is influenced by the Systems Theory. Learning organizations are characterized by five disciplines: systems thinking, personal mastery, mental models, shared vision, and team learning. Participation, in these organizations, is the basis of learning. In order to have a learning organization, a company must have very well-informed employees who are able to contribute through their knowledge with other employees and be able to relate it to a work environment.

1.9.6 Chaos Theory

Several psychologists have emphasized the existence of continuous processes of convergence and divergence, stability and instability, evolution and revolution in every organization (Jeremy C. Short, G. Tyge Payne, and David J. Ketchen Jr, 2008). The major assumption of the chaos theory is that each organization goes through the periods of transition and turbulence. Hence, it follows the cycle of instability to stability to sustainability of growth and so on. Based upon the belief in the uncertainty and unpredictability of the environment. The Chaos Theory asserts that organizations are living, self-organizing systems that are complex and self-adaptive. The system moves between order and chaos and is only stable temporarily. The Chaos Theory takes into account very careful analysis of chaotic situations and business goals with participation from all concerned with the issues at hand.

1.9.7 Diversification Theory

Multi-business firms opt for unrelated and/or related diversification for their survival as well as progress. The diversification theory (Peter G. Klein and Lasse B. Lien, 2009) assumes that diversification is the expansion of an organization into different arenas either by complementing existing services or by moving into areas that differ from the original product or service. Diversification process will have multi-organizational arrangements such as mergers – organizations combining assets to ensure profits and survival; acquisitions – buy-out usually of a smaller facility, and consolidated systems- large regional or national entities. Firms often diversify when they have successful internal resources-allocation system.

1.9.8 Matrix Structure Theory

The Matrix Structure Theory aims to bring together employees and managers from varied departments to contribute towards a common goal. A matrix organization is a popular organizational structure used by project-based teams. Importantly a well run matrix organization creates higher levels of goal and role ownership considering the following concepts (Kevan Hall, 2013).

- Matrix designs have a dual authority structure with both a functional manager and a project manager.
- Product and functional structures are integrated and results in a dual organizational focus.
- Professional practice or self-governance allows staff to govern themselves using specific councils with decision authority.
- Participatory management allows participation in decision making but the power over the final decision remains with the top executive.
- Other designs include project management, collegial management, and the corporate model which has led to mergers, buy-outs, etc.

To sum up, a matrix structure is generally defined as one where there are several reporting lines, that is, people have more than one official manager.

Exhibit 1.1: Some Relevant Definitions of the Concepts Associated with the Organizational Psychology Theories

Organizational Climate and Culture

The climate of an organization is the perceived characteristics including the physical plant, lines of communication, and rule structure. The culture of an organization is the maintained norms and traditions.

Organizational Charts

Resources, departments, and personnel are grouped horizontally and vertically into lines of authority, communication, delegation, and decisions. The chart designates areas of responsibility and areas of specialization. The charts show only formal relationships, the framework in which the management process takes place. Informal structure and personal and social relationships are not depicted on the chart.

Chain/Unity of Command

The chain of command is the formal line of authority and communication. In bureaucratic structures or hierarchies, authority and communication flow from the top downward. Unity of command represents the managerial dictum of 'one person, one boss'. It is represented by the vertical solid line between positions on the organizational chart.

Span of Control

Span of control or span of management is the number of people the manager directs. The optimal span of management is highly variable. In general, managers in bureaucratic structures have a narrow span of control while those in flat structures have a broader span.

Centralized versus Decentralized

Centralization refers to the area where decisions are made. In autocratic structures decisions are made at the top and these flow downward. There is a small span of control resulting in many layers of management and a tall structure. Decentralized structures are flat and decisions are made at the level where they occur.

1.10 MODELS OF OP

Several models of OP dominate the management's thought and action in each organization. Therefore it is important that managers recognize the nature, significance, and effectiveness of their own models, as well as the models of others around them. Douglas McGregor (2006) suggested the management philosophy as below:

Theory X: It assumes that most people dislike work and will try to avoid it if they can. Workers are seen as inclined to restrict work output, having little ambition, and avoiding responsibility. They are indifferent to organizational needs and resistant to change. They are attracted to workplace in order to fulfil their physiological and security needs. Most people have low participation as well as little creativity in solving organizational problems, and they must be controlled for completing organizational targets. Theory X has been a typical management view of employees. Today, of course, there is a transition in management philosophy and action. Theory X no longer holds good as it is criticized badly in employees' cooperatives and associations. In summary, the managers exercise control and authority over subordinates.

Theory Y: This theory is definitely an improvement over Theory X and it assumes that people are not inherently lazy. If management provides proper environment and work conditions are conducive to realize their potential, employees will work for which they are committed. They are attracted to the workplace in order to fulfil their self-esteem, affiliation, and self-actualization needs. They would self-direct themselves and need not be controlled by the managers. They are naturally creative and would contribute towards achieving organizational goals. This theory is obviously humanistic, easy to practise and favourable to both employees as well managements and this is why Theory Y is preferred over Theory X in management practice across organizations. Managers support employees to develop their potential and their utilization towards achieving organizational objectives.

Models such as Theory X and Theory Y are also called organizational paradigms and frameworks of possible explanations about how things work.

The selection of a model by a manager is determined by number of factors. The environmental conditions help determine which model will be most effective. A brief discussion of four models, beginning with the autocratic to custodial to supportive to collegial, roughly follows their historical evolution.

1.10.1 Autocratic Model

Autocratic models depend on power and the managerial orientation is formal authority. The employee orientation is obedience to a boss. The autocratic model actually exists in all shades of grey, from rather dark to light and can be useful under some conditions. This model has been the least preferred as it is unidirectional and does not involve employees in the decision-making process. The manager is the formal and official authority who decides almost everything at the workplace and has the power to hire and fire employees.

1.10.2 Custodial Model

The autocratically managed employees did not interact with their boss and experienced insecurity, frustration, and aggression towards their boss. To satisfy the security needs, companies began welfare programmes to provide employee security by applying a custodial model of OP. Although the custodial model is desirable to provide employee security, it is best viewed as the foundation for growth to the next step. The companies evolved a variety of welfare programmes and fringe benefits to increase a feeling of security among employees in order to motivate them.

1.10.3 Supportive Model

The supportive model of OP had its origin in the principle of supportive relationship (as stated by Rensis Likert) which depends on leadership instead of power or money. Management provides a climate to help employees grow and accomplish in the interest of the organization. The supportive model works best with both employees and managers, and it has been widely accepted. This model cropped out of a series of researches at the Hawthorne plant of Western Electric in the 1920s and 1930s, and it was further led by Professors Elton Mayo and F.J. Roethlisberger. They realized that an organization was an interesting social system having players such as the worker and the supportive supervisor who valued group dynamics. The supervisor acted as a mentor and counsellor to his colleagues.

1.10.4 Collegial Model

The collegial model depends on management's building a feeling of partnership with employees and the result is that those employees feel needed and useful. A sense of partnership can be built in many ways: some firms tried to eliminate the use of terms like bosses and subordinates, some organizations abolished the use of reserved parking spaces for executives, so all employees had an equal chance of finding space close to workplace. Other companies used the same canteen facility both for managers and non-executives. The psychological result of the collegial approach for the employees is fostering of self-discipline and feeling responsible.

1.11 CHALLENGES AND LIMITATIONS OF OP

Owing to the dynamic nature, scope, and goals of OP, the subject confronts three major challenges as well as limitations as given below.

1.11.1 Managers Look for Rapid Solutions

In an extremely competitive business environment, managers are under pressure to deliver best results and complete assignments in the shortest possible time. They often look for quick solutions without deep thought and analysis.

On one side, it is a great challenge especially in large projects, to deliver the outcomes in a measureable fashion by involving a host of contractors fulfilling all legal procedures and meeting deadlines. On the other hand, it requires an immense set of technical and interpersonal skills to manage the large and rotating workforce which practically becomes a big constraint for functional managers even in very professional organizations.

Hence, the field of OP provides an area of understanding human behaviour. It also poses a lot challenge and makes one aware of the limitations of human resource development/management and broadly the practical issues of project work implementations.

1.11.2 Managing the Changing Environments

The greatest challenges that confront OP is determining how applicable its methods and techniques are in a fast changing business environment under changing economic, technological, and political conditions.

The major challenges under such conditions are the stresses that the workplace or the organization undergoes during the times of employee attrition, transfers, acquisitions, and mergers. The organizations take several measures or interventions such as downsizing, re-skilling, competency mapping, stress management methods, organizational surveys, feedback sessions, and the like.

1.11.3 Clear Definitions

Organizational Psychology will have to define more clearly its applications and approaches in terms of behavioural measurements and outcomes especially its major contributions in improving the effectiveness of organizations (H.L. Kaila, 2007).

Essentially, the organizational interventions for improving safety, health, production, quality, environment in terms of employee behaviours across departments have to be operationally definable, observable, modifiable, measurable, and implementable.

1.12 FUTURE OF OP

Workplaces across the world are witnessing a bunch of changes right from the selection techniques to employee appraisals, rewarding approaches, retaining methods, shaping competencies, optimizing potential, maximizing performance, and retirement benefits and so on. All these areas are almost becoming specialized functions and attracting experienced individuals for delivery of best results in business scenario. Looking at this context, the prospects of OP are being positioned in almost all types of organizations such as industrial establishments, hospitals, schools, banks, insurance companies, etc.

The scientific nature of OP provides employers a wide array of applications from this field such as assessment for employees selection, performance appraisals, competency mapping, employee counselling, safety, work-life balance and the like for enhancing organizational effectiveness and business performance. The 16th Congress of the European Association of Work and Organizational Psychology, 2013 (EAWOP) conference emphasized on creating new ideas and future trends for work organizations to enhance organizational effectiveness as well as growth and health of the working people.

Amongst the hospital establishments, there is a strong competition for increasing and measuring the quality and satisfaction of services to the patients and the staff. The satisfaction surveys as organizational intervention provide a very strong base for understanding the underlying factors for the same, hence contributing to the hospital performance and service to the society.

Similarly, the schools (whether traditional or corporate) immensely value the concepts and applications of OP such as leadership, human resource planning/ development, motivation, appraisals, decision making, engagement and participation for all stakeholders (school management, teachers, parents, students and community). All these concepts play an important role for school effectiveness and delivery of education.

Hence, all kinds of work organizations in future would require the services of OP for better understanding and promotion of their employees/partners or members.

It is important to mention here is an application of OP that is behaviour-based safety particularly known as BBS which is the latest technique to deal with accident prevention with a perspective that all workplace accidents have roots in unsafe behaviours and BBS methodology helps in reducing unsafe/at-risk behaviours of employees in organizations. This technique is recognized as per OHSAS 18001: 2007 which is an occupational health safety assessment series. The BBS remains very popular all over the world in organizations.

1.13 CAREER IN OP

The employers need the industrial/organizational psychologists on their roll to perform all functions under the scope of OP such as selection, recruitment, appraisal, training, counseling, and motivation of employees. The study of OP would help all kinds of organizations to understand the basis of behaviour of employees at workplaces. Why and how they behave the way they do? The employers need to be interested to hire trained people in OP to improve their work practices and to understand how they can manage the low performers and retain the high performers.

The organizations are increasingly inclined in hiring the qualified organizational psychologists trained from the universities. The organizations would recruit the psychologists for a variety of important functions: roles and responsibilities such as human resource planning, talent management, human capital index, assessment centres, employee engagement, employee counselling, competency mapping, training needs analysis, motivation and job satisfaction, work-life balance, attrition and retention, organizational commitment, business etiquette, BBS management, delegation in the organization, performance management, leadership styles, research methods and statistics for organizational development (OD) interventions. The execution of these functions and processes are decided by the human resource department of the respective organizations. These functions are dealt with in depth in this book.

To make a career in OP, the students need to complete their studies and programmes such as graduation and masters programme in OP. Many universities across the world also offer a doctorate programmes in OP.

The careers or positions in OP could be enumerated in many ways such as:

All industrial establishments need organizational/industrial psychologist:

(i) Freelancer OD (organizational development) practitioner

(ii) HR departments of hospitals, schools, colleges

(iii) Banks
(iv) Insurance companies
(v) Entertainment companies
(vi) Government institutions
(vii) Teaching positions
(viii) National/international NGOs, etc.

The graduates, preferably post-graduates in psychology who study academic papers of industrial/organizational psychology could enter the above organizations in various functions/departments such as training, HRD, learning, and development. After an experience of about 5 years, one can expect a very good position with a handsome salary package.

Many colleges/universities would require a lecturer/teaching faculty to complete their doctorate in OP for a better teaching–learning process for their students who enrol for masters programme in OP.

In India, the institutions such as Central Labour Institutes (CLIs), Institute of Banking Personnel Selection (IBPS), Defense Institute of Psychological Research (DIPR), departments of psychology in universities/colleges, and the HR departments of industrial organizations and many others have employed freshly trained as well as experienced psychologists in various positions. In United Kingdom, the post-graduates are employed as internal consultants in large commercial and industrial organizations, in HR departments, in the Police, the NHS, and also as management consultants (The University of Manchester, 2014).

SUMMARY

- Organizational psychologists across the world are busy in their respective works with regard to teaching, research, consultancy assignments in the public and private universities and institutions depending upon their socio-cultural requirements and economic context. Understanding this, there is also a need to emerge or evolve the cross-cultural and international OP perspectives. This is the precise reason that OP concepts are seen as leadership, performance management, motivation, human resource planning, and others are being seen as internationally relevant and applicable across nations and contributing to economic development.
- The subject of Industrial/Organizational Psychology provides scientifically researched tools and applications to organizations for improvement in workplace practices for better performance and well being of their employees.
- This chapter is foundational in nature and has introduced the subject of Industrial/Organizational Psychology along with its concepts, approaches, and models. It has also depicted various organizational theoretical frameworks which would help the students understanding the further chapters in this book on OP more clearly.

- The chapter also described why organizational and not industrial psychology is more important by providing the definition and meaning of OP, its history and development, scope and goals, characteristics of OP, challenges and limitations, future of OP, and careers in OP.
- Thirteen more chapters have been added in this manuscript under the scope for a textbook on OP for undergraduate and postgraduate students. These chapters cover the basic concerns and issues to organizations for understanding human behaviour at work situations; hence the students need to sincerely take note of these topics for their understanding on creating more humanized environments for people to work for their job satisfaction and performance.

EXERCISE FOR CLASSROOM PRACTICE

For better understanding of the subject matter of this chapter, please read and check each of the following statements whether True (T) or False (F) or Uncertain (U):

1. Knowledge about human behaviour would not be useful in improving an organization's effectiveness.
2. Employee behaviour may not be generalizable across industries, rather it needs to be studied and understood as organizationally relevant.
3. Organizational Psychology is the scientific study and application of knowledge about how people as an individual and as a group act within an organization.
4. Organizational Psychology suggests ways by which we can motivate employees, reduce stress in workplace, and improve team efforts and productivity.
5. There are numerous academic developments that led to the evolution from personnel to industrial to organizational psychology.
6. The Human Relations Movement did not push managers toward gaining participative support of lower levels of the organization in solving organizational problems.
7. The Hawthorne Studies helped to see that an organization is not only merely a formal arrangement of functions but is also a social system.
8. Organizational psychology is influenced by a complex set of dynamic forces that affect the nature and functioning of an organization. These forces are the people, structure, technology, and the environment.
9. The goals of OP are describing, understanding, predicting and controlling behavior of employees for achieving excellence in quality, safety, health, and environment aspects of an organization.
10. Organizational Psychology has six basic concepts about the nature of people.
11. Organizational Psychology is described as interdisciplinary in nature.
12. The basic approaches of OP such as human resources, contingency, and result-oriented are not interwoven.

13. Several models of OP dominate the management's thought and action in each organization.
14. All the models of OP are designed to build a spirit of mutuality in which every person makes a contribution and is appreciated those of others.
15. Organizational Psychology will have to define more clearly its applications and approaches in terms of behavioural measurements and outcomes.

Answers: All statements are **True** except statement numbers 1, 6, and 12 which are **False**.

REVIEW QUESTIONS FOR DISCUSSIONS/EXAMINATIONS

1. Critically differentiate and define industrial and organizational psychology.
2. Describe different theories of OP.
3. Discuss various approaches of OP.
4. Illustrate upon the scope and goals of OP.
5. How would the study of Industrial/Organizational Psychology facilitate in improving the workplace practices?
6. Critically discuss career opportunities in OP in India.
7. How important are scientifically grounded concepts, empirical findings, and the evaluation for organizational processes?
8. Address the new challenges and strains for individual workers and work organizations in the multinational cultures.

FIELD RESEARCH REPORT

This is a research assignment section for students for their internal assessment by the teacher during the semester. This assignment is for understanding the practical application of the subject.

An action research project: Interview and interact with a group of 15 managers and 15 workers across an organization preferably where you are placed for an internship. Conduct interviews through a closed/open-ended questionnaire to signify the issues and concerns pertaining to organizational behaviours that require immediate attention for improvement. Prepare a report of about 15 pages reflecting an action plan to improve the work practices.

REFERENCES

16th Congress of the European Association of Work and Organizational Psychology, 2013. 22-25 May held in Münster, Germany. http://www.eawop2013.org/

Bertalanffy, Ludwig Von (1962). 'General System Theory: A Critical Review', *General Systems* 7, 1–20.

Bhatia, Sudarshan Kumar (2009). *Contemporary Industrial Psychology*. Delhi: Deep and Deep Publications.

Curado, Carla (2006). 'Organisational Learning and Organisational Design', *Learning Organization*, 13 1: 25–48.

Daft, Richard L. Daft, J. Murphy, and H. Willmott (2010). *Organization: Theory and Design*. Hampshire: Cengage Learning EMEA.

Davis, Keith and John W. Newstrom (1989). *Human Behavior at Work: Organizational Behavior*. New Delhi: Tata McGraw-Hill.

Douglas, McGregor (2006). *The Human Side of Enterprise*. New York: McGraw-Hill. (Annotated edition). 25th Anniversary Printing. (Original work published in 1960).

Fiedler, F.E. (1971). *Leadership*. New York: General Learning Press.

Frederic Winslow, Taylor, (1911). *The Principles of Scientific Management*. New York: Harper & Row.

Ghanekar, Anjali (2001). *Industrial Psychology: Concepts and Cases*. Everest Publishing House.

Greenberg, Jerald and Robert A. Baron (2010). *Behavior in Organizations*. New Jersey: Prentice Hall.

Hall, Kevan (2013). *Making the Matrix Work*. London: Nicholas Brealey.

Kaila, H.L. (2007). *Organizational Behavior & HRM* (2nd edition). Delhi: AITBS Publishers.

Klein, Peter G. and Lasse B. Lien (2009). 'Diversification, Industry Structure and Firm Strategy: An Organizational Economics Perspective'. *Economic Institutions of Strategy Advances in Strategic Management*, 26: 289–312.

Kyle, Bruce (2006). 'Henry S. Dennison, Elton Mayo, and Human Relations Historiography'. *Management and Organizational History*, 1(2): 177–199 May.

Newstrom, John W. and Keith Davis (1998). *Industrial Psychology and Human Behaviour* (10th edition). New Delhi: Tata McGraw-Hill.

Robbin, Stephen P. Timothy A. Judge, and Timothy T. Campbell (2010). *Organizational Behaviour*. New Jersey: Prentice Hall.

Short, Jeremy, C. G. Tyge Payne, and David J. Ketchen Jr (2008). 'Research on Organizational Configurations: Past Accomplishments and Future Challenges,' *Journal of Management* 34: 1053–1079.

The University of Manchester (2014). *MSc Organisational Psychology*. http://www.manchester.ac.uk/study/masters/courses/list/02302/organisational-psychology-msc/careers/. Retrieved on 3 May 2014.

2

Research Methods

Learning Objectives

This chapter would help the readers:

- to understand meaning and various types of research;
- to acquaint with the research methods in psychology;
- to be familiar with techniques for collection of research data; and
- to reflect upon case studies about research cases.

An Opening Story: Challenges in Data Collection

Choosing an appropriate research methodology and its execution is all the time a challenging as well as an interesting experience for organizational researchers. Though research is a planned effort on the part of the researcher, nevertheless with all the research preparations done, the research investigators often face several practical issues during data collection. In one such large research on occupational health of women, the researcher put all his efforts to contact more than 50 organizations employing women for the purpose of data collection. While contacting the organizations individually, out of 50 almost 29 companies refused for data to be collected from them on the grounds that the information is confidential or it is not their policy to allow any outsider for collection of information. It became very difficult for the researcher to collect sufficient data from the remaining 21 organizations. A lot of time was wasted on 29 companies which posed a huge challenge to the research investigator to complete the data collection and meet the time line for submission of research report. The researcher had to work very hard while drawing time from rest of his assignments and put extra efforts to collect sufficient data. It is always advisable for an organizational researcher to visualize such data collection problems and delays, and to keep sufficient time at hand for such eventualities in order to meet the requirements of quality and quantity of data required for research.

2.1 INTRODUCTION

Students in college and university often experience lot of anxiety and questions before they begin delving into any research activity or assignment, contemplating as to what they should be looking for in research, how they should actually begin doing research, how they should write or test hypothesis, how to analyse and interpret data, and most importantly what are the implications and utility of research, etc.

C.R. Kothari (2008) defines research as an art of scientific investigation. It is an academic activity carried out by the researcher which is based on a comprehensive review of the existing literature on the subject of research through published articles in various scientific journals as well as setting objectives of research, sampling, data collection, data analysis, drawing inferences, and suggesting recommendations for improvement based on research findings.

According to Cliffor Woody (Rajendar Kumar 2011), research comprises defining and redefining problems, formulating hypothesis or suggested solutions; collecting, organizing and evaluating data; making deductions and reaching conclusions; and carefully testing the conclusions to determine whether they fit the formulating hypothesis.

Panneerselvam R. (2007) defines research as an organized set of activities to study and develop a model or procedure/technique to find the result of a realistic problem supported by literature and data such that its objectives are optimized and further make recommendations/interferences for implementations. For example, if HR managers are interested in finding out the factors responsible for absenteeism or alcoholism or accidents, a systematic research effort can help in this regard. One can also ascertain which factors need to be controlled or necessary data-based approach be directed in order to reduce such organizational or employee problems.

Research is an interesting field for the researchers who are engaged in exploring various hypothesis and research questions in order to seek new learning/answers from the ground realities about social, political, economic, psychological, and industrial life. There are many methods of research available in literature to pursue, depending upon the research context and its queries to find answers or solutions. Michael and Jerry (2012) provided a comprehensive overview of many methodologies and examined the value and difficulties of particular methods across different fields of research.

The organizational psychologists, research scholars, and the students who study Organizational Psychology at the college level quite often make attempts to ascertain perceptions of employees across companies about organizational policies and procedures, and provide research-based feedback from time to time to organizations for improving/updating organizational practices. For systematic measurement of employees' perceptions, they would need various research methods.

The study of research methods are also important for I/O psychologists for many other reasons such as conducting descriptive or correlational studies and surveys about human behaviours in organizations such as describing or predicating employee motivation, job satisfaction, accident causation, counselling, human resource development issues, measuring the impact of organizational development interventions, and the like.

This chapter provides literature about what a researcher must look for and consider while doing his/her research work, and brings insights into the objectives of research, types of research, research methodology, research design, sampling design, collecting the data, analysis of data, research case examples, Master's/PhD thesis proposal format, Master's/PhD thesis evaluation and finally contents of a completed research document.

2.2 OBJECTIVES OF RESEARCH

Every research is guided by a set of objectives which lay the foundation for its approach and search for query. This is normally the second step in any research after the review of literature on the subject. A careful and comprehensive review of the published literature generally guides formulation of research objectives and questions.

Writing a clear statement of research objectives is very important in the research process, hence, this step must be carefully discussed with teachers, students, and professionals in the field. Normally, the research objectives are drawn on the basis of exhaustive literature survey done on the topic of research by visiting a couple of libraries and the Internet search. Sometimes researchers tend to avoid this step which is a basic error in research. Objectives carefully drawn give us fair opportunity to write good hypothesis. C.R. Kothari (2008) stated that the purpose of research is to discover answers to questions through the applications of scientific procedures.

Though each research has its own specific purpose, the research objectives can be broadly categorized into following four groups:

Exploratory Research: When the objective is to gain familiarity with a phenomenon or to achieve new insights into it.

Descriptive Research: To portray accurately the characteristics of a particular individual, situation, or a group, or an organization.

Diagnostic Research: To determine the frequency with which something occurs or with which it is associated with something else.

Hypothesis Testing Research: To test a hypothesis of a causal relationship between variables.

Good to Know

Normally, hypotheses are developed from the stated objectives of research.

2.3 TYPES OF RESEARCH

Research can be carried out in multiple ways. Years of research by the scholars has brought out various types of research which help researchers to think about what type of research suits them as per objectives and aims of their research inquiry.

A variety of research types would help researchers to choose between the appropriate ones that would go with their research requirements. There are research types such as descriptive, applied, quantitative, qualitative, longitudinal, clinical, and others that would interest the students more as they go through each of these as described below.

2.3.1 Descriptive Vs Analytical

Descriptive research is to describe the situation as it prevails in the present scenario. For example, describing the rate of accidents at workplace, or the attrition rate across different industries in the state of Maharashtra. Descriptive research is also referred as ex-post facto research. It describes the state of facts or variables as it is in the present context. In this method, the researcher does not control any variables. He only takes an account of what has occurred or is happening. In analytical research, the researcher uses the information or data derived from the descriptive method which provides a basis for formulating further hypothesis looking at the different background variables as to the proportion in which they exist, and also which variables can be included for further analysis. So both descriptive as well as analytical researches are very powerful in their own ways to help the researcher find effective solutions to his/her research queries.

2.3.2 Applied Vs Fundamental

Applied research would help finding an immediate answer to the social or organizational issues or problems such as why employees are not satisfied or motivated on their jobs. Applied research method would assist in finding the determinants of job dissatisfaction or low motivation and the like. Fundamental research is basically theoretical in nature. It does not find any solution to immediate issues, rather it extends the theoretical framework bringing different ideas and variables together as to build a more holistic or multidisciplinary basis of research. Fundamental research is very useful and brings together many perspectives on the existing issues whereas an applied research is more practical in its approach.

2.3.3 Quantitative Vs Qualitative

Quantitative research refers to the extent or size of correlation between two or more variables. It is mostly questionnaire-based. It is expressed in terms of number or value or quantity. Qualitative research would give depth or quality to the research. It is mostly interview-based. For example, quantitative research would provide us the degree of stress the employees are experiencing whereas qualitative research would give an idea as to what is the nature of this stress and in which aspects of life and so on. Processes underlying human behaviours, that is, studying the relationship underlying certain critical behaviours and performance of employees, the research would be qualitative in nature (Michael Berkwits 1998). Attitude research designed to find out how people feel or think about a particular subject is quantitative research (Paj Waddington and Bull Ray 2007). Both quantitative as well as qualitative researches would be necessary for an effective and useful research.

2.34 Conceptual Vs Empirical

Conceptual research refers to concept building or conceptualizing about certain problems or solutions. Conceptual research is useful in organizations in order to deliberate upon framing policies, formulating new rules and regulations which require broad conceptual framework, or benchmarking with other national or international companies. Empirical research is more data based or has on experiential research approach to reach certain conclusions which are testable and generalizable from sample to population. It can also be called experimental type of research which can be based on social or organizational experiments. Both these researches are widely practised in organizations.

2.3.5 Longitudinal Vs One-Time Research

Longitudinal research requires thorough planning and implementation by a number of experienced researchers and investigators involved (Elisabetta Ruspini 2000). Generally, it would require assurance of a large funding for travelling, printing of questionnaires, analysis of data, publication support and the like. Based on longitudinal research findings, it is possible to develop behavioural trends across months, departments, cities, cultures, for example, developing behavioural trends of unsafe and safe behaviours responsible for accidents and injuries in organizations or its units. One-time research is of short or long duration but it does not prolong over the years as longitudinal research does.

2.3.6 Clinical/Diagnostic Research

Clinical or diagnostic research as it reflects is a case study and in-depth study about an individual or organization to find out certain relationships between the prevailing issues so that some reasonable diagnosis can be drawn. For example, the studies on children with autistic or learning or behavioural disorders, or employee misconduct or prolonged absenteeism, habitual low performers.

2.3.7 Exploratory Vs Formalized Research

Exploratory research is basically conducted to explore the situation for portraying its features so that it can be understood for drawing further hypothesis. For example, portraying employees' profile in an organization, an exploratory research can be very useful. Formalized research is primarily designed and conducted with a specific hypothesis to be tested.

2.3.8 Historical Research

Instead of the primary sources of data, the historical research largely depends upon archives, documents, and secondary data such as previous accident records. This kind of research is typical in the sense that no other research would utilize such data. Sometimes this research approach is combined with other types of research.

2.3.9 Conclusion Oriented/Decision Oriented Research

For conclusion oriented research, the researcher designs his research problem or enquiry according to his concepts in mind and reaches certain conclusions but in decision oriented research, his purpose of research is arriving at decisions for which his research is funded or supported for practical solutions to the existing problem at hand.

2.4 RESEARCH METHODS/METHODOLOGY

Research is the arrangement of conditions for collection and analysis of data in a manner that aims to combine relevance to the research purpose. Research methods refer to the techniques that are meant for conducting research till it succeeds in answering research questions.

Which of the research methods to follow is an important challenge for research scholars. How are the claims made in the research justified by the methods used is a major question (Association for Psychological Science 2014).

Broadly, research methods can be put into the following three groups:

(a) Those methods which are concerned with the collection of data (as discussed below).

(b) Those statistical techniques which are used for establishing relationships between the data (as discussed in the last chapter of the book).

(c) Those methods which are used to evaluate the accuracy of the results obtained.

Research methodology covers the research process as well as the research design used in the context of any research study (Glynis Marie Breakwell 2006). Research process consists of formulating the research problem that constitutes the first step in any research procedure which can be investigated or descriptive or study the relationship between variables. Research problem is based on an extensive literature survey for which the scientific journals, seminar proceedings, reports, books and online literature must be referred to. Then a set of working hypothesis is developed following literature survey.

Good to Know

The research process includes an outline of what the researcher will do right from writing hypothesis, operational definitions of variables, analysis of data etc.

2.5 RESEARCH DESIGN

Research designs can be of several types such as: Experimental and non-experimental, hypothesis testing. The research design is the conceptual structure within which the research is conducted; it constitutes the blueprint for the collection, measurement, and analysis of data.

The overall research design may be split into the following parts:

- **Sampling Design:** Methods of selecting items to be observed for the given study.
- **Observational Design:** Relates to the conditions under which the observations are to be made.
- **Statistical Design:** Concerns with the question of how many items are to be observed and how the information and data gathered are to be analysed.
- **Operational Design:** Deals with the techniques by which the procedures specified in the sampling, statistical, and observational designs can be carried out.

2.6 SAMPLING DESIGN

Sampling design refers to a procedure adopted in selecting a appropriate sample as drawn from a population for research. While developing sampling design the following points may be considered:

Type of Universe: One should clearly define the set of objects to be studied, that is, the universe. Universe can be:

- Finite universe has finite number of items for example, population of a city, number of workers in a factory, and so on.
- Infinite universe has infinite number of items for example, stars in the sky, throwing of dice and such others.

Sampling Unit: Sampling unit may be geographical, that is, state/district/village, and so on or social unit, that is, family, school and the like, or it may be an individual.

Source List: It is the sampling frame containing features of the universe to be matched for the sample drawn so that sample represents all characteristics of the population for the purpose of generalizability.

Size of Sample: Size of sample should be neither too large, nor too small. In order to control variance, a bigger sample is needed.

Budgetary Constraint: The research funds would vary depending upon the size and type of the sample.

2.6.1 Types of Sample Designs

Sample designs can be of different types depending on two factors, that is, on the representation basis and elemental selection techniques. On representation basis, it can be probability sampling/random sampling and non-probability sampling/Non-random selection. On elemental selection basis, it can be restricted sample or unrestricted sample

Non Probability/Non Random Selection: It is also called as Deliberate Sampling or Purposive Sampling or Judgment Sampling. Since the Non Probability samples are selected deliberately by the researcher, bias needs to be avoided.

Probability Sampling/Random Sampling/Chance Sampling: Under this, every person is so randomly chosen from the population that he/she has an equal chance or probability of being included in the sample.

Complex Random Sampling Designs: Probability sampling under restricted sampling techniques may result in complex random sampling designs. Some of these are:

Systematic Sampling: Sometimes while sampling we select every item on a list using random numbers to pick up the unit.

Stratified Sampling: This technique is applied in case the population is not homogeneous in nature. Here the population is divided into several sub-populations (called strata) that are individually more homogeneous than the total population and then we select items from each stratum to constitute a sample.

Cluster Sampling: Here the total population is divided into a number of relatively small subdivisions which are themselves clusters of still smaller units and then some of these clusters are randomly selected for inclusion in the overall sample. If clusters happen to be some geographic subdivisions, then cluster sampling is known as area sampling.

Multistage Sampling: It is further development of cluster sampling. It is meant for big inquiries extending to considerably a large geographical area such as a country.

Here sampling may be first of states, then districts, then towns, and then families.

Sequential Sampling: This is a complex sample design. The ultimate size of sample here is not fixed in advance but is determined according to the mathematical decision rules on the basis of information yielded as the survey progresses.

Total Sampling: In case the total population of a unit or tiny organization is very small, then one can choose to select all persons in different categories as sample.

2.7 COLLECTING THE DATA

It is important for research students to know how many ways they could collect data as described below:

2.7.1 Collection of Primary Data

It is basically based on direct information and interaction with study respondents.

Primary data could be both quantitative and qualitative in nature. It is collected in more than one way using the methods given below.

Observation Method: It is the direct information gathered by the researchers from the field by direct observation based on some criteria for the purpose of research. The information collected is current happenings, and thirdly the method is independent of respondent's willingness to respond (Charles Stangor 1998).

Observations can be of the following types.

Structured Observation: This is based on defined approach as well the method of observation to prove or meet the objective of research.

Participant Observation: In this the researcher himself/herself is also participating as an observer along with the real study participants. It is a direct in-depth experience to the researcher about observations.

Non-Participant Observation: Here the researcher or the observer is not the direct participant during the study observations.

Interview Method: Interviews are the direct experience with the study participants on one-on-one basis or group or through telephone interactions.

Personal Interview: This type of interview is a direct personal and in-depth experience with the research participants to ask relevant questions as designed to meet the study objectives.

Personal interviews further can be of the following types.

Structured Interviews: Here the questions are pre-set and sequenced in a flow for the purpose of recording the interview. But recording of responses is done with the consent of study participants.

Unstructured Interviews: Flexibility in questioning is the key for the interviewer so that there is greater scope for in-depth interviewing. But this type of unstructured interview is conducted by a senior researcher. Though a scheme of questions is pre-set but the questions are expanded. This type of interview may take more time than the structured interview format.

Focused Interview: This approach is clearly focused on how each of the study respondents would experience the issues that he/she needs to talk about.

Clinical Interview: This interview is feeling-oriented to motivate individuals towards his/her life experiences. This interview experience is more of a counselling intervention for both the study participant as well as the researcher.

Telephone Interviews: This interview method is based on the discretion of the researcher as to how this would meet the research objectives. He/she may limit telephone interview only up to information collection or to initiate an early dialogue for collecting information on a regular basis or may combine it with personal contact with study participants later.

Questionnaire Method: This method is well accepted for research enquiries. The questionnaire consists of a number of questions printed in a definite order on a form or set of forms. The respondents write their answers in the questionnaire format as per instructions. Usually, a questionnaire is considered the heart of a survey operation. If the questionnaire is very long, the participants would find it difficult or boring, hence it is better if it is short and simple to understand. Questions are dichotomous, multiple choice, or open-ended. Open-ended questions require special technique to analyse such as qualitative analysis (Farrall Stephen et al. 1997).

> **Good to Know**
> An effective research study would make combined use of interviews, and structured/unstructured questionnaire methods for data collection.

The questionnaire is of two types:

Structured questionnaire: A questionnaire is structured in the sense that the questions are pre-set by the researcher using a particular scale of measurement, and presentation of questions is easy to follow for the study participants for getting reliable responses.

Unstructured questionnaire: A questionnaire is unstructured as it consists of open-ended questions, or the questions that demand description from the respondents. This approach is used mostly for exploratory studies for new areas of research when the nature and process is not clear as to how the respondents are experiencing the personal or social issues which are to be explored in the study.

2.7.2 Collection of Secondary Data

Secondary data are collected from secondary resources such as health or accidents resources. Here we refer to the data such as past records and historical archives which are useful to show previous trends of behaviours in organizations which could be compared with the present trends. Usually published data are available in:

- Various publications of foreign governments or of intellectual bodies;
- Publications of central, state or local governments;
- Technical/trade journals;
- Books, magazines, and newspapers;
- Reports prepared by research scholars, universities, and such others.

2.8 ANALYSIS OF DATA

After collecting the data, it is analysed using the following processing operations:

Editing: This would mean to remove the inaccurate or incomplete data or any errors in data before analysing so that it helps in proper coding.

Coding: This would mean assigning numerical values to responses for computing data through statistical packages for quick analysis. Coding decisions should usually be taken at the designing stage of the questionnaires.

Classification: This helps in reducing big raw data to certain grouping for meaningful analysis. Thus, classifying the data involves arranging data in groups or classes on the basis of common characteristics. Classification can be done according to the attributes or class intervals.

Tabulation: This is the process of preparing initial statistical tables as per objectives of research for hypothesis-based analysis further.

2.9 TYPES OF ANALYSIS

Analysis means looking for certain patterns or trends among the data for hypothesis testing or forecasting or discriminant analysis by making certain sub-groups of data. Analysis may be categorized as follows:

Correlational Analysis: Studies the degree of relationship between two or more variables. This is more relevant in social and business researches where the interest is in understanding and controlling relationships between variables (Martin Bulmer 1984).

Causal Analysis: This helps to establish cause-effect relationships or path analysis using some sets of variables or factors.

Generally, students or new researcher's are confused over the scheme of data analysis and how to select a particular statistical technique (Karl Knox 2004). Normally, the data analysis is governed by the research questions, hypothesis, and research objectives. One can read through the first hypothesis and understand what analysis does it require, for example, if the hypothesis states that there is no difference or significant difference between two groups, it's understandable that t-test is required here. Thus, one can move on from one hypothesis to another hypothesis and go on conducting analysis of data. There may be as many statistical methods/techniques required for data analysis of the entire research study as the number of hypotheses or objectives.

The data analysis through the Statistical Package of Social Sciences (SPSS) becomes quite easy for researchers, but it requires a thorough familiarity with the SPSS output which means how to read meaningfully and infer from the analysis format of the SPSS. The SPSS is a useful computerized statistical tool for the benefit of researchers for quick analysis of data. With the knowledge of SPSS and support, one can do analysis of data in more than one way. One can imagine different research questions and actually play with the data.

2.10 RESEARCH CASE EXAMPLES

The following four research case examples are presented to help students contemplate over the research methodology adopted in these articles. The students would gain insight discussing about the research methodology (to improve upon the research design) from the viewpoint of an effective application of research findings in an organization for practical implications.

(a) Job Stress and Job Satisfaction in a Software Company

Job satisfaction and occupational stress both indicate workers' appraisal towards the workplace and work itself. This article (H.L. Kaila 2007) attempts to examine the relationship between job stress and job satisfaction among 50 IT engineers of an InfoTech company in Mumbai. It was hypothesized that there is a negative correlation between job satisfaction of employees and occupational stress experienced by them.

To measure job satisfaction, Locke's job satisfaction test was used. To measure occupational stress, a self-constructed questionnaire called Job stress inventory was used. It was found that there is a negative correlation between job satisfaction of employees and occupational stress experienced by them. That is, employees who experience high level of job satisfaction are likely to feel less stressed out at the job and vice versa.

(b) Organizational Culture and Motivation

The purpose of this article (H.L. Kaila 2007) is to explore the nature of relationship between organizational culture and motivation. It was hypothesized that there will be a positive correlation between strong organizational culture and motivational needs whereas there will be a negative correlation between weak organizational culture and motivational needs. The sample size consisted of 50 employees belonging to two different organizations: a power and a mobile company. In each organization 25 employees were tested, that is, 13 males and 12 females, respectively. The tools utilized were two close-ended questionnaires: Organizational Culture Assessment Instrument (OCAI) and McClelland's Motivation (M) questionnaire. Statistical analysis of Pearson's Product Moment correlation (r) [consisting of Strong Organizational Culture and Motivational Needs] of Males in the Power company showed a high positive correlation between Organizational Culture (OCAI-Clan Culture Type) and Motivational need [*n*-Ach] ($r = 0.73$, $p < 0.01$), moderate positive correlation between Organizational Culture (OCAI-Clan Culture Type) and Motivational need [*n*-Affil] ($r = 0.58$, $p < 0.05$), and moderate positive correlation between Organizational Culture (OCAI-Clan Culture Type) and Motivational need [*n*-Pow] ($r = 0.60$, $p < 0.05$). In the case of 'r' of females in the Power company there was a moderate positive correlation between Organizational Culture (OCAI-Clan Culture Type) and Motivational need [n-Ach] ($r = 0.65$, $p < .05$), high positive correlation between Organizational Culture (OCAI-Clan Culture Type) and Motivational need [n-Affil] ($r = 0.80$, $p < .01$), and moderate positive correlation between Organizational Culture (OCAI-Clan Culture Type) and Motivational need [*n*-Pow] ($r = 0.68$, $p < .05$). In case of 'r' [consisting of Weak Organizational Culture and Motivational Needs] of males in the Mobile company showed a high negative correlation between Organizational Culture (OCAI-Market Culture Type) and Motivational need [*n*-Ach] ($r = -0.74$, $p < .05$), high negative correlation between Organizational Culture (OCAI-Market Culture Type) and Motivational need [*n*-Affil] ($r = -0.76$, $p < 0.05$), and high negative correlation between Organizational Culture (OCAI-Market Culture Type) and Motivational need [*n*-Pow] ($r = -0.80$, $p < .05$). In case of 'r' of females in the Mobile company there was a high negative correlation between Organizational Culture

(OCAI-Market Culture Type) and Motivational need [*n*-Ach] ($r = -0.71$, $p < 0.05$), moderate negative correlation between Organizational Culture (OCAI-Market Culture Type) and Motivational need [*n*-Affil] ($r = -0.69$, $p < 0.05$), and moderate negative correlation between Organizational Culture (OCAI-Market Culture Type) and Motivational need [*n*-Pow] ($r = -0.68$, $p < 0.05$). The present correlational study was conducted to assist the organizations to know their prevailing organizational cultures and to successfully deal with their organizational changes by recognizing employees' motivational needs which will ultimately increase employees' job satisfaction, production, organizational growth and development, and decrease attrition rate in the future.

(c) Employee Engagement and Work-life Balance

The purpose of this article is to understand the relationship between work-life balance and employee engagement. The study (H.L. Kaila 2007) hypothesized that there is a positive correlation between work-life balance and employee engagement.

The research design of this study was a non-experimental and correlational one as the relationship between work-life balance and employee engagement was studied. There were two surveys that were utilized so as to gauge the level of employee engagement and work-life balance. Fifty participants were part of this study out of which 25 were males and 25 females. The participants in this study were all employees working in corporate organizations.

The results showed that there was a positive correlation between employee engagement and work-life balance. Additional findings revealed that married females have a low level of engagement as well as work-life balance in comparison to married males.

(d) Effects of Quality of Work Life on Job Satisfaction

Quality of work life (QWL) is one of the major components for the employees' motivation and satisfaction in organizations. The aim of this research (H.L. Kaila 2007) is to find out about the effect of quality of work life on job satisfaction. Review of related literature has been done particularly with a view to locate the possible correlates of the variables studied.

Eight variables to measure (QWL) are examined namely: work environment, organization culture and climate, relations and co-operation, compensation and rewards, facilities, job satisfaction and job security, freedom of work and adequacy of resources. All these variables have correlated with job satisfaction. Questionnaire on quality of work life and job satisfaction was administered to study the effect of quality of work life on job satisfaction. A sample of 50 employees was randomly drawn from different employees working in diverse organizations.

Results showed that each domain of QWL was a predictor of job satisfaction. However compensation (0.7733), work environment (0.694), and job security (0.6027) were more correlated with job satisfaction whereas facilities (0.1652), relations and cooperation (0.4346) were less correlated with job satisfaction.

2.11 AN EXAMPLE OF MASTER'S/PHD THESIS PROPOSAL FORMAT

Many students find it difficult to write a Master's/PhD thesis proposal. They often look for a suitable format for this purpose.

Here below is presented an example of a detailed format which should guide the students. A detailed proposal may have 8–10 pages.

Repercussions of Child Abuse and Therapeutic Interventions in Childhood and Adolescent Behaviour

A
RESEARCH PROPOSAL
SUBMITTED
TO THE
UNIVERSITY OF PUNE
FOR THE DEGREE
OF
DOCTOR OF PHILOSOPHY
In
PSYCHOLOGY
By
Ms SHEELA PRABHU
UNDER THE GUIDANCE OF
Dr S.S. NIRMA
DEPARTMENT OF PSYCHOLOGY
UNIVERSITY OF PUNE
30 March 2014

1. Preamble/ Rationale of the research study
   Review of literature
   What is child abuse?
   The major types of abuses faced by a child in society:
   Sexual Abuse
   Pedophilia
   Physical force
   Emotional Abuse
   Child Neglect
   Female Feticide and Infanticide
   Repercussions of Child Abuse in Childhood
   Repercussions of Child Abuse on Adolescent Behaviour
   Therapeutic Interventions for Child Abuse in Childhood
   Therapeutic Interventions for Child Abuse in Adolescence
   Repercussions of Child Abuse from Childhood to Adolescence
   Child Abuse in Childhood and on Adolescent Behaviour, both need Therapeutic Interventions
2. Objectives of Research
3. Hypothesis

4. Variables
   (a) Independent Variables.
   (b) Dependent Variables.
   (c) Control Variable.
5. Research Design
   (a) Correlational Method
   (b) Survey Method
   (c) Archival Research
   (d) Group Discussions and one-to-one interactions with children
6. Methodology
   (a) Primary Data
   (b) Secondary Data
   (c) Sample: Sample size, locations, study participants
   (d) Tools Used
   (e) Procedure for the therapeutic interventions (including counselling sessions)
7. Scope of Study
8. Utility of Research
9. Limitations
10. References: to be listed as quoted in the text for review of literature as per APA format
11. Schedule/timeframe of the study.

Stage	*Work*	*Duration in months*	*Starting date*	*Completion date*
1.	Defining research problem.			
2.	Review of literature.			
3.	Formulate hypothesis and design the research (including sample design).			
4.	Pilot study (sample).			
5.	Collection of data (full).			
6.	Data analysis (simultaneously).			
7.	Testing of hypothesis.			
8.	Final report preparation/rough print			
9.	Final print and binding/submission			
	TOTAL			

2.12 AN EXAMPLE OF MASTER'S/PHD THESIS EVALUATION

Many students at the masters level opt for a research thesis. It is important for them to know how their research thesis would be evaluated so that they would ponder over and include all the necessary ingredients for research. So is the case for PhD level students. The evaluation criteria would help them prepare their theses better.

Here below is an example of Master's/PhD thesis evaluation which reflects various aspects of research to be taken care of.

Evaluation Report of Master's/PhD Thesis in Psychology

Aldina has selected a very current and relevant topic for her Master's/PhD research. She has used the proper research framework, methodology, and excellently discussed the results of her research.

The detailed evaluation is as below:

The dissertation is well organized.

The methodology chapter is explained well in terms of objectives, reliability, validity of tools, sample, and such others.

Hypotheses are too many; they could have been clubbed together.

The data analysis is quite comprehensively carried out and suitably interpreted.

Scales used for research are proper.

The discussion and conclusions are well presented.

The findings are properly summarized.

Indian references on the topic are missing.

Case studies could have been narrated for better presentation of research work.

Recommendations need elaboration on the utility or applications of the research findings.

Other relevant respondents such as parents and teachers could have been included.

There are almost 400 references listed on about 50 pages. One really wonders whether the candidate had the opportunity to view all of them and having gone through them. One should limit listing the number of references which are quoted in the text of the thesis. One should not list bibliography which one has consulted but not quoted inside text.

2.13 QUOTING RESEARCH WORK/REFERENCES

The students would often use the reference work but not quote or list in proper way. The incomplete references are not accepted. It is of utmost importance that the references must not miss the author name/initials, year of publication, the title of article or book, publisher's name, place of publication, page numbers, journal volume, and issue number.

Here below are some examples as to how the students must quote or list their references:

Journal Reference

Wansoo Park, August (2009). Parental Attachment among Korean–American Adolescents. *Journal of Child and Adolescent Social Work*, 26(4): 307-319.

Book Chapter Reference

Steinberg, L. (1990). 'Autonomy, conflict, and harmony in the family relationship', in: S.S. Feldman & G.R. Elliott (eds.), *At the Threshold: The Developing Adolescent*, pp. 255–276. Cambridge, MA: Harvard University Press.

Internet or Web Reference

Smith, B. (1998). *Communication: The Key to Successful Families*. http://www.family.go.com/Features/family-_1998_09/iowa98talk/iowa98talk.html Retrieved on 9 May 2014.

2.14 CONTENTS OF A COMPLETED RESEARCH DOCUMENT

The students often complete their research and sit back to find a proper packaging to present their research work. Many a times, students wonder about what a completed thesis or document of a research study would contain.

> **Good to Know**
>
> Years of research work if not packaged or presented well would lose its impact.

Here below is a list of contents that would help the student decide about the same.

- Acknowledgements
- List of Tables
- List of Graphs
- Abstract
- Introduction
- Review of Literature
- Research Methodology
- Results and Discussion
- Summary and Conclusion
- Limitations of the Research
- Suggestions for Future Research
- Implications of Research
- References
- Appendix

SUMMARY

- There are hundreds of books and thousands of articles written over a variety of research methods used in organizational psychology studies. However, the students would be keenly interested in conducting new researches on the behavioural issues in organizations if they are explained well and attracted to the subject.

- Organizations are keen to use various methods of research to scientifically survey the existing practices and behavioural trends across departments for production, health, safety, marketing, quality, and so on.
- In this chapter, the various research methods that are available to carry out research in different fields, have been explored and explained.
- It has been observed that irrespective of the field of research, be it sociology, psychology or behavioral sciences, every researcher should choose a set of methods which are unique to the nature and scope of research that he/she has to conduct.
- The types of research, sampling designs, collection and analysis of data, and some research examples are discussed for students to gain insights.
- The chapter has also described the objectives, methods, design of research, and examples of Master's/PhD thesis proposal format and its evaluation.

EXERCISE FOR CLASSROOM PRACTICE

For better understanding of the subject matter of this chapter, please read and check each of the following statements whether True (T) or False (F) or Uncertain (U)

1. Research is an art of scientific investigation carried out by the researcher and is based on a comprehensive review of existing literature.
2. Writing of research objectives is based on the study design.
3. Descriptive research is to portray accurately the characteristics of a particular individual, situation, or a group, or an organization.
4. Longitudinal research requires a thorough planning and implementation by a number of experienced researchers and investigators involved.
5. An objective of exploratory research is the development of hypothesis rather than their testing.
6. Research methods are all those methods/techniques that are used for the conduction of research.
7. Hypothesis directs the researcher to generalize findings from sample to the population.
8. Sampling design depicts methods of selecting items to be observed for the given study.
9. Clinical Interview is concerned with broad underlying feelings or motivations or with the course of individuals' life experience.

10. Analysis means computation of certain indices or measures along with searching for patterns of relationship that exist among the data groups.
11. The data analysis through the statistical package of social sciences (SPSS) becomes quite easy for researchers.
12. Coding refers to the process of assigning numerals or other symbols to answers so that responses can be put into a limited number of categories or classes.
13. Tabulation is the process of summarizing raw data and displaying the same in compact form (statistical tables) for further analysis.
14. Correlational analysis helps to discriminate between two or more variables.
15. Causal analysis is concerned with the study of how one or more variables affect changes in another variable.

Answers: All statements are **True** except that statement numbers 2, 7, and 14 are **False**.

REVIEW QUESTIONS FOR DISCUSSIONS/EXAMINATIONS

1. Reflect upon the significance of objectives of research.
2. Discuss various types of research for use in organizations.
3. Explain the different research methods in psychology with examples.
4. Critically discuss various sampling designs.
5. Evaluate quantitative and qualitative methodologies for collection of data.
6. Critically discuss the research methodology adopted for an article published in a psychology journal.
7. Argue over the proposal format of Master's/PhD thesis in the class.
8. Discuss various aspects of Master's/PhD thesis evaluation.
9. Provide a comprehensive overview of the methods of organizational psychology research with some illustrations.
10. Examine the value and difficulties of a particular research method of organizational psychology.

FIELD RESEARCH REPORT

This is a research assignment section for students for their internal marking by the teacher during the semester. This assignment is for understanding the practical application of the subject.

An action research project: Choose a relevant topic of research based on a comprehensive literature review, discuss with the subject professor, classmates, as well as your mentor in the company. Interview a group of minimum 15 managers and 15 workers across an organization preferably where you are placed for an internship. Conduct interviews with them by using a closed/open-ended questionnaire to signify the issues and concerns pertaining to topic of research. Prepare a report of about 15 pages reflecting an action plan to improve the work practices.

REFERENCES

Association for Psychological Science (2014). Submission Guidelines. Retrieved on 4 May 2014. https://www.psychologicalscience.org/index.php/publications/journals/psychological_science/ps-submissions.

Berkwits, Michael (1998). 'Making Use of Qualitative Research Techniques,' *Journal of General Internal Medicine*, 13: 194–199.

Breakwell, Glynis Marie (2006). *Research Methods in Psychology* (3rd edition). Sean Hammond, Jonathan A. Smith, Chris Fife-Schaw, SAGE, Google Books.

Bulmer, Martin (1984). *Sociological Research Methods: An Introduction*. Chicago: Transaction Publishers.

Hammond, Michael and Jerry Wellington (2012). *Research Methods: The Key Concepts*. London: Routledge.

Kaila, H.L. (2007). *Organizational Behavior & HRM*. (2nd edition), Delhi: AITBS Publishers.

Knox, Karl (2004). 'A Researcher's Dilemma: Philosophical and Methodological Pluralism', *Electronic Journal of Business Research Methods*, 2(2): 119–128.

Kothari, C.R. (2008). *Research Methodology: An Introduction*. New Delhi: New Age International (P) Ltd Publishers.

Panneerselvam, R. (2007). *Research Methodology* (1st edition). New Delhi: Prentice-Hall of India Pvt. Ltd.

Rajendar, Kumar C. (2011). *Research Methodology*. New Delhi: APH Publishing.

Ruspini, Elisabetta (2000). 'Longitudinal Research in the Social Sciences', *Social Research Update*, University of Surrey, Guildford, England.

Stangor, Charles (1998). *Methods for the Behavioral Sciences* (2nd edition). University of Maryland, College Park, Houghton Miffin College Division.

Stephen Farrall et al. (1997). 'Open and Closed Questions', *Social Research Update*, Issue 17, University of Surrey, Guildford, England.

Waddington, Paj and Bull Ray (2007). 'Cognitive Interviewing as a Research Technique', *Social Research Update*, Issue 50, University of Surrey, Guildford, England.

3

Human Resource Planning/Human Resource Management

Learning Objectives

This chapter would help the readers:

- to understand the concepts of HRP/HRM;
- to acquaint with integrating HR into business performance measurement;
- to be familiar with the model of talent management;
- to identify critical issues in talent management;
- to be aware of the objectives of human capital index (HCI);
- to reflect upon case studies about HRP, HCI, and talent management.

An Opening Story: Challenges of an Organizational Psychology Student

How HR management is truly a line function, is demonstrated by this story. As a part of an academic requirement in the college, a student of Organizational Psychology was to undertake a research project on HRM while she was doing an internship in a family-run organization which was a glass factory in Mumbai employing about 350 employees including the workmen. This company did not have an HR department and she was being mentored by the executive director of the company. Her main problem was to select an HR specific topic of research project as part of her internship. She wondered very much and was very eager to know as to how the HR functions are being administered in the absence of a formal HR department in this company. And somehow she took up this challenge and decided to work on this topic. This was appreciated by the executive director. She found out through her research in the organization that all the HR functions in the company such as selection, training, appraisal and so on were being shared formally/informally by the line managers and led by the executive director in a very mature manner with lot of sensitivity and concern for his employees and workmen. This finding was a great outcome of her research as this 'shared model of HR functions' is what should actually take place in any company. This was a great new learning experience for the student as well as the company. Hence, she converted her challenging task into an interesting learning even for other companies to follow and practise this model of HR.

3.1 INTRODUCTION TO HRP/HRM

The study of human resource management includes an introduction to the factors involved in the effective utilization of people within organizations, analysis of the global context for human resource management, the strategic role of HRM, human resource planning, job analysis, staffing, performance management, training and development, remuneration, legal issues in HRM, and occupational health and safety (Monash University 2014).

Human resource planning and management are very functions in any progressive organization that has changed and grown significantly during the last 25 years. Looking ahead we can see the results-based HR strategies and plans for different workforce segments. We can also envision the need for more vital contributions from HR in business strategy and leadership.

Many HR management teams have a well-developed vision of their department's strategic value. At the same time, many CEO's and senior line managers are skeptical of HR's role in the firm's success and they just can't understand how the HR function makes that vision a reality (Becker, et al., 2001). Gary Dessler (2013) has emphasized upon critically analysing and evaluating the human resource management policies and procedures in organizations.

Although many HR models are used today, the managers need to consider the following on the development of human resources as valuable asset.

- The firm hires and pays people but doesn't focus on hiring the best or developing exceptional employees.
- The firm uses bonuses, incentive pay, and meaningful distinctions in pay to reward high and low performers.
- The senior managers see employees as strategic assets, but if they don't invest in overhauling HR's capabilities, the HR system can't influence management's perspective.

The major focus of human resource management is to bring the people and the organization together so that there can be an alignment between the goals of both and each of them can fulfil the same.

3.1.1 Importance of HRM/HRP to a Organization

> **Good to Know**
> The HRM/HRP is both what it is doing today and what it needs to take on for the company in future.

The HR planning and management are of utmost important in the development of an organization and effectiveness of its business and in many ways as to how the HR functions are managed to deliver the business outcomes on a regular basis in the present era of competitiveness across the world for ensuring quality, quantity and cost of products and more importantly the customer care and satisfaction.

The HR function must also anticipate and manage change. This is easier to do if the HR procedure has clarity and has been simplified for practising for employees.

HR should be the guide in monitoring and advising how the business implements its strategies. Some of the best initiatives collapse simply due to inadequate implementation and/or active leadership required (Ulrich 1996). Continuous improvement requires monitoring. This can only start once initial high standards or benchmarks have been established. Monitoring also requires regular review and reporting. Increased monitoring and performance management are closely related.

3.1.2 Combine HR and Company's Performance

The scope of organizational performance being related to the human resource policies and practices adopted has been debated by both academicians and practitioners for a long time (Mila, Michael, and (Shaun 2013). Practically speaking, there remains a difference between organizational practices and policies. All employees don't identify with these policies and fail to follow them.

The HR teams are supposed to regularly emphasize, facilitate, and perform according to the expected results of the company's business policy and strategy.

To combine the HR activities with performance measurement, following aspects are important (Matthewman 2002):

- Managers must identify their deliverables for combining into the organization's strategy implementation plan.
- Human resource managers need to focus on HR performance drivers in order to demonstrate their strategic influence.
- The trustworthiness of HR measures is on the whole important when financial and non-financial performance measures clash.

One kind of model of High-Performance Work System (HPWS) is to build and maintain a talented human capital. An HPWS does the following (Ulrich et al. 1999):

- Connects its selection and promotion decisions to validated competency models;
- Develops strategies and timely support for the skills demanded by the firm's strategy implementation; and
- Enacts compensation and performance management policies that attract, retain, and motivate high performers.

These are vital steps in improving the quality of employee decision-making throughout the organization. HR systems persistently support and reinforce the high performance workforce.

3.1.3 HR and Talent Management

Managing talent as per the needs of an organizational business success on a regular basis is a big challenge which is actually a test of skills of any HR department/team of a company.

Talent management is an upcoming topic with a lot of significance for the organization's strategic goals and their achievement. The capacity of an organization to hire, develop, and retain talent is the most crucial business process.

The term 'talent management' was coined by David Watkins of Softscape (Chris 2011). It refers to the process of developing and integrating new workers, developing and retaining currents workers, and attracting highly skilled workers to work for your company.

> **Good to Know**
> Employees' talents and skills drive the company's business success. Hence, companies develop plans and processes to manage their employee talent.

Talent management is also known as HCM (Human Capital Management), HRIS (HR Information Systems) or HRMS (HR Management Systems), and HR Modules (Chugh and Bhatnagar 2006). Talent management is a key business process and like any business process takes inputs and generates output.

Talent management is a core area of HR function helping an organization to attract, develop, and retain employees. Effective leaders have always resorted to honing the bundle of talent in the organization by knowing and empowering people and transforming them to beings of substance.

3.1.4 Models and Critical Issues in Talent Management

Though there are several frameworks and researches on a variety of issues of talent management, the basic model of talent management for any organization to follow should include six components as operationally defined below (Cappelli 2000):

- **Role and talent design:** This refers to defining roles and expectations of incumbents. It also includes defining what good performance and low or potential performances are.
- **Performance focus:** Performance focus is measuring the performance and potential of individuals in organizations.
- **Career planning:** Career planning is about creating and communicating career plans to all members of the organization that help to sustain and realize individual aspirations for business growth.
- **Succession:** Ensuring critical succession and retention is an integral part of an effective talent management process.
- **Deployment and optimization:** Deployment and optimization refers to the merging or restructuring at organizational or functional level, and the ability to deploy people around the business to capitalize/optimize on business opportunities and available talents.
- **Development:** Development is exercising activities to trigger, deliver, and sustain individual growth on regular basis through learning and development (L&D) schemes.

Despite following the above framework, the critical issues and challenges for the HR department remain to strategically link its HR activities with the organization's goals to achieve the desired results, that is, to attract and retain a competent and motivated workforce, and measure the organization's performance in meeting strategic objectives (Chris and Lynne 2005).

3.1.5 Critical Issues in Talent Management

> **Good to Know**
> Talent Management is a most happening function of Human Resource department.

Talent management is a series of business processes – not a product or solution one can buy. It's a forward-looking HR function. Not only should talent management improve the organization's flexibility and performance, it should give the information and tools to plan for growth of human resource, change, acquisitions, and critical new products and service initiatives.

While most organizations focus on the key elements and build an integrated approach over time, a few mature organizations have dealt with most of the critical processes and issues below.

(a) Talent management requires integration amongst the existing L&D functions:
Learning takes place through training but this learning can become a skill only if what is learnt is practised on the job. Many times the training function does not follow up this link of learning and development; hence there is a loss of learning and no return on investment in training.

Newly hired employees should attend a set of trainings which complement and reinforce their competencies. Training programmes should be developed and updated to continuously address problems related to the performance management process. Compensation programmes should naturally tie to the performance management process.

(b) Competency management:
A difficult part of training and HR, has become critical.

The best practice is for your organization to have a small set of consistent, easy-to-understand competencies which can be applied across the organization. The HR department has to ascertain that the learning through training turns into competencies for use to the organization.

(c) Select approach on the basis of need of the organization:
There is no one right approach for talent management. There are as many approaches as there are organizations. However, the organizations that most successfully implement talent management are those that have questioned their assumptions, articulated the assumptions, discussed with senior management, and translated it into practical steps as below.

- Design a strategy that fits your organization, culture, and business strategy; question your assumptions; and develop a practical action plan to implement, evaluate, and review.
- Employee involvement in the talent management strategy varies. Some organizations involve all staff and allow all to have their skill sets assessed, while others choose only a select group.

3.1.6 HR and Human Capital Index (HCI)

Human capital index shows that the better an organization is doing in managing its human capital, the better its returns for its employees and shareholders (Flamholtz 1990). It is thus a fundamental source of wealth creation. Before we know the objectives of HCI, it is very important for HR teams here to first discover the basic characteristics of HC as specified below.

> **Good to Know**
> Companies with *superior human capital practices* can create more than double the shareholder value than companies with average human capital practices.

3.1.7 Characteristic Features of Human Capital (HC)

- All other forms of capital (land, machinery, buildings, and natural resources) represent potential. Human capital converts that potential into reality.
- Training and development are treated as costs though they have all the attributes of investment in human capital asset.

Managing HC is therefore managing the paradox of containing HC costs while evoking loyalty, motivation, innovation, and extracting value (Crook et al., 2011).

The broad objectives of HCI have been identified by researches (Aldisert 1954; Rao 1993; Scholz 2006) as follows:

- To understand and put in place key measures such as skills and qualifications, rate of innovation, leadership, and employee statistics, that is, demographic composition.
- It involves measuring costs to recruit, select, hire, train, and develop employees and their economic value to the organization.
- It helps in assessing the inner strength of an organization and helps the management to steer the company through most unfavourable circumstances.
- It provides information for investors interested in making investment in the firm.
- It helps employees in improving their performance and bargaining power. It makes each of them understand his contribution towards betterment of the firm vis-à-vis the expenditure incurred by the firm on him.
- To aid in the development of management principles, and proper decision making for future by classifying financial consequences of various practices.
- It helps understanding the measurements of human resource costs; and the measurements of human resource value.

3.1.8 Measuring HCI

Any discussion of human capital implies that people in the organization represent more than just expenditure; that they are not to be seen only in the income statement but more in the balance sheet as an asset (Likert 1971). Employees depict their net worth in terms of contributions by performances over months and years to achieving the targeted business goals.

HCI is a methodology of Watson Wyatt (2002) to calculate the correlation of human capital and shareholders' value. Companies with better quality human capital can create more than double the investor value than the companies with just normal human capital.

> **Good to Know**
> Employees have moved from being a cost to becoming a resource and today they are considered to be an asset or a capital. Any careful management must take care of its assets and try to maximize the return on them.

Below is the (return on investment), RoI for measuring the investments made in people, including recruiting, selection, training, compensation, and benefits. After determining the investment, divide that amount by the profit or revenue that employees bring into your organization to determine RoI.

An RoI measurement can be affected by variables such as the work environment, the economy, and organizational culture. With the ability to understand and measure the effectiveness of human capital programmes, organizations can adapt, change, and optimize their activities to improve the overall performance of their business (Fitz-enz 2000).

$$\text{HCROI} = \frac{\text{Revenue} - (\text{Expenses} - \text{Pay and Benefits})}{\text{Pay and Benefits}}$$

However, HCROI has a limitation, it takes into account only non-human expenses and does not take training costs, contingent, absence and turnover costs, and the like into consideration.

There are three levels at which the human capital investment can be measured. The principal focus must always start at the enterprise level goals including strategic financial, customer, and human issues. The second level of measurement is the business unit including for changes in intermediate-level service, quality, and productivity outcomes. The third level is the effects of the human resource department's work on planning, hiring, compensating, developing, and retaining the enterprise's human capital (CFO Research Services 2003).

3.1.9 Effective HRM/HRP

The most potent action HR managers can take to ensure their strategic contribution is to develop a measurement system that convincingly showcases HR's impact on business performance (Matthewman 2002). Organizations that adopted data based practices to support HR decisions are reaping the benefits in terms of increased employee satisfaction and organizational revenue (Business Manager 2014).

Effectiveness and measurement go hand in hand. The attempt to judge how effective the HR function is, assumes that there is a benchmark or some scale to refer to. The function needs to demonstrate why and how all resources are used but most personnel departments have rarely monitored how they utilize people, time, or money.

As suggested by Gubman (2004), key HR effectiveness measures are central to business successes. HR managers ought to focus on two major issues as their financial colleagues: return and growth by combining HR goals such as attracting, developing, and retaining staff; rewarding performance and reducing HR costs.

Good to Know

HR managers need to become healthier profit-and-loss company leaders.

Tamkin et al. (2008) recommended a number of issues that HR managers must focus on:

- enhancing the quality of the recruitment process;
- effective, long-term development plans;
- aligning employees to the objectives of the organisation; and
- encouraging autonomy, empowerment, and generation of ideas.

3.1.10 Case Studies

Three important research cases (H.L. Kaila 2007) are presented below for discussion and developing better insights.

- A research case on HRP
- A research case on talent management
- A research case on HCI

3.1.11 A Research Case on HRP

Following the literature on HCI, HRP, and talent nanagement presented above, this case on HRP is offered for the objectives as below:

- to know the attitude of employees regarding how HRP helps in business growth;
- to know the attitude of employees towards HR functions like performance appraisal, training, and recruitment;
- to know how much importance they attach to these HR functions;
- to know if the company's business is benefitting from HRP;
- to study the best practice factors in HRP and development;
- to identify and discuss the causes and limitations for HRP and development;
- to study and assess impact of HRP towards organizational performance; and
- to study the application of selective HR tools and techniques in an organization.

Research sample: 50 employees (between 25 and 58 years, males and females) were sampled from all types of organizations. The work experience of respondents was ranging from less than two years to 15 years and above.

Methods of data collection: Open-ended questions to obtain more insight, case studies and a structured questionnaire.

Description of tool: This questionnaire (see appendix) measures the attitudes of employees towards the functions of the HR department in their organization and how it affects business growth.

Section 1 of the questionnaire consists of personal data of the respondent.

Section 2 deals with application of HR tools and techniques. It is divided in 3 parts A, B, and C. Part A deals with organizational planning. It has six statements and they are scored on a 5-point rating scale ranging from strongly disagree to strongly; 1 being strongly disagree, 2 being disagree, 3 being neutral, 4 being agree, and 5 being strongly agree. Part B deals with tools in HRP and organizational planning. It consists of eight statements and is scored on a 5-point rating scale, ranging from very uncommon to very common. 1 is very uncommon, 2 is uncommon, 3 is neutral, 4 is common, 5 is very common. Part C deals with the application of tools and techniques in HRP and team development. It consists of eight statements and is scored on the basis of a 5-point rating scale ranging from very uncommon to very common, as explained above.

Section 3 deals with HRP and development towards organizational performance. It consists of seven statements and is scored on a 5-point rating scale ranging from strongly disagree to strongly agree, as explained above.

Section 4 deals with the causes leading towards failure in HRP and development. It consists of eight statements. Respondents could tick more than one statement which they feel contributes to the failure of HRP and business growth

Section 5 consists of two open-ended questions and qualitative analysis of the same was done.

The least score a respondent could get on the questionnaire would be 29 and the highest score was 145. The score range was divided as 29–51 as very unfavourable, 52–74 as unfavourable, 75–99 as neutral, 100–122 as favourable and 123–145 as highly favourable.

In section 2, Part A, the least score a respondent could get was 6 and the highest score was 30. For part B and C, both, the least score that a respondent could get was 8 and the highest score was 40. In section 3, the least score that a respondent could get was 7 and the highest was 35.

Data analysis (scoring): The tool which was used to measure the attitudes of the respondents towards HRP and business growth, in the light of the research objectives, was scored as follows:

For sections 2 and 3, the raw score of each respondent was calculated on the basis of the rating scale. The scores were converted into percentage for each section and each part. This was done to know what percentage of respondents are having what kind of attitude towards HRP and business growth. Percentage from 1 to 100 was divided as: 1–20 is very unfavourable attitude, 21–40 is unfavourable attitude, 41–60 is neutral attitude, 61–80 is favourable attitude, and 81–100 as highly favourable attitude.

Section 4 has eight causes leading to failure of HRP and business growth. The percentage was calculated to assess what according to the respondents is the cause that contributed most and which contributed least to the failure of HRP and business growth.

Section 5 has two questions and qualitative analysis was done on the same.

3.1.12 Results and Discussion

The total score of the respondents on section 2, part A was 1025. It was converted into percentage form which was found to be 68.33. The total score of the respondents on Section 2, part B was 1319 and the percentage was 65.95. The total score of respondents on Section 2, (Part C) was 1311 and the percentage was 65.55. On section 3 the total score of respondents was found to be 1243 and the percentage thus obtained was 71.03. The same data of percentages was shown in summary data Table 3.1.

Table 3.1 Attitudes of Respondents Towards Factors of Human Resource Planning

Section 2	*% of People*
A	68.33
B	65.9
C	65.55
Section 3	71.03

A graphical representation in the form of a bar diagram was made and is shown as Fig. 3.1 (attitudes of respondents towards factors of human resource planning). As it can be seen in the graph the *X* axis shows the factors of human resource planning and the *Y* axis shows the percentage of people holding the attitudes ranging from very unfavorable to highly favorable.

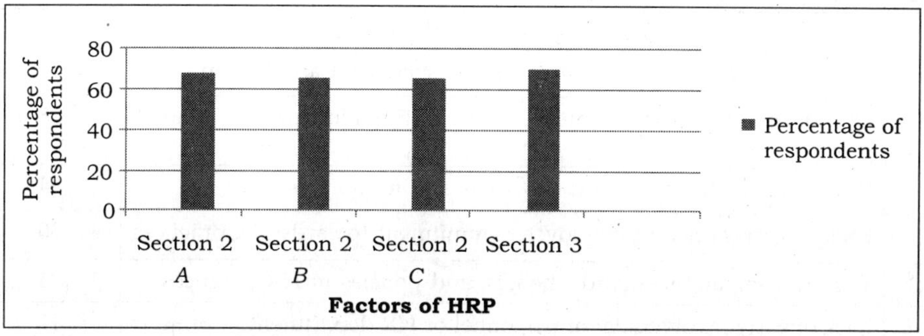

Fig. 3.1 Attitudes of respondents towards the factors of HRP.

Section 2 deals with the application of tools and techniques . Bar A of Section 2 deals with Part A which is related to organizational planning. The height of the bar shows that 68.33% of respondents have favourable attitudes. The height of bar B for part B shows that 65.9% of respondents have a favourable attitude towards the tools used in human resource planning. The height of bar C shows that 65.55% of respondents have a favourable attitude towards the application of tools and techniques in human resource planning (team development).

The bar which is a depiction of Section 3 represents human resource planning and development towards organizational performance. The height of the bar shows that 71.03% of respondents have a favourable attitude.

Figure 3.2 sums up Section 4 and shows the causes of failure of human resource planning and development and the percentage of people who felt that a particular cause is contributing to the failure.

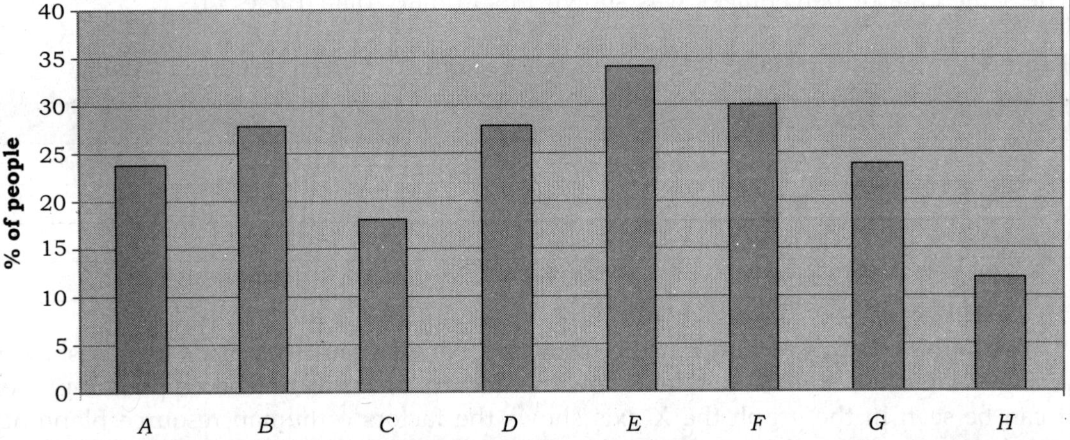

	Causes of Failure	*% of People*
A	Lack of managerial support	24
B	Lack of HR tools and techniques application	28
C	Lack of proven research to indicate the success of application	18
D	Overlooked scope and importance of HR participation in organizational projects	28
E	Resistance to change in new HR tools and techniques	34
F	Lack of employer and employee commitment towards HR practices	30
G	Various company standards, beliefs, and policies in HR practices	24
H	Lack of early involvement of personnel or HR department in projects	12

Fig. 3.2 Causes of failure of human resource planning and development.

Table 3.2 Summary Data Table

Categories	*Very Unfavourable*	*Unfavourable*	*Neutral*	*Favourable*	*Highly Favourable*	*Total*
Number of respondents	0	3	29	16	2	50

Table 3.2 shows the number of respondents in the categories ranging from very unfavourable, unfavourable, neutral, favourable, and highly favourable. As mentioned

earlier total number of respondents is 50. 0 people hold very unfavourable attitude, 3 respondents hold unfavourable attitude, 29 respondents hold a neutral attitude, 16 respondents hold a favourable attitude, and 2 respondents hold a highly favourable attitude.

Figure 3.3 is a pie diagram representation of the data in Table 3.2.

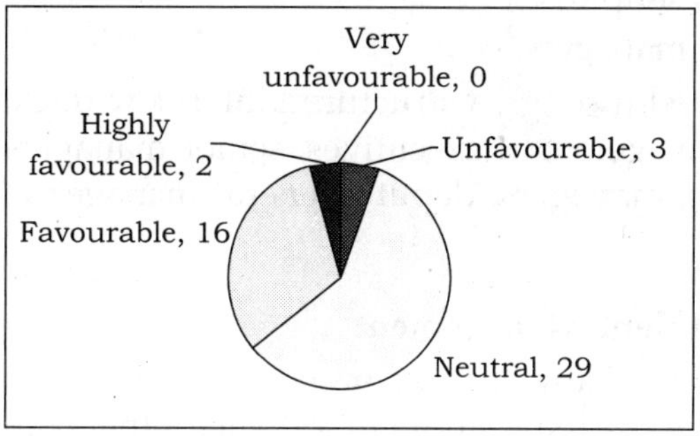

Fig. 3.3 Division of respondents into categories.

Section 5 consists of open-ended questions .The qualitative analysis is as follows. According to the obtained results most people have a neutral and favourable attitude. According to that the respondents have put forth their comments on human resource planning and how according to them it benefits or affects the business growth.

HR brings about confidence in the employee for the employer. It helps to get the best input from the employee in terms of work and morale. Good HR practices help growth of both employee as well as the organization. Only if the employees are happy they will work efficiently towards business growth. HR acts as a middleman between the higher level and lower level management.

HR plays a very important role in the adaptation to new changes taking place in the current market scenario. HR plays a vital role to form a firm organizational structure in the organization. In case a wrong candidate is placed in the structure it may directly/ indirectly contribute to a negative performance to the company. HR helps to enhance good public relations, effective implementation of HR policies and suitable manpower in the industry can contribute to good business growth. HR aides in professional development, minimizes conflict among team members, and motivates people.

3.1.13 A Research Case on Talent Management

An objective of this case study was to review the comparative analysis of talent management processes of four companies as below. The names of companies have been changed for the purpose of confidentiality.

1. Max Limited
2. Nova Pharma
3. Costa Power Limited
4. Benzoic group

Data were collected in terms of interviews, case studies, and examples.

The entire data was analysed qualitatively because it described the processes of talent management in each company, and the process for each company differed in many ways.

Sample description

1. Case study of 12 employees
2. Interviews of 16 managers.

The data was collected through a structured interview questionnaire (see appendix) by interviewing HR managers, HR executives, senior managers, regional manager, HR head, directors, training managers, deputy general manager, VP of operations head.

1. Max Limited

Various Processes of Talent Management

Max Limited does not have any specific process designed for talent management but recruitment, training, succession planning, and such others, are some areas where the talent is considered, developed, and enhanced. As an organization, Max Limited values its employees and provides immense growth and development opportunities to the employees to develop and explore their potential.

Workforce Planning: It is planning and evaluation of the company plans of hiring, compensation, targets, and the life. It has a record of how many employees are required for a particular position and how many have been employed. The compensation structure and planning for scope is included here.

Recruitment: It involves recruiting the best of the talents available in the market by recognizing the individual's capabilities and potential during the selection process through interviews and various other methods and selecting the right candidate for the right job, so that both the individual and organization progress.

Training and Performance Support: Every employee is given a training of 48 hours. A training need analysis is done according to which a training calendar is formed and training for behavioural, technical, and managerial skills is given.

Training ensures the growth and development of every employee, the areas they need to be trained to be competent in their job profile and areas where they lack competency. Training is a continuous process and it ensures growth and development of the employees. It is both external and internal.

On Boarding: The company recruits 14 management trainees every year. These trainees are trained for one complete year in all aspects of the company's working. The knowledge of the company's complete working and functions of every department is provided. These trainees are then taken as assistant manager or operation heads in the company according to their capabilities.

Performance Appraisal: Performance appraisal is done according to the individual's performance. The individual's key result areas (KRA) indicator and performance indicator is determined. For instance an IT manager's KRA would be server management. His performance indicator would be installing operating systems, maintenance, and the like. The total weightage to the given KRA is decided and while evaluating individual's performance the actual weightage given is rated. This is done together by the appraiser and the appraisee.

Appraisal is done on both functional skills and soft skills though more weightage is given to functional skills. Appraisal takes place twice a year. In April, the individual's job analysis sheet is filled and by October the first evaluation is done. Depending on the performance and the criteria of scoring the individual is given incentives or appraised.

In case the individual fails in achieving his KRA to the desired extent that would be due to the fact that

1. he lacks skills, he is then trained to perform well; or
2. he is incapable of handling the position, he may then be terminated

The interviews reflected the talent management process that exists in Max Limited. Following is a review of the interviews in a summarized pattern.

Talent management is creating, enhancing, or modifying talent. It is utilizing talent to the fullest and continuous improvement. It takes place in various ways like cross department, rotation, and hierarchy. Giving training to employees, promoting capable employees, retaining efficient employees, reducing attrition are some other ways. Training can be technical behavioural training, soft skills training, and domain specific training.

Max Limited believes in giving chance to the existing employees as old employees are aware of the company's culture, mission, and vision. Old employees have high level of integrity, loyalty, and trust towards the company. This benefits the company, as the efforts to recruit a newcomer are reduced, training is saved, and the cost to hire a new employee is also reduced.

It is the individual potential, capabilities, performance, and talent that leads to the need of talent management as well the departmental needs. Potential is recognized by PMS, observing work, references, supervisor's feedback, and a detailed review of the employee's performance. Once the potential or talent is recognized the management, the department head or the HR manager takes the initiative to promote the employee. At times the employees approach their managers and convey that they want a promotion. In such cases the management reviews the employee's performance and takes the decision.

Max Limited believes in talent management as it is a way to give opportunity to employees to prove themselves; it is a challenge for employees and helps them to climb the ladder. Employees are motivated to work, are satisfied, and think that the company cares for them. Though talent management has been very successful in Max Limited, there are times when failures in talent management have to be encountered. These failures are due to misjudged talent, miscommunication, recruiting employees who are not efficient, or promoting employees who are not capable.

The employees who have been promoted or retained are getting a good exposure and experience. They are being imparted training at different levels so that they can enhance their talent and improve their performance.

Failures are managed in the following ways:

- Training the employee in the respective area.
- Before promoting the employee his performance is observed in the new position and then he is given confirmation.
- Formulating talent management, which is promotion and increment in salary, everything should be in writing.
- Taking feedback of employees who are leaving.
- Re-evaluating the perception about talent.

Max Limited is an organization with a pool of talented people. It is like a melting pot where people from various departments, with varied potential, capabilities, and talent come together, become one and have one aim, which is of contributing to the organizations, success and growth.

2. Costa Power

Talent management is an ongoing process that starts right from attracting talent in terms of recruitment and even after that. Here, the focus is on attracting the right talent for the right job and cultural fit.

Costa Power employees are given a lot of internal movement opportunities or job rotation. Since the company is growing and executing huge power projects in India and abroad, the job vacancies are published within the company through internal ads and applications are invited. Interviews are held and subject to selection, the employees are then moved to the new positions as soon as replacements for their current position are hired.

The company has also taken in a lot of skilled retired employees as consultants to guide us and train and monitor the project.

It's being used in many ways like identifying the experience of the employees and engaging them as trainers in various in-house training programmes. One employee for example had 23 years' experience in our Trombay power plant. He now is our trainer for the 'basics of power plant' programme.

Costa Power has an HR strategy that looked at TM as a tool to help our company grow. The company is growing at a rapid speed and this growth will not be possible unless supported by qualified manpower.

The company's strategy is to become the world's leading power project company. The first largest Asian power project is being implemented here. Thus, we have to develop our existing talent since the manpower with experience in large enough projects would not be available outside.

It contributes to the competitive advantage. For example, our in-house trainers help cost reduction in terms of hiring external trainers. We believe a penny saved is a penny earned.

Our PMS system is integrated with our training and job requirements. Thus, we know who our talents are.

It happens quite a few times internally in the company. Not all though. We needed a mix of internal and external talent.

Recruiting is based both on merits or competencies. We believe both cannot be separated.

Costa Power tries to meet different job descriptions with a person who responds to that description and meet all the requirements when recruiting a new person. We need employees with very niche qualities.

Through job descriptions and talking to the senior, Costa Power finds out what skills to look for when filling important positions. We try and understand the nature of the requirement from whatever source possible.

The company is familiar with the concept of employer branding. It is an epitome of stability, growth, good working environment, trust, and mutual respect.

The brand has been built over years and for Costa Power also, we are consciously building it.

Costa Power has a performance appraisal system. The goals or the KRA of every employee are cleary and mutually decided at the beginning of the year. Then at the end of the financial year, performance is measured against these goals and ratings are given on a 6-point rating scale.

O – Outstanding

VG – Very good

G+

G – Good

M – Marginal

U – Unsatisfactory

Employees are developed through an LD team in place that looks after this function.

There is no difference in the level of development resources allocated for different employees. It is need-based. Some may need more development than others.

As yet there is no concrete plan for future supply of key competencies. But we, being a power company, are very clear as to the future requirements.

Key personnel are of utmost importance, not only for the success of the project but also in terms of retaining leadership for the company as a whole.

The company has not lost too many key personnel as yet. One key position is vacant but is being looked after by a Costa Power employee at a highes position till a new person is recruited.

3. Nova Pharma

Summary of what the managers said: HR manager, Sr manager, head HR, regional manager, HR executive.

Benefits of talent management at Nova Pharma:

- Talent-related issues within the sales organization
- Build capability by way of identifying development opportunities for the target population.
- Identification of high potentials and their grooming will support the company's business growth in future.
- Succession planning: An enhanced 'path for success' for each.
- Participating leader to support their careers.
- Creation of development centres.

At an organizational level:

- Achieving business goals.
- Developing good leadership for the company.
- Acquiring the best talent and retaining them for better profits for the company.

4. Benzoic

Basic tools for talent management:

- Behavioural interviews
- Role plays
- Group discussions
- In-tray exercises
- Motivational tests and other psychometrics
- Personal assessment reports
- Individual feedback and coaching.

3.1.14 Comparative Analysis of Talent Management Processes

A research was conducted to study the processes of talent management of four different companies.

1. Max Limited: Entertainment industry
2. Costa Power: Power industry
3. Nova Pharma: Pharmaceutical company
4. Benzoic: Oil company

Max Limited believes in developing and enhancing the existing talents, rather than hiring new employees. It gives great importance to the employees as they are the ones who carry the culture of the organization and maintain it whereas Costa Power hires employees from the multinational companies so that the employees are exposed to new projects and in this way efficient employees are retained.

Nova Pharma is a multinational pharmaceutical company which believes in talent management very strongly. It gives opportunities to its employees if they are high potential employees. Benzoic believes in a very detailed and systematic process, it has scope for both existing and new employees.

Max Limited emphasizes on promotion, retaining efficient employees, and giving training to enhance talent, whereas Nova Pharma places importance in recruiting efficient employees from outside the company and encourages talent (retention) within the company itself. Costa Power is a growing company and has recently implemented talent management. Benzoic is a established company and the talent management begins from the recruitment level itself.

The common feature existing in all the above processes is that the organizations believe in retaining employees as they carry the culture of the company and promoting them increases their motivation and satisfaction. The employees are well aware of the vision and mission of the company.

3.1.15 A Research Case on HCI

This model was used by a big chemicals company for calculating the HCI. Value of human capital depends of two major factors:

1. Competence of the employees
2. Value realized form competencies

Competence comprises of functional competencies and managerial/generic leadership competencies. Value realized for the organization is reflected in consistency in performance and expertise in variety of domains.

The HCI was calculated as follows:

The first step was to define the weightage and rating scale for the above factors and rate each employee on a scale of 1–10 for each factor. Next step was to multiply the rating by the weight and the third step was to divide the sum of weighted ratings by the maximum possible score of 1000 to arrive at index of human capital.

The company model was based on company leadership practice (CLP) ratings, managerial generic competencies, experience level, and performance of the employee in variety of domains (CWL). Individual scores were given to the employee and the individual value was given to the organization. The total value given to the organization was the HCI.

Based on the employees' education, experience and managerial generic competencies certain scores were given to them. Those employees who had experience of less than five years were given the score of 2, employees having an experience of 5–10 years were given a score of 4, between 11–15 years were given a score of 6, between 16–20 years were given a score of 8, between 20–25 years were given the score of 9, and those who had an experience of more than 25 years were given the score of 10.

Those employees who had the educational qualification of a diploma or a undergraduate was given a score of 2, a score of 4 was given to those who were graduates, a score of 6 was given to those who were professionally qualified, postgraduates were given a score of 8, and those holding a PhD qualification were given a score of 10.

The company leadership practice ratings (CLP) was taken into consideration when giving scores on the managerial and generic competencies. Those who had a rating of 5 were given a score of 10, those who had a rating of 4 were given a score of 8, those who had a rating of 3 were given a score of 5, those who had a rating of 2 were given a score of 3, and those who had a rating of 1 were given the score of 1.

Consistency of performance was also taken into consideration. Those who were on Tier 1 were given a score of 10, those on Tier 2 were given a score of 8, those on Tier 3 were given the score of 5, those on Tier 4 were given the score of 2, and those on Tier 5 were given the score of 1.

Gears	0	1	2	3	4
Performance in variety of domains-CML					
Year of exp.	*G*	*F*	*E*	*D*	*C*
<5	6	7	8	9	10
5-10	5	6	7	8	9
11-15	4	5	6	7	8
16-20	3	4	5	6	7
21-25	2	3	4	5	6
>25	1	2	3	4	5

High CWL needs high competencies to handle more width and depth of domains

There is scope for org to realize more value from employees in higher CWL but with lesser experience than from employees needing more experience to deliver same value

Below is the format used in calculating the HCI using the Company Model:

Factor	*Weightage*	*Rating*	*Score*	*Max rating*	*Max score*	*Value*
Variety of Domains	20	5	100	10	200	0.5
Consistency of Performance	40	10	400	10	400	1.0
Education	10	8	80	10	100	1.0
Experience	10	10	100	10	100	1.0
Generic Competencies	20	5	100	10	200	0.5

As the number of domains increased a higher rating was given to the employee with an increase in CWL. This too was calculated SBU-wise and class work level-wise. The index or the value was obtained for all the employees individually.

3.1.16 Towards a Better HRM/HRP

Every organization looks forward to its workforce being managed so well through the best available HR planning and practices so as to meet the competitive scenario and ever-growing challenges in business performance. Based on the literature review and researches, the suggestions towards a better HRM/HRP are considered below:

(a) To make HR the backbone of the company there must be transparency in decision making of the top management.

(b) HR departments should interact with departmental heads to tap and exploit the core competencies of the individual by taking them into confidence.

(c) Reorientation programme in functional disciplines should be organized for effective and pursuit of excellence
(d) There should be a regular evaluation and upgradation of staff skills as it benefits the company as well as motivate the employees.
(e) Regular training programmes and evaluation of employee skill must be conducted.
(f) HR has to motivate the employee to keep him interested by opening new avenues for him so that he continues the same job.
(g) HR must contribute in collating the right candidate for the requirement of the positions in the company.
(h) The duty of the HR is to bring comfort and confidence in the employee's mind for the organization.
(i) HR has to involve and create an interactive platform for better understanding and grooming in the ever evolving market.
(j) Standard HR practices should be laid down and communicated to each employee.
(k) Reinforcement should be given in the form of rewards and incentives for following rules and punishment as a negative reinforcement for not following the same.
(l) HR should be a catalyst for healthy employer and employee relationship.
(m) HR should see to it that there is no employee discrimination taking place in the company.

Most things that are important to an organization are hard to measure objectively. Competitors can steal your products, services, distribution channels, often just about anything we do, except for fuzzy things such as your culture or people. Traditional HR metrics fail to tell an organization about the level of performance or knowledge of its employee base.

It is often useful to calculate indices several different ways for a year or two to find the right formula that best depicts overall business performance levels.

It is also important that the HCI has face validity with your employees. One must be prepared to do some evaluation and refinement of the index over time.

It's definitely worth the effort if this type of data can help make more balanced management decisions regarding the company's human resources.

There is no single measure which is independent of context and which accurately represents the impact of competencies on business performance.

It is also important that the index has face validity with your employees. One must be prepared to do some evaluation and refinement of the index over time.

Company accounts currently record the costs with people but not the benefits they bring. This is despite the fact that most organizations accept that people represent the key driver of value in organization.

The more people who have input to the ratings, the more bureaucratic the system will become so one must carefully select an approach that will really stick. The more rigour one tries to put into the index, the more complicated it becomes. While giving scores to the ratings one must make sure that there is a relatively even distribution of scores.

The human capital management enhances performance through raising the skills base of employees, e.g., appropriate recruitment and retention, comprehensive training and development activities, enhancing the employee's motivation and ability to use their skills through measures such as design of jobs to promote autonomy and challenge.

By giving regular training and motivating the employees through rewards and recognitions one can increase the human capital index or the worth of the employee as well as the organization.

In addition to proving value, of training budget, the human capital measurement provides the cornerstone for making improvements. To optimize learning investments, these improvements apply to the larger talent management process, including measuring workforce competencies and then developing training programs to fill in gaps that might otherwise go unnoticed and hinder achieving performance goals.

The value of human capital and the conventionally defined stock allocation are directly related. People with high levels of human capital can generally afford to take more risk with their financial investments. Thus, management has to sit up and take notice whenever high value employees leave irrespective of the years of service.

There is an opportunity for practitioners to improve their clients' decision making by valuing human capital and representing it on the balance sheet. Most things that are important to an organization are hard to measure objectively.

Many companies in India and abroad have opted for e-HRM which means most aspects of HRM such as leave, appraisal, time office, selections, etc., are manageable by computer and the Internet for the ease of employees as well as employer.

SUMMARY

- Human resource planning (HRP) and human resource management (HRM) both are inevitable for professional growth of employees and the company's business development.
- The influence the human resource planning in business growth is being increasingly realized in organizations. Employees believe that HR functions like performance appraisals, training, recruitment, and various tools used for implementing the same are used beneficially to a great extent.
- Resistance to change in new HR tools and techniques and lack of employee and employer commitment towards HR practices are the two major causes leading towards failure.
- The common features of talent management processes in most of the companies are that they believe in retaining the existing employees and enhancing their talents as they carry the culture of the company and are more committed to the organization.
- Talent management is a process to acquire new talents so that the organization is ready for competition and growth. It is a mutual process in which both the

organization and employee benefits. Dependent on culture and need, organizations should select a talent management strategy that works for them.

- HCI is a methodology to calculate the correlation of human capital and shareholders' value. A person has a set of competencies and a value is assigned to each of these competencies. The sum total of it is the value of an employee and the sum total of the value of all the employees is the human capital of the organization. Since there is no single measure which is independent of context and represents impact of competencies and commitment on business performance, the HCI is calculated. The results obtained are used for further action planning in areas of selection, recruitment, training and development, rewards, communication, and integration.
- In short, this chapter introduced the concept of HRP/HRM, emphasized the importance of HRM/HRP to organization, combined HR and company's performance, explained the concept, models, and critical issues in talent management and also provided case studies and recommendations for better HRM/HRP.

EXERCISE FOR CLASSROOM PRACTICE

For better understanding of the subject matter of this chapter, please read and check each of the following statements whether True (T) or False (F) or Uncertain (U):

1. The HR department needs to identify both what it is doing today and what it needs to take on for the future.
2. Human resource managers need to focus on HR performance drivers in order to demonstrate their strategic influence.
3. Managing talent as per needs of an organizational business on regular basis is a big challenge of any HR department/team.
4. Companies have realized that their employees' talents and skills drive their business success.
5. Performance focus is measuring the performance and not the potential of individuals in organizations.
6. Career planning would mean to reward and promote all members of the organization.
7. Development is exercising activities to trigger, deliver, and sustain individual growth on a regular basis through learning and development schemes.
8. HCI shows that the better an organization is doing in managing its human capital, the better its returns for its employees and shareholders.
9. HCI is a methodology of Watson Wyatt (2002) to determine the organizational resources and shareholders' value.
10. The most potent action HR managers can take is to ensure HR's impact on business performance.
11. At last, HR managers need to become healthier profit-and-loss company leaders.

12. One of the major causes of failure of human resource planning and development is lack of managerial support.

Answers: All statements are **True** except that statement numbers 5, 6, and 9 are **False**.

REVIEW QUESTIONS FOR DISCUSSIONS/EXAMINATIONS

1. How would you define the human resource planning in business growth?
2. Discuss how to integrate HR into a business-performance measurement system.
3. Reflect upon the importance of HRM/HRP in an organization.
4. Critically discuss critical issues of talent management in an organization.
5. Describe the HR strategic approach for talent management in the Indian context.
6. Discuss the relationship between HR and a company's performance.
7. Critically comment upon the effectiveness of HRM in your organization.
8. Describe the objectives of human capital index.
9. How is human capital index calculated?
10. Compare and contrast organizational case studies on HRP/talent management and HCI.

FIELD RESEARCH REPORT

This is a research assignment section for students for their internal marking by the teacher during the semester. This assignment is for understanding practical applications of the subject.

An action research project: Identify a group of minimum 15 executives and 15 non-executives across an organization preferably where you are placed for an internship. Conduct interviews with them by using a set of closed/open-ended questionnaires to signify the issues and concerns pertaining to the HRP/HCI/talent management. Prepare a report of about 15 pages reflecting an action plan for better work practices.

REFERENCES

Aldisert, M. Lisa (1954). *Valuing People: How Human Capital can be Your Strongest* Asset. Chicago: Dearborn Trade Pub.

Becker, B., M. Huselid and D. Ulrich (2001). *The HR Scorecard: Linking People, Strategy, and Performance*. Boston: Harvard Business School Press.

Business Manager 'Driving Business through Data-Driven HR policies', (2014). 17 (4): 38–39.

Cappelli, P. (2000). 'A Market Driven Approach to Retaining Talent', *Harvard Business Review*, 78(1): 103–11.

CFO Research Services (2003). 'Human Capital Management: The CFO's Perspective', February p. 28 (www.mercer.com).

Chris, Ashton and Lynne Morton (2005). 'Managing Talent for Competitive Advantage: Taking a Systemic Approach to Talent Management', *Strategic HR Review*, 4(5): 28–31.

Chris, Uba (2011). Talent Management Strategy, Business School, 3 January.

Chugh, S. and J. Bhatnagar (2006). 'Talent management as high performance work practice: emerging strategic HRM dimension', *Management and Labour Studies*, 31(3): 228–53.

Crook, T.R., S.Y. Todd, J.G. Combs, D.J. Woehr, and D.J. Ketchen (2011). 'Does Human Capital Matter? A Meta-analysis of the Relationship between Human Capital and Firm Performance,' *Journal of Applied Psychology*, 96(3): 443–456.

Dessler, Gary (2013). *Human Resource Management* (13th edition). New Delhi: Prentice Hall.

Fitz-enz, J. (2000). *The ROI of Human Capital: Measuring the Economical Value of Employee Performance*. New York; AMACOM Publication.

Flamholtz, E.G. (1990). *Growing Pains: How to Make the Transition from an Entrepreneurship to a Professionally Managed Firm*. San Francisco: Jossey-Bass.

Gubman, E. (2004) 'HR Strategy and Planning: From Birth to Business Results', *Human Resource Planning*, 27(1): 13–24.

Kaila, H.L. (2007). *Organizational Behavior & HRM*. (2nd edition). Delhi: AITBS Publishers.

Lazarova, Mila Michael Morley, and Shaun Tyson (2013). *International Human Resource Management: Policy and Practice*. London: Routledge.

Likert R. (1971). 'Human Organizational Measurements: Key to Financial Success'. *Michigan Business Review*, May pp. 1–5.

Matthewman, J. (2002). *Human Resources Effectiveness*. Mumbai: Jaico Publishing House.

Monash University (2014). Human Resource Management. Retrieved on 5 May 2014. http://www.buseco.monash.edu.au/unit-guide/archive/2014/s1/mgc2430.html

Rao D. Prabhakar (1993). 'Human Asset Accounting: An Evaluation of the Indian Practices', *ASCI Journal of Management*, 22.

Scholz, C. and Volker Stein (2006). *Human Capital Management, the Saarbruecken Formula*. Germany: Saarbruecken.

Tamkin, P., M. Cowling, and W. Hunt (2008). *People and the Bottom Line*. London: Institute of Employment Studies.

Ulrich, D. (1996). 'Organizational Capability as a Competitive Advantage: Human Resource Professionals as Strategic Partners'. *Human Resource Planning*, 10(4): 41–54.

Ulrich, D., R. Halbrook, D. Meder, and M. Stuchlik (1999). 'Employee and Customer Attachment: Synergies for Competitive Advantage'. *Human Resource Planning*, 14(2): 89–102.

Wyatt, Watson (2002). Human Capital Index: Human Capital as a Lead Indicator of Shareholder Value. Research Report. http://www.watsonwyatt.com/research/printable.asp?id=W-488.

APPENDIX

Structured Interview Questionnaire on Talent Management

(a) Describe talent management.
(b) How does it take place in your organization?
(c) How are these practices linked to the company strategies?
(d) What leads to talent management, departmental needs, or the individual's potential.
(e) Give examples of talent management that has taken place in your department.
(f) How do you recognize potential?
(g) Who takes the initiative of the same for recognizing potential?
(h) How do you form a talent pool?
(i) What are the benefits of talent management?
(j) Failures in talent management.
(k) How do you improve them?

Questionnaire on HRP

Section 1: Personal information

Please fill in the blank or tick (✓) in the box as shown.

Organization's/Company's Name (optional): ________________

Type of organization: ________________

Name: ________________

Age: ________________

Job Position: ________________

Years of experience in the company:

- Less than 2 years
- 2 to 5 years
- 5 to 10 years
- 10 to 15 years
- 15 years and above

Section 2: Application of HR Tools and Techniques

The purpose of this section is to study the factors considered in human resource planning (HRP) and development, and applications of HR tools. Please answer the statements based on your experience and knowledge by a tick (✓) in the box as shown using the rating scale below.

(a) HR Planning (Organizational Planning)

Rating Scale (1-5)

1–Strongly disagree

2–Disagree

3—Neutral
4—Agree
5—Strongly agree

1. The company focusses and considers all stakeholders and has a corporate strategy.

☐ 1 ☐ 2 ☐ 3 ☐ 4 ☐ 5

2. The company has a proper organizational structure/chart.

☐ 1 ☐ 2 ☐ 3 ☐ 4 ☐ 5

3. The organizational structure, chart has suitable people to enhance reporting, recording, decision making, and informational flow.

☐ 1 ☐ 2 ☐ 3 ☐ 4 ☐ 5

4. The company evaluates the current resources—people, skills, interests, abilities, and experiences.

☐ 1 ☐ 2 ☐ 3 ☐ 4 ☐ 5

5. The company analyses internal availability such as demand and supply of the HR required for projects undertaken by the company now and in the future.

☐ 1 ☐ 2 ☐ 3 ☐ 4 ☐ 5

6. The company makes job analysis and design to ensure the right people in the right job.

☐ 1 ☐ 2 ☐ 3 ☐ 4 ☐ 5

(b) Tools in HRP (Organizational Planning)
Rating Scale (1-5)
1—Very uncommon
2—Uncommon

3–Neutral
4–Common
5–Very common

7. Your organization uses standard procedures in performing job activities and marking individual responsibilities.

☐ 1 ☐ 2 ☐ 3 ☐ 4 ☐ 5

8. Your organization practices HR guidelines and procedures for project teams in running company projects.

☐ 1 ☐ 2 ☐ 3 ☐ 4 ☐ 5

9. Your company analyses constraint factors in organization such as organizational structure, type, preferences in project management teams.

☐ 1 ☐ 2 ☐ 3 ☐ 4 ☐ 5

10. Your company analyses and prioritizes the benefit of stakeholders and shareholders.

☐ 1 ☐ 2 ☐ 3 ☐ 4 ☐ 5

11. HRP would bring better delegation in roles and responsibilities.

☐ 1 ☐ 2 ☐ 3 ☐ 4 ☐ 5

12. Your company improves staffing management plan that reduces cost and improves motivation.

☐ 1 ☐ 2 ☐ 3 ☐ 4 ☐ 5

13. Your company has a proper formal and informal reporting relationship being produced as outcome of HRP.

☐ 1 ☐ 2 ☐ 3 ☐ 4 ☐ 5

14. Your company has a proper supporting document such as job specification.

☐ 1 ☐ 2 ☐ 3 ☐ 4 ☐ 5

(c) Applications of tools and techniques in HRP and development (team development) rating scale (1–5)
1 – Very uncommon
2 – Uncommon
3 – Neutral
4 – Common
5 – Very common

15. Your company's project document includes project plan, project staff record, performance reports for all respective projects.

☐ 1 ☐ 2 ☐ 3 ☐ 4 ☐ 5

16. You have attended any team-building activities that led to improve team members' skills and competencies.

☐ 1 ☐ 2 ☐ 3 ☐ 4 ☐ 5

17. Your company has general management skills' training to develop individual and team performance.

☐ 1 ☐ 2 ☐ 3 ☐ 4 ☐ 5

18. Your company rewards and recognizes employees accordingly to improve individual and team performance within the company projects.

☐ 1 ☐ 2 ☐ 3 ☐ 4 ☐ 5

19. Your company uses appropriate interaction processes in conducting meeting or discussion.

☐ 1 ☐ 2 ☐ 3 ☐ 4 ☐ 5

20. Your company puts the project team members in any formal or informal training (on the job, off the job).

☐ 1 ☐ 2 ☐ 3 ☐ 4 ☐ 5

21. Your organization looks into the aspect of improving the team performance in terms of individual skills, team behaviour and competencies in enhancing project efficiency.

☐ 1 ☐ 2 ☐ 3 ☐ 4 ☐ 5

22. Your company does employee assessment by recording the project team members' performance (skills and behaviour).

☐ 1 ☐ 2 ☐ 3 ☐ 4 ☐ 5

Section 3: Human Resource Planning and Development towards Organizational Performance

The purpose of this section is to study the application of HRP and HR development tools and techniques in relation to organizational performance.

Please answer these statements based on your experience and knowledge by a tick (✓) in the box as shown using the rating scale below:

Rating scale (1:5)

1–Strongly disagree

2–Disagree

3–Neutral

4–Agree

5–Strongly agree

23. Appropriate HR tools and techniques (staff management plans, employment assessment) used in the organization may bring about 'efficiency of project execution' in achieving target time, cost, and quality standard.

☐ 1 ☐ 2 ☐ 3 ☐ 4 ☐ 5

24. Effective HRP and development helps in improvement in 'technical performance and innovativeness' such as minimizing human error, low skills level, and possible delay; and improves ability in problem solving.

☐ 1 ☐ 2 ☐ 3 ☐ 4 ☐ 5

25. HR helps team performance and interferes in lowering the risk in conflict, improves decision-making process, and increases motivation level and team cohesiveness.

☐ 1 ☐ 2 ☐ 3 ☐ 4 ☐ 5

26. Efficient HRP and development may also affect the personal growth of the team such as challenge and professional development.

☐ 1 ☐ 2 ☐ 3 ☐ 4 ☐ 5

27. Effective HR may contribute to managerial and organizational competencies in promoting team motivation and long-term attachment with the company.

☐ 1 ☐ 2 ☐ 3 ☐ 4 ☐ 5

28. Effective HR helps in business performance such as gaining repetitive business, low cost in operations, and low staff resignation rate.

☐ 1 ☐ 2 ☐ 3 ☐ 4 ☐ 5

29. Your organization does enough to attract people with multidimensional skills and experiences that suit the present and future organizational strategies.

☐ 1 ☐ 2 ☐ 3 ☐ 4 ☐ 5

Section 4: Causes Leading Towards Failure in HR Planning and Development

Please tick (✓) which factors are relevant as the limitation and causes for failure in efficient HR planning and development (answer can be more than one)

30. Failure factors in HRP and Development

Lack of management support	
Lack of application of HR tools and techniques	
Lack of proven research to indicate the success of application	
Overlooked scope and importance of HR participation in organizational projects	
Resistance to change in new HR tools and techniques	
Lack of employer and employee commitment towards HR practices	
Various company standards, beliefs, and policies in HR practices	
Lack of early involvement of personnel or HR department in projects	

31. Your frank and open comments on HR practices and how it affects business growth.

4

Employee Recruitment and Selection

Learning Objectives

This chapter would help the readers:

- to understand the process of employee recruitment and selection;
- to acquaint with the techniques and factors affecting recruitment;
- to be familiar with the procedures of applicant assessment;
- to know how organizations apply recruitment and selection function; and
- to reflect upon case studies about recruitment and selection.

An Opening Story: Challenges of Recruitment and Selection

Recruitment and selection are always tough decisions to make for managers as well as psychology consultants especially when the company location is far off from the city or in rural areas where it becomes difficult to attract candidates and make a choice for high performers. In one such occasion, a company started its business almost 200 kilometres in the outskirts of Mumbai. Though the company used the best recruitment and selection methods including the psychological tests, it could not find many candidates having high potential or attitudes. Then the company, along with the organizational psychology professional, took the challenging decision to select the candidates having middle or even low aptitudes in order to fill the vacancies and start the project activities. But the company managers also decided that if we are considering people with low or average potential in such a remote area, then it is essential to provide sufficient training by the best trainers (internal and external) so that the selected candidates could perform up to the desired expectations. This is how the challenges of recruitment and selection combined with first-rate training brought excellent results for the company as well as employees.

4.1 INTRODUCTION

Recruitment has been regarded as the most vital function of human resources administration. Unless the right people are hired, even the best planned organization and systems would not do much good (Jonathan 2013).

Recruitment is like searching diamonds in a coal pit. Average recruiters quite often come out of the pit with artificially shining stones misjudging them as real diamonds. At the same time, many organizations fail to pay attention to establishing and maintaining an effective recruitment process. When the business moves on fast track, managers are given hardly any time to sit, rethink, and make this process rewarding (Anil Kaushik 2013).

Good to Know

To be successful in business, it is crucial to have the right people in the right job roles.

The proper start to a recruitment effort is to perform a job analysis in order to document the intended requirements of the job to be performed. This information is captured in a job description format and provides the recruitment effort with the boundaries and objectives of the search. Each company will have job descriptions that represent a chronological collection of tasks performed in the past. These job descriptions need to be reviewed prior to a recruitment exercise to reflect present requirements. Initiating recruitment with an accurate job analysis and job description ensures that the recruitment process starts off on an appropriate track for success.

Though recruitment is a very common human resource function, it has many aspects that are quite different from theory in actual practice. It is important to actually see them at work to understand the full scope of the concepts of recruitment, selection placement, and motivation.

Recruitment relates to all the activities and practices of attracting and identifying potential employees from a pool of applicants (Barber 1998).

Recruitment and selection are the most important functions of human resources management. 'Right person for the right job' is the basic principle in recruitment and selection. Recruitment involves the utilization of organizational practices to influence the number and types of individuals who are willing to apply for job vacancies (Rynes and Cable 2003) whereas selection involves the process of differentiating between applicants in order to identify those with a great likelihood of success in a job (Ashwathappa 1997).

In India, organization groups such as L&T, Reliance, Tata, and Birla have implemented best recruitment and selection methods in a very professional manner using psychological tests and an assessment centre approach. Institute of Banking Personnel Selection (IBPS) and many other individual recruitment consultants have popularized the use of professional and scientific approach to recruitment and selection of employees in the industry.

4.2 PURPOSE OF RECRUITING

Recruitment refers to the process of attracting, screening, and selecting qualified, trained, and experienced people for a job. For some components of the recruitment process, large-size organizations retain professional recruiters or outsource some of the processes to recruitment agencies and/or train their HR managers for the same.

Edwin B. Flippo (1961) defined recruitment as the process of searching prospective employees and stimulating them to apply for jobs in the organization. The function of recruitment includes developing the sources of prospective employees and attracting them to submit an application for jobs.

> **Good to Know**
> The HR staff gets themselves trained by the professionals for the use of personality profiling and assessment centre approach for tapping human potential.

The recruitment industry has four main types of agencies: employment agencies, recruitment websites and job search engines, headhunters for executive and professional recruitment, and niche agencies which specialize in a particular area of staffing. Some organizations use employer branding strategy and in-house recruitment instead of agencies. Recruitment functions are generally carried out by the organization's human resources personnel.

Recruiting the right person for a right job is a time consuming and lengthy process especially for senior positions. Recruiting must start with a thorough assessment of immediate staff requirements. It is important to ensure best fit for the position.

> **Good to Know**
> Hiring the right candidate especially for senior positions is a hilarious task for employers.

The stages in recruitment include sourcing candidates by advertising or other methods, screening potential candidates using tests and/or interviews, selecting candidates based on the results of the tests and/or interviews, and to ensuring that the candidate is able to fulfil his new role effectively.

4.3 PROCESS OF RECRUITMENT

Depending on the position, right sourcing strategy needs to be adopted. Sourcing strategy includes the decision of choosing one or more of the sources of recruitment mentioned below. Identifying a wrong source for recruitment would often delay the process. Hence, the HR/functional managers need to take active interest in identifying the right sources at the first stage which would then begin the process of recruitment.

4.3.1 Sourcing Involves

1. Advertising, a common part of the recruiting process, often encompassing multiple media, such as the Internet, general newspapers, job advertisement in employment special newspapers, professional publications, and campus recruitment programmes; and
2. Recruiting research, which is an identification of talent who may not respond to job postings and other advertising methods. This initial research for passive prospective candidates results into a list of persons who are then contacted to seek their interest in the position, obtain a resume, and be screened.

4.4 TECHNIQUES/SOURCES OF RECRUITMENT

The process of recruitment would rely upon the identification of right sources of recruitment. The entire recruitment is based on the goal of providing a candidate to a client for a cost. There are agencies that are paid only if they deliver a candidate that successfully stays with the client beyond the agreed trial period. There are other agencies that are paid a retainership amount to focus on a client's needs in search for the right candidate, and then again are paid a percentage of the candidate's salary when a candidate is placed and stays with the organization beyond the training period.

4.4.1 Types of Agencies

Also known as *employment agencies,* recruitment agencies have historically have a physical location/office. A candidate visits a local branch for a short interview and an assessment before being taken to the client. Recruitment consultants work to match their pool of candidates to their clients' open positions. Suitable candidates are shortlisted and put forward for an interview with potential employers.

Compensation to agencies takes several forms, the most accepted are:

- A contingency fee paid by the company when a recommended candidate accepts a job with the client company (typically 20% to 30% calculated on the candidates' first-year base salary).
- An advance payment that serves as a retainership money (for example, 40% upfront, 30% in 90% days, and the rest once a search is completed). This form of compensation is generally reserved for high level executive search.
- Hourly compensation for temporary workers which is normally pre-negotiated.

Specialized recruiters exist to seek staff with a especially fine area of expertise or specific skill set. These special firms tend to be more focussed on building ongoing relationships with their candidates as the same candidates are placed many times throughout their careers. Niche firms also develop knowledge on specific employment trends within their industry of focus (for example, energy, oil & gas, electronics industry, chemical, automobile and so on).

An employee referral programme is a system where existing employees recommend prospective candidates for the job offered, and if the suggested candidate is hired, the employee who referred, receives a cash bonus only if the referred employee stays with the organization for 3–6 months duration.

A *headhunter* is an industry term for a third-party recruiter who is generally considered more aggressive than in-house recruiters or may have industry experience and contacts. They may arrange a formal interview between their client and the candidate and help negotiate the salary.

To reduce costs, employers tend to undertake their own in-house recruitment, using their HR department and functional managers. One example of a successful practice of in-house recruitment is L&T group of companies. In-house trained recruiters advertise job vacancies on their company's website as well as newspapers, coordinate internal employee referrals, and work with external associations, industry groups, and focus on campus graduate recruitment.

> **Good to Know**
> Social recruiting is the use of social media such as linked-in, facebook for recruiting.

Some large employers choose to outsource all or some of their recruitment process. However, a much more common approach is for employers to introduce referral schemes where employees are encouraged to source new staff from within their own social media/network. This recruitment approach is found to be more useful as the concerned managers from the department (where the vacancy exists) are actively involved to look for what they actually searching for in the prospective candidates.

Executive research firms are the firms in the recruitment profession which are able to discover passive candidates and combine them to make new hires for their clients. They generate varying degrees of candidate information a company is looking to fill.

The sources of recruitment in public sectors are employment exchange, open advertisement, deputation from other government departments, promotion from within, transfer from other units and the like.

Despite trying all sources of recruitment, sometimes the employers are not likely to get the right candidates they are looking for, or they land up getting the poor performers, or those who quit very soon. Hence, recruitment remains an all time demanding exercise for HR departments to balance the manpower requirements across the organization.

4.5 FACTORS AFFECTING RECRUITMENT

> **Good to Know**
> The first thing to start with the recruitment is to go through the recruitment policy manual of the company.

There are several factors that would influence recruitment depending upon its three phases as mentioned below. The recruitment of the employees is done as per the procedure explained in the policy manual of the company. To understand the effectiveness of the recruitment procedure, it is essential to know the different stages involved before and after the recruitment.

Phase I: (Before Recruitment)

- Sanction of the post.
- Calling in for CVs.
- Shortlisting.
- Written Test Mathematical/Psychological/English/General Knowledge
- Interview Calls.

Phase II: (Recruitment Process)

- Shortlisting/Selection.
- Medical check-up.

- Filling up of salary data.
- Antecedent check.
- Appointment letter.
- Collection of required documents/certificates.

Phase III: (After recruitment)

- Induction and orientation of the employees.

All these three stages affect the quality of recruitment, hence this needs to be followed very stringently.

4.5.1 Campus Recruiting

Campus recruitment is a popular practice in industry each year but a great challenge for employers as well as candidates. Competition is expected to be focussed on students with degrees in business, engineering, and computer-related fields. The competitive environment makes it critical for companies to sell themselves as an employer of choice among institutions and students.

Finding the right candidates is another big challenge; positions that require stringent qualifications are difficult to fill. For example, some positions require a specific skill set, while others require that a candidate has completed specific coursework.

Attracting students to specific locations and industries is a real challenge of concern. Some employers have the difficult task of attracting candidates to locations (rural/ remote areas and areas with a high cost of living) or places which don't have adequate infrastructure such as proper roads, communication network, housing and so on.

For both employers as well as candidates, campus recruitment proves to be beneficial. Within a short span of time, the companies can explore and hire the best talented youth for them.

Instead of spending big amount on advertising vacancies, screening, and eventually selecting applicants for employment, campus recruitment offers an opportunity to hire personnel in the most cost-effective way.

It is a dream of every student to get placement after his graduation and this process of recruitment offers him an opportunity to work with some of the best industries for fulfilling their dreams. Companies come to the campus to introduce themselves and the opportunities they have to offer to the professional students.

Campus recruitment provides a platform for the organizations to meet the qualified aspirants and pick up intelligent, committed youth who have the requisite enthusiasm and zeal to prove them.

4.5.2 Applicant Assessment

Suitability for a job is typically assessed by looking for a set of skills, for example, communication, technical, social, and computer skills. Qualifications may be checked through résumés, job applications, interviews, educational or professional experience, the testimony of references, or through in-house testing or software

Good to Know

Computerized software is used by many recruitment agencies to automate the assessment process.

for assessing knowledge, typing skills, numeracy, and literacy, through psychological tests or employment testing. Other resume screening criteria may include length of service, job titles, and length of time at a previous job. In some countries, employers are legally mandated to provide equal opportunity in hiring.

References should be sought routinely as part of the selection process for all the organization´s appointments. References should never be used as the sole ground on which to base a recruitment decision as they provide a limited perspective of an individual´s abilities and performance (The University of Sheffield 2014).

Many recruiters and agencies are using an applicant tracking system to perform many of the filtering tasks, along with software tools for psychometric testing such as personality, interests, and aptitudes.

On boarding is a term which describes the process of helping new employees become aware of an organization. The young people often wish to know, before an offer of employment, various things about the company such as salary package, working environment, leave, and training opportunities. A well-planned introduction helps new employees become fully operational quickly and is often integrated with a new company environment. Many companies have on boarding campaigns to retain new talent; the campaign may last anywhere from one week to six months.

Role of Assessment Centre in Applicant Evaluation

Assessment centre typically involves the participants completing a range of exercises like psychometric testing, group exercises, and interviews and such others that are used to assess particular competencies in individuals.

Organizations select employees in a number of different ways. They will all be looking for someone who has a variety of skills (competencies), abilities, and personal qualities to do the job well but the method of selection used will vary from perhaps a single interview to an extended form of assessment generally known as an assessment centre.

A well designed assessment centre is the most effective tool available for assessing individuals in both individual and group-based environments for selection or development.

There is no such thing as a 'standard' assessment or development centre; some can last as little as half a day, while others can go on for three days or more (Iain Ballantyne and Nigel Povah 1995).

What is an Assessment/Development Centre?

Traditionally, an assessment centre consists of a set of exercises designed to assess a bunch of personal characteristics. Assessment centres typically involve the participants completing a range of exercises which simulate the activities carried out in the target job/environment. There are numerous possible competencies and the ones which are relevant to a particular job are determined through job analysis.

A development centre is a forum where a group of participants experiences simulated situations, and their preferred behaviour styles are observed by trained facilitators. Multiple trained observers and techniques are used for the participants. Observations about behaviours are made from specifically developed exercises. These observations are pooled in a meeting amongst the assessors (The British Psychological Society, 2010).

Why is G-Company Conducting Development Centres: A Case Study?

In order to meet the challenges of a constantly changing business scenario, G-Company (name changed) has always focused on strengthening and developing its human talent.

Development centres (DC) will provide an opportunity for participants to focus on and enhance their unique capabilities and at the same time explore areas of further development. These DCs will also provide a focus and direction for G-Company's people development initiatives.

The activities of assessment centre at G-Company are as follows:

- Psychometric test
- In-basket exercise
- Case study preparation
- Group discussion
- Management game

Psychometric Test

1. Aptitude tests taken under exam conditions and designed to measure thinking and reasoning skills such as numerical, verbal, and diagrammatic reasoning.
2. Personality inventories not usually timed and with no right or wrong answers, used to assess what you are like as a person and how you might react in different situations.

The assessor introduced a psychometric test in the assessment centre named Wechsler's Adult Intelligence Scale (WAIS) which is divided into two parts, i.e., one as verbal IQ (WAIS) and the other as performance IQ (WAPIS).

The Wechsler Adult Intelligence Scale (WAIS) was developed by Wechsler in 1955. An updated version of the scale (WAIS-R) was developed in 1981. WAIS measures global or general intelligence and is commonly used by psychologists. It is divided into two parts: the verbal scale and the performance scale. Each of these parts is further divided into subtests each of which taps a specific verbal or non-verbal skill. Each subtest has items ranging from easy to increasingly more difficult.

The WAIS is composed of eleven tests—six verbal and five non-verbal. The verbal and non-verbal groups may be administered separately or together to yield, respectively, a verbal, and a performance section of a full scale IQ. This feature permits one to use the performance section of the scale alone with subjects who are unable to comprehend or manage language, or the verbal section alone with subjects who are visually or motorically handicapped. More importantly, the use of both verbal and performances tests together afford those additional ways to demonstrate their capabilities, and their examiners a greater opportunity to assess the abilities which the tests are designed to appraise.

The individual tests below are grouped according to the scale to which they are assigned.

Verbal Scale	Performance Scale
Information	Picture completion
Digit span	Picture arrangement
Vocabulary	Block design
Arithmetic	Object assembly
Comprehension	Digit symbol
Similarities	

The verbal IQ is derived from scores on seven of the subtests: information, digit span, vocabulary, arithmetic, comprehension, similarities, and letter-number sequencing. Letter-number sequencing is a new subtest added to the most recent edition of the WAIS (WAIS-III).

The performance IQ is derived from scores on the remaining seven subtests: picture completion, picture arrangement, block design, object assembly, digit symbol, matrix reasoning, and symbol search. Matrix reasoning and symbol search are new subtests and were added to the most recent edition of the WAIS-III.

In-Basket Exercise

In the in-basket technique, the participant is presented with numerous background materials so that he may become familiar with the organizational situation. They may include such items as financial statements, organizational chart, job description, formal position papers, and informal items such as descriptions of the personalities and performance of other characters in the test situation. Once a player is familiar with the situation, the exercise itself is started. Each player is presented with a group of letters, reports, notes, and related items which have presumably accumulated in the in–basket of the hypothetical manager. He is then asked to take any actions he deems appropriate with the in–basket items within a limited time period.

The in-basket game also includes a procedure which allows players to explain their actions. The player's actions are either (1) scored in some manner, or (2) reviewed with him by an interviewer or instructor, or by a group fellow player, or both.

One of the advantages of the in-basket game is that it can be designed either to focus on the activities that are part of all executive positions, or to emphasize certain specific aspects (Gary, Groth-Marnat 1997).

In-basket Interview

There are many ways for assessing an in-basket exercise such as games or role-play, whereas G-Company uses an exercise called in-basket interview in which the candidates have to prioritize their things from the in-box in 30 minutes only. The interview is conducted to see how they prioritize the items and how well they can express themselves during the interview.

Case Study Preparation

A case study samples real-life incidents or cases for the primary purpose of learning.

A case study presents a sample of business environment, so that it may be studied in detail. Trainees learn to get the most out of sometimes limited data by asking effective questions. The objective diagnosis of causes and alternative solutions broadens participants' understanding and provides an improved guide to action.

A case study analyses and debate, as well as exposure to the experience and opinions of other trainee managers, helps participants to realize that there are several ways of looking at, thinking about, and acting in a particular business situation.

Using case studies is a convenient means of exposing candidates/participants to a diversity of business situations and problems during a training course.

Group Discussion (GD)

As the term itself suggests, a group discussion is a discussion on a topic. But most candidates misconstrue it to be a debate and that is precisely where they falter. Consequently, you find a fish market kind of situation in most GDs. What is however expected is a candidate's participation in a systematic discussion on a particular topic. GDs are to be conducted to find out whether you possess the critical qualities to become an effective manager. GD measures:

- Ability to interact in a team
- Communication skills
- Reasoning
- Leadership skills
- Initiatives
- Assertiveness
- Flexibility
- Nurturing ability
- Creativity
- Ability to think on one's feet
- Body language
- Self-confidence
- Team skills
- Listening skills
- Ability to present the views logically
- Time management

At G-Company there are different topics for GD which are used according to the candidate's level or cadre. Here is an example of deputation abroad.

Deputation Abroad

G-Company is planning to expand its operations in European Union and is thus keen on deputing its good performing employees to be a country manager in Germany with a view to developing takeover responsibilities in its foreign business.

You are a member of the screening committee appointed to select one person. Your committee has to decide and recommend the most appropriate person. There are four persons recommended for deputation and their belief details are attached.

You will have 10 minutes to read this material and another 20 minutes for the meeting. Please note that you cannot make any assumption that is not based on the facts provided here.

Also the case for group discussion which is - The nuclear war problem which says that India and Pakistan are currently at war and there are situations and some data are given. The group has to decide or suggest on which Indian city would Pakistan attack with the nuclear weapon.

Case for Group Discussion: The Nuclear War Problem

India and Pakistan are currently at war. You are all members of the war cabinet of Pakistan, reporting to General Musharraf. Given that the war with India is not going very well for him, the General has decided to use the nuclear option.

Unfortunately for him, Pakistan has only one nuclear warhead and the General has to decide which Indian city he will use this weapon on. In order to help him with this decision, he turns to his war cabinet — you all.

The data available for making such a decision is in terms of probability of success for each city (what are the chances that an attack be successful) as also the percentage of destruction that will be wrought on the city if the attack is successful.

Name of city	*Probability of success*	*Percentage of destruction*
New Delhi	60%	75%
Mumbai	70%	65%
Chennai	50%	90%
Kolkata	40%	80%
Bengaluru	80%	100%
Hyderabad	60%	100%
Ahmedabad	90%	100%
Kanpur	60%	100%
Pune	70%	100%
Ambala	100%	100%

Based on the above data, the task before your group is to arrive at a consensus advising General Musharraf on which Indian city he should attack with the nuclear weapon.

Management Game

This is a training technique in which participants, grouped into teams, consider a sequence of problems and organize themselves to make decisions. It is defined as a sequential decision-making exercise structured around a hypothetical model of an organization's operations, in which participants assume roles in managing the simulated operations. It's most crucial aspect is an attempt to reproduce the social, psychological, and economic dynamics of organizational behaviour in an artificial setting.

1. The purpose of management games is to increase a person's understanding of specific organizational problems (marketing, production, and others).
2. The interrelatedness of the functions and parts of an organization and its relation to its environment
3. The problems of organization policy and decision making
4. The problems of working in a team.

Management Games at G-Company

G-Company has many management games which they normally use in the assessment centre (H.L. Kaila 2007). Some of them are as follows:

- Straw game
- Mela (attract the people)
- Egg game

The candidates were given some material such as newspapers, balloons, threads, and such others, and then were told that they would be given 15 minutes and their task was to make something such that if the egg is thrown from the first floor it does not break.

Also they had to make a tower of those materials such that if egg is placed on it then the egg should not break.

Interviews at G-Company

Interviews at assessment centres can be one-to-one or panel interviews. Questions may refer back to your first interview, to the assessment centre activities, or to the aptitude test results. The interviewer may be from the department to which you are applying and the questioning will be more in-depth and probing at this stage.

Assessment Rating

G-Company assessors rate the candidates on general basis for the simplicity as follows:

2 marks: If the candidate is poor.

4 marks: If the candidate is ok.

6 marks: If the candidate is good.

8 marks: If the candidate is excellent.

A study done by A. Keenan (1976) on the 'Effect of non-verbal behavior of interviewers on candidate's performances' is an important aspect in recruitment. In order to have an optimal or an effective evaluation of an candidate, it is important to create approving non-verbal cues from the interviewer's point of view because it helps to evaluate the candidate in a much better way. A. Keenan's study proves that by allowing approving non-verbal style it helps candidate to be at ease and talk more about them.

In his study it is observed that non-verbal approval was operationalized as smiles, positive head nods, and eye contact. Non-verbal disapproval was defined as frowns, head shaking, and avoidance of eye contact. This study has shown that the non-verbal style of interview in a mock selection interview can influence the behaviour of the candidates as perceived by neutral observers. Non-verbal approval results in a candidate being better able to create a good impression, perhaps because he feels more relaxed and at ease under these circumstances. Although creating a good impression only on non-verbal approving style is possible because the candidate is not only at ease but also feels confident in order to put across his point of view. He thinks that he has created a positive impact on the interviewer and the probability of him getting selected will be high because of the approval style of non-verbal recruitment technique that has been used. But creating a good impression and the candidate's competence are two different things. Creating a good impression is based on or rather it's an outcome of the recruiting style used by interviewer but competence is the utmost base of the selection over which the other aspects build up.

Why employers use assessment centres

The companies use assessment centres for the following reasons:

- They are considered to be the fairest and most accurate methods of selecting staff.
- Selectors are able to see you over a longer period of time than in a single interview.
- The wide range of activities and situations enable them to see what you can do rather than what you say you can do.
- Each exercise is designed to assess a clearly defined set of competencies, for example, technical knowledge, leadership, creativity, and flexibility. You are measured on these competencies and not against the other candidates.

Some important psychometric tests are listed below along with their diverse use/ application in organizations.

List of psychometric tests	*Use of these tests*
16 PF by Cattell [16 Personality Factors]	This test can be used for pre-employment testing as well as a tool for assessing training and development needs in an individual. This helps one to become more aware of one's strengths and weaknesses and work on them accordingly.
FIRO- B	The instrument helps define your leadership style and show how one might develop it by examining the following three aspects of your interpersonal relationship—how much you include others and want them to include you, your need for control, and your need for warm and affectionate relationship.

ASUFA [Attribution of Success and Failure]	This test is usually used for training and development purposes. This measures whether the individual attributes his success and failure to internal or external factors. This then helps the trainer to help the individual change his attribution in a way so as to take responsibility, thus having a higher degree of internal locus of control.
M.B.T.I. based on the theory of Jung	This instrument is most widely used in the organization. It is used to form teams with people who have different personalities and preferences so that there is sufficient diversity to solve group problems.
B.D.I. [Brain Dominance Inventory]	This test is a measure of creativity in a subtle way. The hemisphere of the brain that is dominant in an individual will help determine his innovation and also his style of thinking. The trainer can then focus on attaining whole brain thinking by pointing out the pros and cons of either of the dominant hemispheres. This test can also point out why the person is not functioning to the point in a certain area, due to lack of creativity.
OCTAPACE	This is an organization culture test and is very useful for team building. This test assesses the individuals view on light organizational parameters. The areas where the individual rates the team low are the areas where they could work in order to enhance team effectiveness. This test can also be used by the organization to assess the employee's view of the organization.
SPIRO-M. [Styles Profile for Interaction Roles in Organizations for Managers]	This test is based on the theory of transactional analysis. It determines the dominant ego state in which the individual works. This helps to understand the reason for the individual's reaction in a particular situation. If the test is also filled in by subordinates keeping the manager in mind, it can make one aware of the perception gap that may exist in the way the manager views himself and the way the subordinates view him.
MAO-B. [Motivational Analysis of Organizational Behaviour]	The behaviour of a manager or employee can be analysed not only in terms of the six primary motives but also from the perspective of positive approach or negative avoidance reflected by hope or fear, respectively. For HRD purposes, the result can be used to help individuals and the group plan the increase in effectiveness in their respective roles.
J.S.S. [Job Satisfaction Survey]	This test can be used by the management to check if the employee is satisfied with the job. This exercise done by the management will show the employee that the management is interested in the employee and respects the employee. This, in turn, will boost the employee's morale and will also reduce the attrition rate in the organization.

TEAM [Team Effectiveness Assessment Measure]	This test measures the way the team is performing and also gives an idea of the way the members view the team. The team also sees which members are unable to perform and also gives a brief view of the reason of the underperformance.
M.L.Q. [Multifactor Leadership Questionnaire]	This test helps to assess the dominant leadership style in which the individual functions. Taking this into consideration the organization can determine which would be the team in which one's leadership trait would be most effective. It also helps rationalize the way the individual behaves with the internal and external customers and the subordinates.

Some of these tests can be used for recruitment purposes as they help in screening the right candidate along with other tests such as general intelligence (GI), which assesses the candidate on his/her intelligence. The other tests which can be used while selecting the candidate is a test which measures his core competencies, that is, his competency in the area for the field that he is to be chosen for. Other psychometric tests can also be used to assess the training and developmental areas of candidates. These tests are to be used as a background to identify the specific areas where training is needed.

4.5.3 Nature and Importance of Selection

The employee selection in organizations is considered to be one of the most relevant of HR processes. What to look for in an applicant and how to assess that is very important so as to select the right person. Selecting a high performer for the job is tough for any assessor. At the same time, the rationale for not selecting an applicant is equally relevant.

The important parameters to be looked for in an individual candidate for selection are as follows:

Sr. No	*Personnel specifications*	*Technical knowledge*	*Others*
1.	Educational qualification	Knowledge related to job	Social awareness
2.	Emotional quotient and intelligence quotient	Experience in particular field	Past service records
3.	Ethics and values	Knowledge of systems and procedures	Reason for leaving previous job
4.	Personality and attitude	Areas of interest	Teamwork
5.	Confidence level		

In addition, attention to the following aspects could help the management in making the selection procedure even more effective.

- Involve members from other related departments other than HR in order to check the candidate's competency in that related field so as to get the right person as per the job description.

- At least three people should conduct the interview and it should be pre-decided who will look after what aspect of the candidate. For example, the HR will look after his presentation, ability to answer, and other soft skills. The others should look after his knowledge related to that specific field and knowledge about that field in general.
- The questions asked during the interviews (see Interview Assessment Form in appendix) should deal with a variety of skills and the technical knowledge which he/she possesses and should also give emphasis on the personnel specification/ candidates profile (in terms of physique, intelligence, aptitude, qualifications, experience and so on) in order to make interpretations about a person's behaviour and personality and arrive at a proper decision.
- The interview time, date, and venue to be intimated to the interviewer and interviewee at least three days in advance.
- The interviewers should be given a list of all those to be interviewed on a particular day at a particular time and no candidate should be entertained after that.
- Security and reception offices should be informed in advance to make necessary arrangements.
- Proper communication to be given to the interviewee pertaining to travelling expenses in cases where they are not borne by the company.
- Shortlisted candidates should be communicated the date of final interview at least three days in advance.
- Once the candidate is shortlisted after the final interview the other formalities should be completed in a day and all his/her certificates should be verified properly.
- Referred cases to be accepted only if they are able to meet the minimum level and job requirement.

4.5.4 Selection Process/Procedure

Selection is the most crucial activity in organizational HR processes in which all those people are involved to whom the selected person would matter, which means the specific department where he/she is going to work, the HR department who is coordinating the selection process.

Specifically, selection process is a procedure for filling a vacancy. Whenever a position falls vacant in an organization, the following procedure is observed:

1. Sanction for the post should be checked up with the organization chart.
2. Locate suitable human resources from the following sources:
   - Advertisement in newspapers.
   - Scrutinizing application bank.
   - Placement consultants.
   - Employment exchange.
   - Any other source.

3. The text of advertisement (qualification/experience) should be consulted with the respective department head.
4. Management's sanction should be obtained for releasing the advertisement.
5. Check up whether funds exist in the budget for releasing the advertisement in newspapers.
6. Code number and description of the post should be given in the advertisement, if necessary.
7. Release advertisement: The advertisement as released in the newspaper should be checked with the approval given to the advertisement agency/newspaper.
8. The bill for advertisement agency/ newspaper should be passed as per the terms and conditions of the company's advertisement agency/newspaper.
9. Check-up for budgetary provision for giving placements, consultants' fee.

The applications received should be scrutinized with respect to qualifications, experience, age and the like. Some selected applications will be shortlisted and be called for interview.

Candidates selected for the interview will be sent telegram/letter/orally requesting them to attend interview. Travel allowance/dearness allowance will be paid as per company policy.

Interview schedule should be prepared and the concerned HoD should be intimated about the interview candidates.

The following papers should be kept ready:

Application form filled by candidates.

1. Bio-data of candidate.
2. Xerox copy of Certificates in support of educational qualifications/experience.
3. Appraisal Form (filled in by personnel).

When candidates are interviewed, suitable endorsement on the appraisal form as to the suitability or otherwise should be obtained from concerned HoD/DGM (P&A). The applications with endorsement 'Keep Pending' should be maintained by the personnel department.

The selection board members should sign in the appraisal form.

Candidates selected should be given a appointment order detailing the terms and conditions upon which they are appointed.

Candidates should be given an appointment letter in duplicate. One copy will be retained by the candidate and acknowledging receipt of the other copy in token of the receipt of the appointment letter will be kept by the organization. The candidate should mention the likely date of joining.

All associates joining the company should submit a joining report. The requirements in the joining report should be complied with.

Appointment letter should be sent to the selected candidates by registered post or by courier.

Training of associates has acquired importance in the context of change of technology, change in consumer behaviour and the like. The personnel department should educate the associates throughout the company. 'Training' is not a one-time activity. It is an on-going activity.

The object of training is to enhance knowledge, skills, and attitudes of associates. Keeping this in view the company should formulate 'training policy' which aims at enhancement of human potential. Trained employees are assets of a company.

Every good organization on its part must employ a selection process in which justice is not only seen to be given, but it is given. Selection must be fair, unbiased, and above all in tandem with the requirements of the company's goals.

4.5.5 Orientation of New Employees

Once the selection process is complete, the new employee must be inducted in order to make a productive contribution to the organization. An induction or orientation programme is a must as it makes a new employee comfortable in the new situations.

It covers all the newly joined employees at managerial and staff category. The Induction Training Manual giving complete information of the company, is given to the employees who join the company. Manager (HR) is responsible for the implementation and governance of this procedure. The MR (management representative) and manager (HR) reviews the procedure and its amendments prior to its approval.

Procedure for orientation of new employees: HR department completes all the joining formalities as per the checklist below:

- It gets all the legal formalities such as PF nomination and Declaration form, gratuity nomination forms, superannuating forms and such other completed.
- A communication mentioning brief details about the new employees is prepared and circulated to all the HoD's by HR department.
- HR department introduces the new employees to the HoD's and other staff of the company.
- New employees are provided with the information about the company such as product range, product features, competitor, market, volumes, future plans, and so on.
- HR department provides information on policy matters, systems, and procedures of the company to the new employees.
- New employees are introduced to the CEO.
- The HR department makes an arrangement of providing orientation to various departments.

4.5.6 Recruitment and Selection Process at a Power Company in Mumbai: A Case

In the earliest stages of recruitment decisions, right people are selected for long-term roles including middle and senior management. The integrity of the recruitment and selection process helps to ensure sustainability by building a strong and balanced team, demonstrating the organization's neutrality, promoting its good name, and serving as an example for partners (H.L. Kaila 2007).

The six-stage model used at the power company for its recruitment and selection process was:

1. **Defining the Requirement**

   Decide what vacancy you have. If you need to fill a new role quickly you might find it helpful to adapt one of the models provided here.

   Task analysis: Draw up a detailed list of tasks that the person will have to do. This helps in determining the qualities and qualifications genuinely required for the job.

   Job description: Produce an outline of the broad responsibilities (rather than detailed tasks) involved in the job.

   Person specification: Decide what skills, experience, qualifications, and attributes someone will need to do the job as defined in the task analysis and job description.

2. **Attracting Applications**

   Your file of previous applicants can be a good place to start.

   Advertising: Phrase your announcement in a way that makes clear what the job involves and the type of person needed. You can display a notice internally and/or at your gate, in the local newspaper, or with a message on the local radio station.

   Application form: A well-designed form can elicit information about the person's ability and willingness to do the job. Make it clear on the form that applicants should consider the points in the job description and person description when applying.

3. **Selection**

   Select your candidate. Be objective and unbiased. Choose the person who best fits your specification.

   Shortlisting: Assess applications on the basis of the person specification (standard forms can be very helpful at this stage). Guard against bias and discrimination – ensure that you select for interview those who match the specifications, regardless of age, sex, race, and other parameters and that the specifications are not themselves discriminatory.

   Interviews: Interview your shortlisted candidates. Remember that your job is not only to assess the best candidate for the job, but also to create a great impression of your organization.

   The amount and quality of the information will be largely due to the effectiveness of your questions. Use open questions (for example, tell me about...how you... why did you...talk me through...do) and probe from the general to the specific.

4. **Candidate Assessments**

   The interview will provide you with some information but check it out before offering a job. Ways in which you could do this include:

- Ask the candidate to show you examples of previous work, do a presentation, a case study, some tests or full assessment. Tests can be done before the interview or after the interview. It depends on the number of candidates being interviewed and the type of job.
- Taking up references: You must have the specific permission of the applicant to do so, particularly if you wish to contact their current employer. If you need them quickly, try phoning.

5. Making a Job Offer: Job offer is made through a letter of appointment. Such a letter generally contains a date by which the appointee must report on duty.
6. Induction: To help your new recruit to settle in quickly and become productive as soon as possible.

4.5.7 A Case of Recruitment Process at an Electrical Engineering Industry

Bharat Limited is one of the leaders in the electrical engineering industry in India. A multi-product, multi-divisional organization, its main business segments are transformers, projects, electric motors, elevator systems and drives. The company's manufacturing facilities are located in Mumbai (H.L. Kaila 2007).

The recruitment process in Bharat Limited starts with the manpower requisitions provided by the respective heads of the departments to the HR. These are forwarded to HR head, VP, and Divisional VP for their approval. Based on their approvals, final manpower plan is prepared, with the final sanctioning of the MD. As per the priority and need of the departments, HR decides the sources from which the candidates are to be searched. They usually opt for walk-ins and the Employment Exchange for worker class. For the skilled employee mostly walk-ins, job portals, and advertisements are used. To recruit higher level managers, consultant agencies are used. Job portals were the best source for recruitment. The resumes are then shortlisted by the department heads of the respective departments and the HR, and then the candidates are called in for an interview.

The interview process consists of two rounds. The first round is with the HR and the HoD where there is a technical interview, and general HR interview. The second round is the panel interview with the VP of the division, HR, and HoD. In case of a senior position, the MD also joins the panel in the second round. For the finance department recruitment, a written test for mathematics is taken. An individual assessment sheet for the interview is maintained. Accordingly, the person who is most suited for the position is selected and the position is considered closed when the new employee joins. The target recruitment cycle is of 90 working days.

Medical check-up of the selected candidate is conducted by the company before he/she joins, but for senior level managers it is conducted in certain hospitals. All the formalities related to the physical resources like sitting arrangement, system allocation and such others are taken care of by the respective departments one day prior to the day of joining.

On the first day of joining the new joinee is given information of the organization, its history, its departments and the like. The new joinee has to fill certain forms like application form, employee data form, PF, insurance. Then over a week's time the new joinee is taken to all the departments of the organization and given information and trained by the respective departments for different processes.

SUMMARY

- Employee recruitment and selection in organizations is an all time challenging process and a profound concern for HR as well as functional managers.
- This chapter comprehends the importance and implications of one of most important functions – the employee recruitment and selection – of HR department in organizations.
- The main aspects included are the purpose, the process of recruiting, the sources/ techniques of recruitment, the factors affecting recruitment, campus recruiting, and the applicant assessment (including assessment centre), the nature, process and importance of employee selection, and the importance of orientation of new employees.
- The cases of recruitment and selection process are also included.
- A detailed interview assessment form is appended.

EXERCISE FOR CLASSROOM PRACTICE

For better understanding of the subject matter of this chapter, please read and check each of the following statements whether True (T) or False (F) or Uncertain (U):

1. The proper beginning to a recruitment process is to perform a job analysis and to document the intended requirements of the job to be performed.
2. Recruitment relates to all the activities and practices of attracting and identifying potential employees from a pool of applicants.
3. Recruitment and selection are two of the most vital functions of human resources management.
4. Identifying a wrong source for recruitment would often delay the process.
5. The first thing to start with the recruitment is to go through the Recruitment Policy Manual of the company.
6. Attracting candidates to specific locations for employment is a real challenge for companies.
7. Campus recruitment provides a platform for the organizations to meet the qualified aspirants.
8. 'On boarding' is a process of helping new employees move upward in an organization.
9. Assessment centre would mean to train people for psychometric testing and interviews.

10. The development centre is a forum where a group of participants experience simulated situations.
11. The companies use assessment centres as they are considered to be the fairest and most accurate methods of selecting staff.
12. Training is a one-time activity, not an on-going process as it is costly.

Answers: All statements are **True** except that statement numbers 8, 9, and 12 are **False**.

REVIEW QUESTIONS FOR DISCUSSIONS/EXAMINATIONS

1. Critically discuss the purpose of recruiting in organizations.
2. Describe various techniques of recruitment.
3. Write a short note on the factors affecting recruitment.
4. Discuss the process of recruitment and the applicant assessment (including psychological tests, assessment centres).
5. Briefly describe the nature and importance of employee selection.
6. Compare and contrast the selection process of three organizations.
7. Critically emphasize the importance of orientation of new employees.
8. Address the specific skills to conduct selection interviewing.
9. Reflect upon how to *select* and retain the best talent for your organization
10. Investigate the processes of recruitment practised in your organization.

FIELD RESEARCH REPORT

This is a research assignment section for students for their internal marking by the teacher during the semester. This assignment is for understanding practical applications of the subject.

An action research project: Identify a group of minimum 15 executives and 15 non-executives across an organization preferably where you are placed for an internship. Conduct interviews with them by using a set of closed/open-ended questionnaire to signify the issues and concerns pertaining to the recruitment and selection processes. Prepare a report of about 15 pages reflecting an action plan for better work practices.

REFERENCES

Anil, Kaushik (2013). 'Editor's Note: Becoming Better', *Business Manager*, October.

Ashwathappa, K. (1997). Human Resource and Personnel Management, (4th edition). New Delhi: Tata McGraw-Hill.

Ballantyne, Iain and Nigel Povah (1995). *Assessment and Development Centres.* London: Gower Publication Ltd.

Barber, A.E. (1998). *Recruiting Employees. Thousand Oaks,* CA: Sage Publications.

Busby, Jonathan (2013). Recruitment and Selection of Employees. 1, February 2013. Retrieved 9 June 2013. http://www.studymode.com/essays/recruitment-and-selection-of-employees-1433763.html

Flippo, Edwin B. (1961). *Personnel Management.* New York: McGraw-Hill.

Groth-Marnat, Gary (1997). *Handbook of Psychological Assessment,* 3rd edition. New York: John Wiley and Sons,

Kaila, H.L. (2007). *Organizational Behavior & HRM.* 2nd edition, Delhi: AITBS Publishers.

Keenan, A. (1976). 'Effects of the Non-verbal Behavior of Interviewers on Candidates' performance'. *Journal of Occupational Psychology,* 49, 171–176.

Rynes, S.L. and D.M. Cable (2003). Recruitment Research in the Twenty-first Century. Borman, in W.C. and D.R. Ilgen (eds.), *Handbook of Industrial and Organizational Psychology,* 12: 55–76. New York: Wiley.

The British Psychological Society (2010). *Assessment & Development Centres: Best Practice Guidelines.* London.

The University of Sheffield (2014). Human Resources. Retrieved on 6 May 2014. https://www.sheffield.ac.uk/hr/recruitment/guidance/references.

APPENDIX

Interview Assessment Form

Name of the Applicant: Age:

Position Applied For: Qualification:

Interviewer's Name:

Date and Venue:

Please tick mark in the columns possible. Only mark in one column. Scale ranging from 1 to 5, 1 being the highest and five being the lowest.

Selection criteria	*Excellent*	*Good*	*Average*	*Below average*	*Comments*
Marketing Skill					
Job Knowledge					
Computer Savvy					
Arithmetic					
Customer Orientation					
Organize Planning					
Attention to Detail					
Innovative					
Decision Making					
Team Player					
Problem Solving					

Result Oriented					
Communication Skills					
Adaptability					
TOTAL					
Overall Assessment					

Suggested Areas of Improvement:

FINAL RECOMMENDATION (please tick)

( ) Selected ( ) Wait-listed ( ) Not suitable for the post

Signature of Panel Members:			
Division/Dept.			

Notes

1. Arithmetic refers to mathematical power.
2. Communication skills refer to both written as well as oral communication. It refers to articulated ideas that are clear and concise. It also includes listening skills.
3. Adaptability refers to be flexible with people around and in situations.

Some Key/Relevant Questions for Selection Interview

1. When competition is tough in the market regarding the same product you are dealing with, what will be your business strategy?
2. A customer is upset with you and our company and wants to deal with your competitor. How will you deal with him?
3. Why this job is important to you and what do you know about this job?
4. Do you know how to use Microsoft Office?
5. What is PPT and MIS XL?
6. What is rate of interest, insurance and loan?
7. You had an argument with our potential customer and he is denying dealing with our company? How would you handle?
8. Customer and boss are always right. Who is important for you to survive in the company?
9. How important is time management for you? Give us some situations where you were an effective time managers.
10. A customer submitted a few documents and they are not available and this particular customer is very important to us as well as documents. How would you manage?
11. Give us five important things you noticed while coming to office.
12. How will you generate business with your x-customer?

13. You are already busy with work and you are asked to handle another project. How would you deal with this situation?
14. Why the team is important or sometimes it's best to work alone?
15. Give us a scenario that was challenging for you. How did you manage it?
16. Why it is important to be a patient listener?
17. One of your important team member is sick and you have a deadline to complete your task, how will you deal with it?
18. Is MBA quite hyped up in India?
19. Studies or money, what is your choice?

Scoring Key for these Questions

Questions	*Competencies/Attributes/Traits*
questions 1 and 2	Marketing skills
question 3	Job knowledge
questions 4 and 5	Computer savvy
question 6	Arithmetic
questions 7 and 8	Customer orientation
question 9	Organize planning
questions 10 and 11	Attention to detail
questions 12 and 13	Innovative and decision making
question 14	Team player
questions 15 and 16	Problem solving
questions 17 and 18	Result oriented, communication, adaptability

Each competency is mapped as the above question ratings were given on scale ranging from 1 to 5, 1 being the highest and 5 being the lowest. Then sum the rating followed by getting the mean of each candidate's benchmark of 3.5 and above is taken to next level. Extra care is taken in order to avoid personal interviewer's biased judgment. Mean value is taken into consideration based on the rating a candidate receives on the assessment form.

5

Training and Development

Learning Objectives

This chapter would help the readers:

- to be familiar with the concepts of identifying training needs;
- to acquaint with methods for conducting training needs assessment;
- to understand the business values and etiquette in organizations;
- to recognize various techniques of training;
- to be aware about evaluation of training; and
- to reflect upon a case study about identifying training needs.

An Opening Story: Challenges of a Training Professional

A newly trained postgraduate in Organizational Psychology, who had no experience in industrial training, joined his first job in a national training institute in Mumbai. He was asked to take training classes but every time he felt inadequate while interacting with experienced industry engineers from various organizations who were nominated for training in psychology areas such as employee counselling, psychological testing, employee motivation, and other fields. Though these topics are not new to any Organizational Psychology professional, a fresh trainer would lack in experience and exposure to the real work life practices, hence would fall short in giving any industrial work-related examples. Therefore, he experienced frustration in fulfilling his job tasks with much low satisfaction. Since he was open to learn the art of training, one day he approached his senior colleague and asked him as how best to deliver a training class. He explained that a trainer must prepare his presentation in a particular order and sequence and rehearse thoroughly, and he should follow this presentation order in the class. He must prepare the slide material what he is confident about to explain and should not put any material what he cannot justify to the training participants. He followed this advice but it took many years for him to develop the confidence level to deliver in class while interacting with a variety of participants right from workmen to executives to senior to top management level. After many years of training experience, now he enjoys every training class as much as the people who attend it. It requires a lot of preparation such as training methodology, use of videos, practical examples, and field observation in order to make a training presentation an interesting and truly meaningful and useful for organizations.

5.1 INTRODUCTION

There are three main elements for the success and excellence in training and development: the trainees, the trainers, and the training materials. In addition, the sub-elements of training are important such as time, place of the training programme and the logistic services related to multimedia training tools, room facilities, training tools and such others (Reference-rcd 2014).

Training and development (T&D) or training for development is a value perception which helps any trainer or organization to set and achieve training goals. Training and development are inseparable entities. Many organizations now regard T&D function as learning and development (L&D). Some organizations would like to be labelled as learning organizations such as Larsen & Toubro (L&T) which is widely known as learning and training organization as it believes in this concept so much so that learning and training is a regular experience for its employees and contract workmen. L&T management want training to be more stimulating, engaging, and motivational.

Training becomes learning only when it is implemented during the course of work, failing which people who undergo training tend to forget it fast and it results into loss of training and loss of investment on part of an organization.

Even the best training plan or package loses its value if it does not get the management emphasis, which means that all the training initiatives must have the involvement and leadership from the HoDs as well as everyone whom this training matters right from the level of the design of training so that it gets implemented smoothly for better results pertaining to business performance goals. Many managers have the habit of not devoting time in developing their team members and, in turn, expect outstanding results.

From the organizational viewpoint, training shortens the time required for the employees to reach peak efficiency levels. Essentially, training contributes significantly in increasing the quality and quantity of work. Thus, we can see that training and development remains an integral part of a company. But in order for training to be effective, not only should it be well planned but it should also be result oriented and based on identification/analysis of training needs (Chaterjee 1999).

According to Elaine Biech (2012), the successful and the best organizations are those that happen to be the ones with the highest commitment to training and development.

5.2 TRAINING NEEDS ANALYSIS

> **Good to Know**
> A training need exists when the organization requires a change in performance.

The needs assessment process can be thought of as a type of organizational intervention (Muchinsky 2000). To design an effective training system, the training department requires information from various departments to understand the performance gaps or changes. Cooperation of employees is of utmost importance in a needs assessment exercise.

According to French and Bell (1999), if top leadership does not clearly understand the goals and strategies of the needs assessment, then the procedure may become vulnerable to the natural ups and downs that accompany any organizational intervention.

Thus, it would not make sense for either an outside consultant or a member of the in-house training staff to design a plan for the training department without understanding the organization's future goals.

Bennis (1969) emphasizes that it is extremely important to gain a hierarchical umbrella of acceptance (from top to bottom) if the needs assessment process is to succeed. One way to achieve this umbrella of acceptance is to set up a liaison team consisting from the organization who serves as the primary contact between the assessor and the organization.

Training needs analysis forms the first step before designing any training programme.

For carrying out an objective identification of such training concerns or areas, McGhee and Thayer's model (Saiyadain 2009) advocated a multi-pronged approach such as organizational analysis, task analysis, person analysis, resource analysis, and requirements analysis as described below:

5.2.1 Organizational Analysis

Organizational analysis refers to an examination of organizational goals, resources of the organization, climate for training present in the environment, and the like (Davis 1990).

Many organizations seek organizational climate surveys to assess this stage to decide training intervention. Normally, organizational development (OD) consultants are invited for this purpose.

The scope of the organizational analysis depends upon a number of variables including who is to be trained, what type of training is contemplated, the size of the organization, and so on.

5.2.2 Task Analysis

Task analysis results in a statement of the critical activities or work operations performed on the job and the conditions under which the job is performed.

The organizational analysis and task analysis provide a picture of the task and the environmental setting. However, task analysis provides a specification of the required job operation but does not provide information concerning the KSAs required to perform the tasks. (Torrington and Hall 1998).

> **Good to Know**
> The content and method of delivery of training for KSAs are likely to differ for each work-unit.

Knowledge (K): It is the foundation on which abilities and skills are built. It should be noted that possession of knowledge does not ensure that it will be used.

Skill (S): Skill refers to the capability to perform job operations with ease and precision. Most often skills refer to psychomotor activities required for effective job operations.

Ability (A): Ability usually refers to cognitive capabilities necessary to perform a job function. Most often abilities require the application of some knowledge base.

5.2.3 Person Analysis

As opposed to the task analysis, the concentration here is on the individual employee, his abilities, his skills, his knowledge and attitude, as also the inputs required for the job performance.

The difference between the desired performance and actual performance can be assessed (Sarma 2000) by a variety of indicators such as:

- Individual performance data
- Observation at place of work
- Performance records
- Interviews with superiors/supervisors
- Work sampling
- Diagnostic psychological tests

5.2.4 Resource Analysis

This analysis should include a description of the equipment and financial resources available for implementation of training. Every training project shall have manpower and financial implications.

More important, human resource needs to include personnel planning that projects future requirements.

If the training is organized company-wide, it requires a very stringent scheduling failing which the number of participants required for each training batch may not meet and in such cases training programmes may get under-utilized.

5.2.5 Requirements Analysis

Requirements analysis is basically an examination of the details that must be made clear in order for the assessment procedure to function properly. The points that must be addressed in a requirement analysis (Muchinsky 2000) include the following topics:

The first goal of the requirements analysis is to understand the organization so that decisions concerning how phases of the needs assessment should be conducted can be determined.

Information on previous needs assessment of many series of jobs is available from government sources and from other work organizations, if they have needs assessment materials available.

There is also substantial material describing training programmes and other aspects of the organizations. It includes catalogues and descriptions prepared by the organization itself.

While the training needs are being identified so meticulously, there is a serious concern here for managers who put too much effort into the acquisition of knowledge/

skill and not enough in what happens afterwards in terms of development. To find out whether individuals were behaving in a manner consistent with the training depends largely upon organizational support, climate, and leadership of the management at all levels.

> **Good to Know**
> A training needs analysis identifies performance areas within an organization where training should be applied for development of employees for fulfilment of business objectives.

5.3 METHODS FOR TRAINING NEEDS ASSESSMENT

Each method for training needs assessment (TNA) has unique characteristics that can affect both the kind and quality of the information obtained.

Following are the methods that can be utilized to collect information regarding the existing knowledge, skills and abilities of employees (Peterson 1999):

- **Observation:** This method can be used normatively to distinguish between effective and ineffective behaviours, organizational structures, and/or processes by observing individuals or group of people.
- **Questionnaires:** The questionnaires can be made keeping in mind a specific audience with specific content and a use of both open and closed questions. Normally, this method is used for organizational climate surveys.
- **Consultations:** Data can be gathered from the key people who are in a position to know what the training needs of a particular group are, by using techniques such as interviews, group discussions, and focus group discussions.
- **Work Sampling:** It is like observing people at work. Work samples generate written responses from the workmen, supervisors, managers and other employees.
- **Document Review:** Documents such as a performance reviews, accidents data, injury records, absenteeism/production statistics, and job description may be utilized.
- **Group Discussions:** The group discussions may use group facilitating techniques such as brainstoming, organizational mirroring, simulation and such others.
- **Management Requests:** Training facilitator may be requested by heads of departments or top executives to design a specific training programme, which they perceive to be useful, and would fulfil the training requirements assessed by them.

5.4 IMPORTANCE OF TRAINING REQUIREMENT

Training is a central tool to achieve the difference or the change between the present status of business performance (at all levels from top to bottom in the organization) and the desired standard or the higher global benchmark for the organizations for excellence in every respect whether it is quality, production, costing, marketing, environment, health, safety, or technology.

The Difference or Gap Analysis: In this stage, the current situation is measured against the desired situation (Peterson 1999).

Current Situation: It determines the current state of skills, knowledge, and attitudes in the context of the organizational goals and constraints.

Desired Situation: Analysis focusses on the necessary job tasks/standards as well as skills, knowledge, and abilities needed to accomplish these successfully.

> **Good to Know**
> The gap between the current and desired situation will identify the organizational development needs.

Training is essentially required for a more detailed investigation of people, their jobs, and the organization to determine:

- Are people doing their jobs efficiently?
- Do people have adequate KSAs for their job performance?
- Do they know how to do their job safely?
- Whether the performance problem is a question of any technical process or a soft skill?
- Whether anything has changed recently that might be affecting people's performance?
- Whether it is possible to compare best and worst performers to find the difference in their methods of working?
- If the gap between the current and desired conditions may be large, it may be because of a lack of knowledge or skills, and technical training may be a solution. In such cases, a training programme can be devised to fill the knowledge/skills gap.
- It is very important to analyse whether the gap in performance can be addressed by training or whether a change in the management style or organizational restructuring is the solution.

The benefits to the organizations for conducting training (Mitchell 2010) are as follows:

- It allows the organization to examine itself from the point of view of its organizational effectiveness.
- It reveals inadequacies in locations, machines, work designs, safety, health, communications, organizational hierarchies, financial controls, personnel policies and so on.
- A good training needs analysis process provides an early warning sign system for protecting the organization's health, safety, and environment (HSE) because a thorough analysis deals with a cross section of the employees in an organization.
- The usefulness of training needs analysis goes far beyond the requirements of the training department.

5.5 TRAINING TECHNIQUES AND TYPES

Human beings vary in their ways they grasp and learn. Some people learn by observing, others by hearing, experiencing, and insights. So the trainers must be prepared for presenting the learning in such a way that the participants practically observe, experience, and are encouraged to think critically.

> **Good to Know**
> Generally, a combination of training techniques is used by the trainer delivering the learning material for the desired change in KSA (knowledge, skill, and attitude) of employees.

There are a variety of training techniques that are used to make learning meaningful and joyful for the participants.

(a) **Lecture technique:** Lecturing is a cost-effective training method because it permits coverage of a considerable amount of knowledge and information for a number of people. Many people learn more from hearing lectures than from reading.

While training through good lectures aids understanding and learning, they are of little value in changing attitudes, developing job skills, or training in human relations skills.

Though generally the lecturers have a difficulty in holding attention for more than 90 minutes, but an experienced and motivational, professional speaker can engage the audience for a full one week training with joyful learning and insight.

Some companies have their officials talk to their new employees and present their company history and policies to them.

There is also a trend around the world for internal trainers within an organization who know their working conditions, culture, and the job processes.

Classroom lectures clubbed with field tour for training participants within the organization for practical observation would be very useful for a viewpoint of active learning.

(b) **Reading material and training handouts:** An exclusive advantage of reading material is that it permits repetition. An active reader can read as often as he wishes.

Booklets and other reading material have immense value for conceptual understanding of the subject matter provided such material is sufficient and in order as per topics of the training presentation.

The distribution of such materials at the time of the training programme in hard copy as well as softcopy through email or CD/pen-drive by a company does indicate importance of organizational issues in the direction of improving work situation.

(c) **Video films:** Though original cost of the videos is high, since it can be used with a larger audience and for a long-term perspective, it is relatively a learning investment for big companies. Many companies make their own films and also purchase films, relevant to their business, made by other media companies.

Screening of short and specific videos maximum of 15 minutes followed by group discussion can be very impactful for the training participants towards developing insights into the concepts for job applications of what they learned.

A rationally selected film library is likely to teach philosophy or values that are consistent with a particular company's point of view. It will be a useful resource for training.

> **Good to Know**
> A relevant video/clip has its greater value in visual learning.

(d) Visual aids, PPT and film strip, clips: Relevant visual aids and sound film strips are less expensive ways of accomplishing what is achieved by a movie. Their main value is in aiding visual learning which is specific to the industry and job. PPT is the most popular amongst all training techniques.

Visual aids permit somewhat greater flexibility, since they can be adapted to the interest and level of the audience.

Every training programme has some limitations on visual arrangements; hence the trainer must be an accommodating type and be flexible to ensure learning for the participants.

(e) On-the-job training: A supervised training on the job is best when the workmen demonstrate low performance.

When workmen have low or medium aptitudes for the job as found in the selection records, they would need more rigorous training on the job by the supervisors and co-workers.

A distinctive feature of on-the-job training is that it is training through doing. Another feature is that it is primarily individual instruction. Even if some persons are trained simultaneously, each receives opportunities to practise and each should receive help on his particular difficulty or weakness. Because of the individual nature of coaching, this type of training is costly and time-consuming and should be reserved for those who require skill-upgradation along with personal touch.

This kind of training requires a lot of patience on the part of the internal trainers as trainees would vary in their style of learning especially when some learners are fast and others are slow in grasping.

(f) The case method: The case method was developed at the Harvard Business School. This method assumes that the teacher or trainer is not the source of knowledge but he/she is only a facilitator. The basic premise of this method is that learning occurs through participation in discussion and problem analysis. The objective is using facts effectively and developing a rationale for a collective decision.

Executive training programmes frequently use the case method. A complex situation, typically of a real-life problem, is presented to a small group with a bunch of leading questions. The case becomes the theme for discussion about: What to do? How the problem could have been prevented? What are some of the policy issues involved?

The case method gives trainees practice in problem solving and utilizes the benefit of discussion. One important insight gained from case discussion is discovering that there is no one correct answer and the best solutions are a matter of professional opinion and not a personal preference. The employees should develop interest and skills in group problem solving.

(g) **Discussion method:** Many a times, the participants don't get actively involved in a discussion unless they find the subject interesting and useful. Hence, it is a skill of the trainer that he/she stimulates understanding and gives practice in problem solving.

Discussion method demands systematic organization of content and control for discussion on the part of the trainer. Discussion method is to be led with utmost care and professional touch when the participants confuse the issues with their personal emotions and attitudes.

(h) **The incident process:** The incident process is to describe an event that requires action. This method offers training in getting vital details and becomes a game in exploring the work situation. Investigations of accidents, injury, theft, fire, sexual harassment at work, and other such incidents are the problems that can be discussed for deciding an action plan for improving the work situation. The incident process requires skill in asking the relevant questions. The next stage of the discussion requires the participants to make the decision and supply a rationale for it. These may be individual or group reports which become the subject of discussion in the third stage. Finally, the leader tells what actually happened or went wrong and why.

(i) **Business games:** The groups/clusters across organizations meet together and brainstorm over business issues and take a critical look at the current situations with the help of business games. Business games create a good deal of emotional involvement.

Business games simulate a complex realistic solution in which groups compete with one another and the effects of decision made by one group have an effect on the others.

The learning thus gained is the development of a better appreciation of the range of factors that should be considered in making wise decisions, with a concern over risk-taking and conservativeness. The focus is on gaining intellectual sophistication.

(j) **The in-basket exercises:** The in-basket refers to a series of matters a manager finds on his desk. How will he dispose them of? A trainee is confronted with a rush situation, partial information, and a list of actions demanding items, he may find in the basket. He disposes of the matters by replying to mails, delaying action, setting up meetings, deciding who should do some of the urgent things, delegating, or takes any action that seems sensible under the circumstances.

This technique reveals the kinds of decisions executives make under stress and could serve a useful purpose in the training and selection of personnel.

(k) Role play: The role play technique requires trainees to project themselves into a simulated interpersonal situation and play the roles under situations assigned to them.

Role play can be limited to practice in the skills of human relations and team building. The benefits of the case or discussion methods are combined with the benefits of role play. Role play can be used to develop insights over almost all situations an organization may face.

Role play can also be used as reverse role play in which the participants who played first in favour of some issues would then take a role and oppose the same issues. This way the groups in discussion get wider insight over pros and cons of issues being discussed.

(l) T-group training: The T-group or sensitivity groups had its origin at the National Training Laboratories (NTL) in Maine, and are a product of group dynamics.

The basic objective of the T-training is to improve group interactions and interpersonal communication by having participants develop an understanding of the influence they have on others. The major goal is to learn how adults learn from each other.

This technique is also recognized as a human laboratory. The procedure is to organize groups of about 12 persons and have them meet daily for 2/3 hours for a period of two or more weeks. T-group training and some of the role-play methods have similar objectives which are to facilitate interpersonal and group relations.

5.6 BUSINESS ETIQUETTE

In the present times, companies look for managers trained with not just the latest technical competencies; they must also acquire contemporary social graces and cross-cultural understanding, to effectively find the way through the global business environment.

> **Good to Know**
> Organizations are increasingly interested in Business Etiquette training for managers.

Etiquette is a code of behaviour based on kindness, consideration, and unselfishness – something that should not, and will not, ever change. Etiquette governs our relationship with others in both social and business settings. Business etiquette particularly refers to a set of rules governing the way professional people in business conduct themselves (Post 1992).

The concept of courtesy is also rooted in Chinese culture. Courtesies and ethical norms of behaviour are a part of what the Chinese call *li*. Respect, appropriate conduct, and correct attitude are the marks of cultured, well-bred ladies and gentlemen (Chew 1992).

Here below is a listing of key business values, that is, physical, organizational, and psychological values (Gael 2011).

Physical	*Organizational*	*Psychological*
Cleanliness	Discipline	Pleasing the customer
Orderliness	Accountability	Respect for the individual
Punctuality	Standardization	Innovation
Regularity	Systemization	Decisiveness
Safety	Authority	Growth of the individual
Efficient use of money and materials	Coordination of departments	Loyalty
Quality of product	Integration of levels	Service to society
Quality of service	Communication	Integrity

The five most important chosen business values that the employees must adhere to are:

- Good manners
- Assertiveness
- Truth
- Self-respect
- Happiness

The then Prime Minister of Singapore in June 1979, Mr Lee said: 'It is interaction between people, each of us watching and responding to each other's behaviour that will influence our children as they grow up during their most impressionable years. It is an effort worth the making. Money cannot buy courtesy.'

5.6.1 Business Etiquette Statements

Etiquette, formal conduct, mannerism, decorum and so on are unwritten rules and regulations of behaviour and the practised protocols to be followed by employees as established by organizations. Business etiquettes govern our relationship with others in both social and business settings. There is certain level of awareness present among employees about how they are practising etiquette in their work lives. Yet, the awareness has not reached the optimum level and thus employees require some formal training on business etiquettes.

Following are the 15 statements of the business etiquettes, each with three options. These statements form part of the business etiquettes training for employees to be developed so as to fit into formal business environment. So read the statements carefully and choose the option which you feel is apt in that particular situation. The five questions at the end are open-ended questions. Please feel free to answer them in as many words as you like.

1. When you are being interviewed, at that time:
   (a) If your cell rings, you will take the call and say 'Please call me later.'
   (b) If your cell rings, you will take the call and talk out there and then.
   (c) Keep your phone switched off.
2. While out for a business meeting in a restaurant, your cell phone, glasses, and handbag will be kept:
   (a) On the table, beside your plate.
   (b) Cell and glasses in the bag, cell will be kept on silent mode and bag will be on your lap.
   (c) Bag will be kept on the chair beside you and the cell and glasses on the table beside your plate.
3. As a boss, while taking an interview, your phone rings, you would:
   (a) Pick up a call without requesting the interviewee to stop speaking.
   (b) Not pick up the call and let it go on voicemail.
   (c) Say 'Excuse Me' and answer the call.
4. If you were going for a job interview, you would be:
   (a) Arriving 10 to 15 minutes before time and settling down.
   (b) Arriving in for the interview just on time and handing the bag to the secretary.
   (c) Rushing late and barging into the interviewer's cabin without acknowledging anyone outside.
5. At the end of the first job interview, the person taking your interview asks you whether you have any questions to ask, you would answer:
   (a) None.
   (b) Ask about your salary and leave structure.
   (c) Ask about the job timings and the company's projects.
6. While at an interview if the interviewer asks you a certain question to which you don't know the answer, you would:
   (a) Pretend you know the answer by giving a sort of related explanation.
   (b) Say I'm not aware about this topic.
   (c) Say 'That's an interesting question' and avoid answering it by changing the topic.
7. As a telemarketer, when you call a client to sell a product, and you receive 'no' for an answer, you would:
   (a) Say 'Thank you for your time, it's all right, may be some other time.' and end the call.
   (b) Go on talking and asking for personal details.
   (c) Hang up without saying thank you.
8. When you have called someone over to your office for an official meeting and you are already in a conversation over the phone, you would:

(a) Keep talking simultaneously to both the parties, making each one wait while talking to the other.
(b) Hang up and attend to the person who has come in.
(c) Put the phone on hold and try to wrap up your conversation as soon as possible.

9. Your co-worker smells of bad breath, do you:
(a) Tell him/her that your mouth stinks badly.
(b) Pretend that you are getting an odour from somewhere close and expect him/her to understand your signal.
(c) Don't say anything.

10. While meeting people from other nationalities, if you don't get to understand a person's name during introduction, you would:
(a) Clear the confusion in the next meeting.
(b) Address the person with whatever name you have understood and let the person say it right if you are wrong.
(c) Clear the confusion there only, by asking the person to spell it out.

11. While getting introduced, you give a handshake:
(a) With eye contact and grip your hand firmly.
(b) Give a handshake with no eye contact.
(c) Give a light (loose grip) handshake with eye contact.

12. Someone has done a business favour for you, do you:
(a) Take out time and immediately send a 'thank you' note.
(b) Don't feel the need to send a 'thank you' note, because a verbal thank you is enough.
(c) Send in a 'thank you' note, but after a long time since the incident has occurred.

13. While giving your business card to someone and receiving it from someone, you:
(a) You throw your card on the table, and accept his/her card, fold it and put it in your bag.
(b) Accept the other person's card, give yours, and comment on the card details trying to appear that you have noticed the details on it.
(c) Give and accept the card gracefully in the person's hand.

14. When someone complimented you and you know it's not genuine, would you:
(a) Smile and accept it by saying 'thank you'.
(b) Stare at the person sarcastically and walk off.
(c) Pass a compliment back to the person which is also not genuine.

15. You are already in an interview, but have to go for another interview following the same, you would:
(a) Tell the interviewer/s to hurry up the questions as you need to go for another interview.

(b) Get up in the middle of the conversation and make an excuse to go away.

(c) Give all your time to the interviewer to get to know you well, even if it means rescheduling the next interview or missing it altogether.

16. Choose any five values which you feel you practise in your daily life out of the list given below: (please put a tick on the answer chosen)

List of values:

Achievement	*Friendship*	*Growth*	*Power and authority*
Affection (love and caring)	Cooperation	Helping other people	Recognition (respect from others and status)
Honesty	Efficiency	Involvement	Time freedom
Knowledge	Competence	Privacy	Work under pressure
Fame	Self-respect	Fast living	Order (tranquillity, stability, conformity)
Responsibility and accountability	Loyalty	Truth	Creativity

17. Do you think personal values and business etiquettes are related? If yes, can you explain how?
18. How important are business etiquettes for business growth and business communication?
19. Do you think etiquette training is required in any leading organization in today's times? Does your company provide it?
20. How do you think parental upbringing matters when it comes to practising etiquette (mannerisms) in society in general? So can etiquettes be learnt while growing up or is it something in born?

The above business etiquette questions are the important behaviours which are expected to be formally or informally conducted by the employees of an organization during their routine business meetings, functions or events, and that can be used for training of employees, especially during the induction training for new employees.

5.7 EVALUATION OF TRAINING

To evaluate training, we must systematically document the outcomes of training in terms of how trainees/participants actually behave on the job in terms of the relevance and applications of those behaviours towards the objective of the organization.

The most central questions related to industrial training is the effectiveness, usefulness, or impact of the training programmes devised for employees with a defined purpose towards business improvements.

The effectiveness of a programme depends on many factors, like design of training, the coverage of contents, the selection of trainees, motivation, stress, practice, feedback, method and delivery of training and practice, and transfer of learning and so on which may together make a programme or training intervention more or less effective.

To evaluate the utility or value of training, we search for answers to questions such as the following:

- Have trainees achieved the desired level of improvement in KSAs?
- Did change in KSAs occur and how much?
- Is the change in KSAs due to training?
- Is the change in KSAs positively related to the achievement of the organizational and business goals?
- Will similar changes occur with new participants in a similar training programme to be repeated in future?
- What is the level of effectiveness of the programme faculty or trainers?

Kirkpatrick's model describes four different kinds, or levels, of criteria that can be used to evaluate a training programme effectively (Kaufman 2000). These are usually referred as 'reaction, learning, behaviour and result' criteria as mentioned below.

Reaction Criteria: These are the responses and opinions of the participants about the perceived effectiveness of a training programme to the questions such as 'was the training relevant', what 'do you think of the training contents' 'or how do you rate the faculty in terms of his/her delivery of training and the like'?

This method does not really reflect whether or not a change in KSAs has occurred. Reactions can be very favourable or unfavourable depending upon the subjective evaluation of trainees. This method provides an overall feedback and quick idea about the immediate opinion of participants if asked both on an evaluation sheet as well as orally to state in a free and frank manner. Mostly it is observed that participants give fair feedback and reactions.

Learning Criteria: It is development over the reaction criteria. These responses are straight away collected following the conclusion of training, and are intended to reveal whatever trainees learned sufficiently during the programme. This method is one of the most common forms of learning criteria. The difference between trainee's pre- and post-training scores on learning would emerge if planned by the trainer beforehand.

Behaviour Criteria: This method addresses the question of transfer of learning acquired through training to the job or work setting. The behaviour criteria of training effectiveness are measures of job performance that are collected after the participants have reported back to their respective jobs. Yet it is not an easy task to establish the improvement in job performance as a result of training due to many factors involved at workplace.

> **Good to Know**
> Most organizations are now interested in return on investment in training. This precisely means training for development.

Result Criteria: This technique deals with the organizational business performance needs identified during training needs assessment. This criterion goes beyond the measurement of job performance, and assesses the surfacing outcome changes in the KSAs that are translated into the broad changes in the organization as a training intervention. Normally, the criteria changes are expected as an organizational development (OD) intervention. Most progressive organizations would be concerned about this approach as a return on investment (ROI) in training.

5.8 A RESEARCH CASE

It is important for students to gain insight over how organizations identify training needs.

The purpose of this case (H.L. Kaila 2007) is to study the training need identification at Fabon India Ltd. (Name changed for the purpose of confidentiality.)

Employees were asked to fill the questionnaire about training need identification (see Appendix). This questionnaire was administered to 38 employees including both genders, having different designations and from various departments.

The information was collected with the help of the questionnaire method. The questionnaire includes questions regarding behavioural as well as technical trainings (on the basis of company policies).

5.8.1 Organizational Context

Fabon India is a global specialty chemical and materials company producing carbon black, a material used in the production of tyres, industrial products for the automotive industry, inks, plastics, and specialty products.

It is also a leader in the production of nano-structured, sub-micron particles, comprising carbon, metals, and metal oxides. These particles enhance the performance of a variety of products, including rubber reinforcement, pigmentation in inks, polishing and capacitance for microelectronics uses, and UV protection and electrostatic dissipation in plastic and rubber products.

In Fabon India, usually, the HoDs of the concerned departments judge the performance of their subordinates and accordingly recommend which particular training they need to undergo to enhance their performance. This is the only method they adopt to identify the training needs. When we approached Fabon India regarding the project on training needs identification they immediately granted us permission for the study.

5.8.2 Case Findings

The behavioural training programmes were conducted in-house whereas for the technical training, the employees were deputed to external training programmes. The target employees were from the following departments:

- Laboratory
- HR
- Customer service
- Production
- SH and E

The questionnaire handed over to the target employees was majorly focussed on:

- Past trainings attended and their effectiveness.

- New skills and competencies to be developed and trainings expected on the same.
- Trainings to enhance efficiency and effectiveness in the present job.

5.8.3 Department-wise Findings

5.8.3.1 Laboratory

Most of the employees from this department have attended rubber application training in the past. Some of them have also attended team building and leadership training.

They wish to attend following trainings in the future:

- carbon black application in rubber/plastics
- effect of CB parameters on them
- advance training on lab data entry software
- personality development
- team building
- advance training related to current job
- communication skills
- assertiveness
- time management
- problem solving tools and techniques
- computer training

5.8.4 Human Resources

Employees in this department have attended safety related training in the past. They have also attended trainings such as team building, leadership, 5s, and RCA training.

They wish to attend the following trainings in the future:

- Business written communication
- Motivation training
- Stress management
- Current practices in HR

5.8.5 Customer Service

Employees working in this department mentioned that they have undergone leadership, team building, hearing conservation, 5s, and supervisory development in the past.

They wish to attend the following trainings in the future:

- Problem solving tools and techniques
- Supply chain forecasting and planning tools/processes
- Communication skills
- Advance training in computers
- Marketing skills

5.8.6 Production

Most of the employees in this department have attended ISO, 5s, and energy conservation training in the past.

They wish to attend the following trainings in the future:

- Assertiveness
- Safety related training
- Stress management
- Financial awareness programmes
- Time management

5.8.7 Safety Health and Environment

Trainings attended by employees in this department are CIP, SH and E audit, leadership and motivation.

They wish to attend the following trainings in the future:

- CB manufacturing process training
- Refresher in CIP
- Time management
- Microsoft office – advanced
- Photo editing software
- Lotus notes features
- Environment related training
- Effluent treatment
- Process safety
- Preparing high impact PowerPoint presentations.

Employees as well as supervisors (HoDs) were provided with a list of behavioural training programmes and they were asked to give ratings to each training.

The ratings were:

1-a lot

2-moderate

3-little

Every employee and supervisor was asked to rate each training as 1, 2, or 3.

Results depicted that:

1. Most of the employees have given top priority to time management and problem solving tools and techniques.
2. The next priority given is to the training on stress management.
3. The third important topic mentioned by the employees was communication skills.

However, it is interesting to note that the supervisors' opinions differed from these inferences. According to the supervisors:

- The first priority is to the training on communication skills.
- The second priority was training on assertiveness.
- The third important topics were time management and problem solving tools and techniques.

If we compare both the inferences, there is a gap between what employees prefer and what their superiors want them to undergo.

Overall, if the supervisors are the sole decision makers regarding the training to be given to their subordinates, there may be some loops left out. Whatever training the employees expect may not be given to them and it would lead to dissatisfaction in their mind.

The companies should care that needs of the employees and recommendations of the superiors are analysed and then the training needs of each employee are finalized so that no bias gets created in any case.

SUMMARY

- Effective training enables employees to learn to do their jobs better and perform more proficiently.
- Training needs analysis forms the first step before designing any training programme.
- The needs assessment process can be thought of as a type of organizational intervention.
- The process of determining the organization's training needs is to answer the question whether the organization needs, objectives, and problems can be met or addressed by training.
- This chapter has also emphasized the importance of training requirement, business etiquette, training techniques and types, evaluation of training, and included a research case on identifying training needs.

EXERCISE FOR CLASSROOM PRACTICE

For better understanding of the subject matter of this chapter, please read and check each of the following statements whether True (T) or False (F) or Uncertain (U).

1. Training becomes learning only when it is implemented during the course of work, failing which people who undergo training tend to forget it.
2. Best organizations are the ones with the highest commitment to training and development.
3. Training needs analysis forms—the first step before designing any training programme.
4. The content and method of delivery of training for KSAs are not likely to differ for each work-unit.
5. The first goal of the requirements analysis is to understand the organization so that decisions concerning how phases of the needs assessment should be conducted can be determined.

6. Gap analysis means the current situation is measured against the desired situation.
7. Training is the only tool to find the difference between the present status of business performance and the desired standard.
8. It is very important to analyse whether the gap in performance can be addressed by training or whether a change in the management style or organizational restructuring is the solution.
9. Training removes inadequacies in machines, work designs, safety, health, personnel, communications, organizational hierarchies, financial controls.
10. Classroom lectures clubbed with field tour for training participants within the organization for practical observations would be very useful view point for active learning.
11. Discussion method demands systematic organization of content and control for discussion on part of the trainer.
12. Kirkpatrick's model described four different kinds of criteria to evaluate a training programme effectively referred as 'reaction, learning, behaviour, and result' criteria.

Answers: All statements are **True** except that the statement numbers 4, 7, and 9 are **False**.

REVIEW QUESTIONS FOR DISCUSSIONS/EXAMINATIONS

1. Critically argue over the concepts of identifying training needs.
2. Describe methods for conducting needs assessment.
3. What are the benefits of training to the organizations?
4. Discuss the business values in organizations.
5. Describe the importance of business etiquette for organizations.
6. Critically discuss various techniques of training.
7. Reflect upon the importance of training requirement in your organization.
8. Address the critical issues pertaining to evaluation of training in an organization.
9. Develop a research case on the outcomes of a training programme.
10. Compare the training and development practices in two Indian companies.

FIELD RESEARCH REPORT

This is a research assignment section for students for their internal marking by the teacher during the semester. This assignment is for understanding practical applications of the subject.

An action research project: Identify a group of minimum 15 executives and 15 non-executives across an organization preferably where you are placed for an internship. Conduct interviews with them by using a set of closed/open-ended questionnaire to signify the issues and concerns pertaining to the training needs and development practices. Prepare a report of about 15 pages reflecting an action plan for better work practices.

REFERENCES

Bennis, W. (1969). *Organization Development: Its Nature, Origin and Prospects*. MA: Addison-Wesley.

Biech, Elaine (2012). The 2013 Pfeiffer Annual: Training. November, Pfeiffer.

Chaterjee, B. (1999). *Human Resource Management: A Contemporary Text*. New Delhi: Sterling Publishers Pvt. Ltd

Chew, S. (1992). *Business Etiquette: An Essential Guide for Executives*. Singapore: Times Books International.

Davis, K. (1990). *Human Behavior at Work*. New Delhi: Tata McGraw-Hill.

French, Wendell and L. Cecil Bell (1999). *Organization Development: Behavioral Science Interventions for Organization Improvement*, 6th Edition. New Jersey: Prentice Hall.

Gael, O'Brien (2011). Leadership, Common Purpose and Shared Values. Retrieved on 15 January 2013. http://business-ethics.com/2011/03/17/1709-leadership-common-purpose-and-shared-values/

Kaila, H.L. (2007). *Organizational Behavior & HRM* (2nd edition). Delhi: AITBS Publishers.

Kaufman, R. (2000). *Mega Planning: Practical Tools for Organizational Success*. Thousand Oaks, CA: Sage Publications.

Mitchell, Peter L. (2010). The Advantages of a Training Needs Analysis. Retrieved on 12 January 2013. http://ezinearticles.com/?The-Advantages-of-a-Training-Needs-Analysisandid=3825598

Muchinsky, P.M. (2000). *Psychology Applied to Work* (6th edition). New Delhi: Belmount Thomas Learning.

Peterson, R. (1999). *Training Needs Assessment*. London: Kogan Page Limited

Post, E. (1992). Emily Post's Etiquette (15th edition). New York: Harper Collins Publishers.

Reference-rcd (2014). Training Development. Retrieved on 7 May 2014. http://www.reference-rcd.com/english/index.php?option=com_content&task=view&id=57&Itemid=105

Saiyadain, M.S. (2009). *Human Resources Management* (4th edition). New Delhi: Tata McGraw-Hill.

Sarma, A.M. (2000). *Personnel and Human Resource Management*. Mumbai: Himalaya Publishing House.

Torrington, D. and L. Hall (1998). *Human Resource Management*. New Jersey: Prentice Hall.

APPENDIX

Training Need Identification Questionnaire

Name:

Designation:

Organization:

Department:

1. What types of trainings have you attended in this organization till now?

____

____

2. Did you find them helpful? (Yes/No. Give reasons.)

____

____

3. To what extent are the you expecting to apply new skills or competencies in your present or future responsibilities?

____

____

4. Do you need any specific training in those areas?

____

____

5. Which are the different types of training you wish to undergo to enhance efficiency and effectiveness in your current job?

From the given list, please prioritize the training that you would like to attend (please rate on 1–3 scale. 1-A lot, 2-Moderate, 3-little)

Behavioural Trainings:	Individual's rating	Supervisor's rating
1. Stress management	☐	☐
2. Communication skills	☐	☐
3. Assertiveness	☐	☐
4. Time management	☐	☐
5. Team building	☐	☐
6. Personality development	☐	☐
7. Business written communication	☐	☐
8. Health awareness programmes	☐	☐
9. First aid	☐	☐
10. Problem solving tools and techniques	☐	☐
11. Safety related trainings	☐	☐
12. Financial awareness programme	☐	☐
13. Computer training	☐	☐
14. Leadership		

6

Employee Engagement and Organizational Commitment

Learning Objectives

This chapter would help the readers:

- to understand the concept and benefits of engaged employees to the organization;
- to know the stages of employee engagement;
- to be familiar with the concept of organizational commitment; and
- to reflect upon the researches and managers' interviews on organizational commitment.

An Opening Story: Benefits of Employee Engagement

When an employee is meaningfully engaged in his role, he would reflect increased commitment. In one such organizational intervention, the company started a project on behavioural aspect of occupational safety training and involved a senior employee as chief coordinator for this project activity for all-India locations. This employee found this work very interesting and professionally very fulfilling which also boosted his self-esteem. So after a few rounds of implementing this project over a period of six months in a few locations by a professional organizational psychologist, he showed such an increased level of commitment that he took up this project forward to other locations on his own without much consultant's support which saved a lot of cost to the organization that it might have paid to a consultant. This reflects very clearly that when employees are meaningfully engaged, they not only find it personally motivating, but also tend to show a higher level of initiative and commitment for meeting organizational goals. This initiative of behavioural aspect of occupational safety was found very satisfying by different locations of the company and they statistically reflected the improved safety standards and practices.

6.1 INTRODUCTION

The term employee engagement has been often misunderstood or poorly implemented by HR professionals. It is mainly for this reason that HR could not link with business.

Employee engagement movement should be based on business needs. It is time and again disputed that employee engagement is one of the most efficient instruments towards achieving lasting business success. The organizations with employees to share thoughts on regular basis are more likely to have an effective programme. Employee engagement programnme can go wrong if it lacks genuineness or legitimacy. The straightforward but challenging steps to follow for an unbeaten employee engagement program are: connect engagement efforts to core business vision and policy; leverage peer-to-peer influence to create social synergy; persuade employees to choose goals related to their own lives achievable on a daily basis; promote involvement and allow all employees to contribute; and push continuous success as a drive through weekly meetings, recognition and annual awards ceremony. A grand engagement programme is a positive way to retain talent in an organization.

Over the last couple of decades, employers' focus has moved from employees who are satisfied with pay, benefits, and working conditions to those who are genuinely and meaningfully engaged in the work and mission of the organization and to those who are committed to the organization (Armstrong 2006).

Commitment to an organization, a relationship, a goal, or even an occupation involves emotional attachments. Porter, Steers, Mowday, and Boulian (1974) proposed that organizational commitment includes three elements:

- A sense of identification with the organization's goals.
- A feeling of involvement in organizational duties.
- A feeling of loyalty to the organization.

Lee and Mitchell (1994) characterized commitment as a shared belief and acceptance of the values and goals of the organization as well as the desire to maintain membership within the organization.

The positive outcomes of organizational commitment (OC) have been well documented in management literature. People who are committed are less likely to quit and accept other jobs and are less likely to be tardy or absent from work (Angle and Para 1981).

Organizational commitment has also been found to be positively associated with higher work motivation, greater organizational citizenship, as well as higher job performance (Meyer et al., 1989). The findings of a study revealed a significant positive relationship between employee engagement and employee commitment. Employees of private organizations have a higher level of employee engagement and organizational commitment than employees in public organizations, and long-tenured and short-tenured employees did not differ in commitment levels (Collins 2014).

6.1.1 Employee Engagement

Employee engagement is defined as a heightened emotional connection that an employee feels for his or her organization that influences him or her to exert greater discretionary effort to his or her work (Melcrum 2007).

According to Derek Stockley (2005), employee engagement refers to the extent that employees believe in the mission, purpose, and values of an organization and demonstrate that commitment through their actions and their attitude towards the employer and customers.

Employee engagement is a state of mind in which employees feel a vested interest in the company's success and are both willing and motivated to perform to levels that exceed the stated job requirements (Landy and Conte 2005).

Job involvement also refers to employee engagement or work engagement. It is a concept that is generally viewed as managing discretionary effort, that is, when employees have choices, they will act in a way that furthers their organization's interests.

An engaged employee is a person who is fully involved in, and enthusiastic about, his or her work. It is a belief about one's current job and is a function of how much the job can satisfy one's wishes. Highly job involved individuals make the job a central part of their personal character. Besides, people with high job involvement focus most of their attention on their job. The engagement-performance potential which is present in the organization means 'delivering the results in a shared effort' (Holbeche 2013).

Job involvement is defined as psychological identification with a job. This definition implies that a job-involved person sees her or his job as an important part of his self-concept (Lawler and Hall 1970). 'Jobs are defined as one's self concept in a major way' (Kanungo 1982).

Factors influencing involvement within the workplace include the following:

- Employer engagement
- Employee perceptions of job importance
- Employee clarity of job expectations
- Career advancement/improvement opportunities
- Regular feedback and dialogue with superiors
- Quality of working relationships with peers, superiors, and subordinates
- Perceptions of the ethos and values of the organization
- Effective internal employee communications
- Reward to engage.

Job involvement has been clearly linked to absenteeism (Blau 1986; Farrell and Stamm 1988; Shore, Newton, and Thornton 1990; Scott and McClellan 1990), and to turnover or intent to leave (Baba and Jamal 1991; Huselid and Day 1991; Ingram, Lee, and Lucas, 1991; Shore, Newton, and Thornton, 1990).

A Review of the Most Current Research by Melcrum (2007), a research and information company surveyed 1000 corporate communications and HR professionals and conducted 40 case studies and found that many respondents credit offering employee engagement programmes with the following benefits:

- More than 50% report improvements in employee retention and customer satisfaction.
- 33% report higher productivity

- 28% report improvements in employee advocacy
- 27% report improved status as a 'great place to work'
- 27% report increased profitability
- 25% report improved absenteeism.

Steve Crabtree (2004) reported in the *Gallup Management Journal's* semi-annual Employee Engagement Index and puts the current percentage of truly 'engaged' employees at 29%. A slim majority, 54%, falls into the 'not engaged' category, while 17% of employees are 'actively disengaged.' Engaged employees are much more likely than others to say that their organization 'encourages close friendships at work.' Eighty-two per cent of engaged employees showed agreement by rating the statement a 4 or 5 (on a 1–5 scale where 5 is 'strongly agree'), compared to 53% of those who are not engaged and just 17% in the actively disengaged group. This connection shouldn't come as a surprise, considering several of the 12 items used to gauge engagement test for positive relationships (one statement is 'I have a best friend at work.') - But even taking that into account, the correlation is very high.

6.2 A RESEARCH CASE ON EMPLOYEE ENGAGEMENT

Objectives of this engagement study (H.L. Kaila 2007) was to understand the dimensions of employee engagement at Origin India that consistently drive business outcomes, learn about workplace strengths and review weaknesses, benchmark workplace quality against other organizations, build a stronger workplace, determine local accountability versus intervention areas where senior management or HR support is required, and review process of manager education, team feedback, and action planning and workplace improvement.

Sample description: Sample size (N) = 2182. The sample consisted of employees working with Origin India; a software multinational organization, between the age range of 22 to 55, males and females.

A survey method used was: interviews and case studies and a standardized questionnaire (also known as Q12) designed by Gallup Consulting was used (see appendix). This questionnaire was in the form of a 5-point rating scale which consisted of 34 items. It gauged employees' perceptions on various parameters given below which are considered being the *drivers of employee engagement.*

- Leadership
- Management
- Career development
- Communication
- Work environment
- Alignment
- Performance Measurement System (PMS)
- Infrastructure

- Recognition
- Training
- Overall satisfaction

6.2.1 Qualitative Analysis

In order to better understand employees' perceptions, some of them were also interviewed. Employees put forth their opinions on number of issues ranging from administrative and IIM (internal infrastructure management) functions like food and transport facility, issuing of ID cards on time, availability of workstation up to the leadership and management strategies like branding of Origin India in Indian market, etc.

6.2.2 Administration

Most of the employees reported the need of transportation facility to and back from office. This would save their travel time. Also, because some of the employees work in shifts, having a company transport would be more feasible than public transport. They also demanded that employees should be able to get to work from the preferred location.

Some of the employees also recommended improvement in the canteen facilities and demanded a consistent food quality across all the locations of origin India. They also reported that canteen food was rather costly and the food costs should be cut down. Need for automation was also another unanimous demand. Employees reported that the procedures should be automated instead of depending too much upon Word or Excel files and face-to-face interaction. Such automation would make things happen faster and on time.

Induction process, issuing of photo ID cards, and landing process should be made faster.

Many of them also reported that there should be a smooth co-ordination and functioning between support functions of HR, finance, and administration. Also support functions should be more proactive to employees' demands.

6.2.3 Training

Another unanimously demanded programme was increase in technical and soft skill training. They reported that the technical trainings, provided especially to the freshers in the organization, were not sufficient. Also, trainings should be given on the basis of technologies that employees were working upon. With technical skills training, soft skills training at managerial as well as team leader level should be provided.

Apart from playing the role of the leader and guide, they also don the roles of facilitators, coaches, communicators, and team members. Managers should be taught leadership skills and grooming skills to bring out the best from their subordinates.

6.2.4 Career Development

Oigin India employees also demanded a proper career path. Once they enter the organization and start working on a particular project, they should not be made to work on the same project, get stuck with the same technologies throughout. Moreover, employees should at times be given the freedom to choose a project which is compatible with their interest instead of putting them into a particular project without their consultation. Job rotation opportunities after an appropriate time interval should be made available and also optional. If employees are willing to shift from tower to tower or willing to learn and work on different technologies than what they have been working upon, the transition should happen smoothly. They reported that managers should not only be concerned about getting their jobs done but also the career path that their subordinates follow.

6.2.5 Leadership, Management, and Recognition

Employees reported that there needs to be proactive communication from the leaders' side to the employees. Efforts should be made to bring down the level of bureaucracy which leads to delays in action. Leaders should be more transparent and objective during appraisals and promotions. The management and leadership at Origin India 'need to practice what they preach'.

With these unanimous demands, some of the employees also reported that good work should be praised at regular intervals and performance appraisals should be carried out in a more objective and transparent manner. Promotion and increments should be given on the basis of experience and performance and no other criteria. Project level awards should not only be based upon the customers' feedback but also feedback from managers and colleagues. Quantifying qualitative feedback is important in employee engagement.

6.2.6 Recreational Facilities

Last but not the least, many of the employees reported that they wanted more number of recreational facilities such as availability of a gymnasium, carom or any other sport. They stated that since employees spend almost half of their day in the office, having such facilities would act as a stress buster and in fact would refresh them and they would be able to work more effectively.

Some of the employees also expressed their concerns with the politics taking place in their project groups and reported certain incidences of favouritism and biases operating in the group. On the other hand, there were also employees who reported to be extremely happy with the way their career had been shaped in Origin India. They perceived their company as an organization taking care of its employees and being concerned for the well-being of its employees.

Thus, the opinions expressed by the employees varied from expression interest in the organization, improvement suggestions, concerns, cynicism to frustration.

6.2.7 Organizational Commitment

By definition, organizational commitment refers to an attitude that reflects the strength of the linkage between an employee and an organization (Stephen P. Robbins and Judge 1988). The level of commitment has implications as to whether a person would stay with an organization. Commitment can be identified as three very different types, which include: affective, continuance, and normative. Organizational commitment can be ranked as: high, moderate, or low. Thus, managers are interested in maximizing their workers' level of commitment.

There was a survey conducted by Trimble and E. Douglas in December 2006 in order to examine the relationship between organizational commitment, job satisfaction, and turnover intention of missionaries. Around 468 missionaries were surveyed and they found that 70% of the samples were dissatisfied with their jobs and thus the level of organizational commitment was also low and in return the probability of turnover was very high. Needless to mention that high employee turnover tends to cost an organization not only in terms of money but heavily on time and productivity.

Analysing the relationship between job satisfaction and organizational commitment is particularly crucial nowadays, as people often do not work at the same organization or job throughout their lifetime. It is also sometimes hard to find suitable people for certain positions. So once an ideal candidate is chosen, organizations like to make a great effort to retain the employee. If two employees exhibit different levels of job satisfaction and that job satisfaction can be proven to lead to organizational commitment, the employer will likely hire the employee with the higher level of job satisfaction (Cascio Wayne 1995). This is because the employer can expect the more satisfied individual to stay with the organization. Another reason as to why satisfaction will lead to commitment is that a higher level of job satisfaction may lead to a better family life and a reduction in stress. The reason is because an employee's feelings of jobs satisfaction may affect his or her emotions. This feeling will affect the worker's behaviour inside and outside the organization.

When a worker is dissatisfied with the job, he or she may have negative emotions. The consequence is that she or he may start to think about quitting. The decision process will begin with the individual identifying and evaluating alternatives, about whether to quit or to stay on in their job (Robbins and Judge 2008). The sequence of decisions will change the employee's commitment level. Managers would be most interested in knowing about the relationship between job satisfaction and organizational commitment, because it would become clear as to how important and worthy it would be to retain their most satisfied employees. In turn, having this knowledge would motivate managers to satisfy their employees. This would ultimately benefit the organization, as it is expected that these same employees will be highly committed.

Good to Know

When employees are satisfied, they tend to be more committed in the sense that their personal goals may go in line with those of the organization that they work for.

The relationship between job satisfaction and organizational commitment has been studied from various other aspects as well. For example, there was a research conducted in 2008 by RN and Mahmoud AL-Hussami (Professors, Faculty of Nursing, University of Jordan) in order to study the job satisfaction of nurses in relationship to organizational commitment, perceived organizational support, transactional leadership, transformational leadership, and level of education. This study investigated two distinct paths to job satisfaction, organizational commitment, and perceived organizational support. Results indicated that there was a strong correlation between the dependent variables and the independent variables. Of the five independent variables, organizational support was most strongly related to job satisfaction. The researcher chose randomly four nursing homes from a total of 53 Medicare certified nursing homes located in Miami-Dade County. This study provides new support to previous research about the importance of nurses' commitment and satisfaction for organizational effectiveness and performance.

Apart from this, the relationship between job satisfaction and organizational commitment has also been studied in relation to the psychological climatic dimensions (autonomy, cohesion, trust, pressure, support, recognition, fairness, innovation). This study was carried out by Bob Delaney and Gary Johns in 2001 of New York State University. The results of the study clearly demonstrated that psychological climate as a perceptual multidimensional phenomenon can render toward better understanding of a person's functioning in an organization.

The job attitude and, organizational commitment varies from culture to culture also. 'Are employees from different cultures committed to their organizations in similar ways?' was the objective of the research carried out by Y. Cheng and M. S. Stockdale in 2003. This study compared the organizational commitment of Chinese employees to the commitment of Canadian and South Korean workers. Although results revealed that the three types of commitment— normative, continuance, and affective—are present in all three cultures, results also showed that there are some differences among the three countries in how important each type of commitment is. It appears that although all three countries experience normative, continuance, and affective commitment, the degree to which each form of commitment is important differs across countries.

Another research revealed that there is a positive correlation between cohesion at workplace and organizational commitment. This was consistent with previous researches by Riordan and Griffeth (1995) who found the association between work friendships and organizational commitment, as well as factors such as job satisfaction, and so on, which have been associated with organizational commitment (Allen and Meyer 1991). Organizational commitment has been defined as 'the psychological state that binds the individual to the organization and makes turnover less likely' (Allen and Meyer 1990). According to Allen and Meyer organizational commitment consists of three components (Meyer and Allen 1991) as below.

Continuance commitment is an awareness of the costs associated with leaving the organization. It is also the willingness to remain in an organization because of the investment that the employee have with non-transferable investments as retirement, relationships with other employees, years of employment, or benefits that the employee may receive that are unique to the organization.

Normative commitment is defined as a feeling of obligation to continue employment. A person may feel like he/she has a moral obligation to the organization.

Affective commitment refers to an employee's emotional attachment to, identification with, and involvement in the organization. Porter et al. (1974) further characterized affective commitment by three factors: (1) belief in and acceptance of the organization's goals and values, (2) a willingness to focus effort on helping the organization achieve its goals, and (3) a desire to maintain organizational membership. Mowday et al. (1979) further stated that affective communication is: when an employee identifies with a particular organization in order to maintain membership to facilitate achievement of its goals.

They further maintained that these three components either characterize the employee's relationship with the organization or have the implications to affect whether the employee will continue with the organization. Meyer et al. (1993) continue to say that generally the research shows that those employees with a strong continuance commitment remain because they have to, those with a normative commitment remain because they feel that they have to, and those with a strong affective commitment will remain with the organization because they want to.

Allen and Meyer (1990) defined affective commitment, as proposed by their model, as the employees' emotional attachment to, identification with, and involvement in the organization. There are marked similarities between the definitions of affective commitment and cohesiveness. The identification with the organization in case of affective commitment runs parallel to the identification with the social group at work in case of cohesiveness. This makes a valid point to argue that the two aforementioned concepts are correlated.

Most of the researches on organizational commitment focus on the emotional aspect or the affective orientation of the commitment. The term commitment is used to describe an affective orientation toward the organization. Kanter (1968), for example, defined what she called cohesion commitment as the attachment of an individual's fund of affectivity and emotion to the group. Likewise, Buchanan (1974) described commitment as a partisan, affective attachment to the goals and values, and to the organization for its own sake, apart from its purely instrumental worth. Porter and his associates (Mowday, Steers and Porter 1979) described commitment as the relative strength of an individual's identification with and involvement in a particular organization. Employees who are affectively committed to an organization remain with it because they want to do so (Meyer, Allen, and Gellatly 1990).

Previous researchers have found a correlation between perceived group cohesion and concepts like job satisfaction, organizational citizenship behaviour, productivity, and such others. Charles Greene (1989) found evidence of the central role of group acceptance of organizational goals in determining both productivity and cohesion. Greene's research (1989) also suggests that the relationship between cohesion and productivity is reciprocal. The relationship between cohesion and absenteeism and turnover, performance, and interpersonal attraction has been well researched. When cohesion is evident within a work group it usually leads to effectiveness within a group and the job becoming more enjoyable. However, if the opposite situation exists and colleagues are difficult to work with, this may have a negative impact on job satisfaction.

Losh (2001) explains that highly cohesive groups can enforce group norms, whatever they are, far more effectively than less cohesive groups. Because people value their membership in cohesive groups, they are willing to adjust their behaviour to group standards.

> **Good to Know**
>
> If the work group is highly cohesive, the employees will be more likely to remain with the organization in order to maintain their group membership.

Riordan and Griffeth (1995) examined the impact of friendship on workplace outcomes; their results indicate that friendship opportunities were associated with increases in job satisfaction, job involvement, and organizational commitment, and with a significant decrease in intention to turnover. Wech et al. (1998) found research evidence for work group cohesiveness explaining variance in performance and organizational commitment beyond what was explained by perceived task competence. Other authors researching this area have linked organizational commitment to friendships (Ellingwood 2001). In sum, the research suggests a positive relationship between a cohesive work environment and organizational commitment.

Wright and Duncan (1986) however give a different view which incorporates the context in which friendships occur. According to them, the commitment towards the organization may be hampered when juxtaposed with commitment towards the true friendship. He states, '*... the commitment of the individuals to one another usually takes precedence over their commitment to the contexts in which the interaction takes place.*' (p. 94) This notion is important when conceptualizing workplace relationships, as it implies that the boundaries of genuine friendships supersede the role boundaries that may exist in a particular organizational context.

While assessing organizational commitment and cohesion as correlates, one should also take into consideration that there are other factors which may moderate both the aforementioned concepts and influence their effect on the employees. Organizational commitment is also affected by the status of employee in the organization, understandably, a top level employee may have a higher degree of commitment to the organization, this may not be in case of a lower level employee. Similarly, the vice president or such a higher authority will be less likely to have relationships with the co-workers which are equivalent to what executives or such employees may have with their co-workers. Even cohesion is likely to change subject to the authority hierarchy an employee belongs to. It therefore becomes important that the context in which organizational commitment and cohesion are studied is clearly specified with other moderating factors such as job tenure, authority hierarchy, power distance and the like. In the present study, not all moderating factors are considered, only the time that the employee has been working with the organization and the age group is controlled.

Managers once sensitive to the existence or non-existence of commitment in the organization might want to know what causes it. Managers may be able to alter the level of commitment by understanding its antecedents such as: personal characteristics, job/ role-related characteristics, structural characteristics, and work experiences (Huselid and Day 1991).

Research shows that age and tenure are personal characteristics of employees and are positively correlated with commitment. As people get older and remain in their organizations, or it may be, quite simply, that more committed employees stay with the organization longer.

> **Good to Know**
> It is in the organization's best interest for managers to understand what might influence a worker's commitment to the organization.

Higher education is associated with lower commitment, perhaps because educated people have expectations the organization cannot meet or it may also be that work opportunities are greater.

A variety of personal attitudes are related to commitment, among them work-oriented life interests, achievement motivation, and a sense of competence.

Several job role characteristics are correlated with commitment. Job scope is positively associated with commitment, perhaps because broad jobs challenge people more than narrow jobs or because people with broader jobs often have already demonstrated their commitment, which is why they have been given the broader jobs. Role conflict and role overload are negatively associated with commitment; role ambiguity has mixed associations. Thus, when people have broad and clear jobs, commitment may increase, but if their jobs are ambiguous, commitment decreases. Managers need to watch their top performers; the temptation to load them down with additional tasks could result in lowered commitment (O'Brien, Akroyd, and Richards 1993).

> **Good to Know**
> Characteristics of organizational structure such as formalization, functional dependence, and decentralization are related to employee commitment in the organization.

Managers should think about how the structural arrangements of their organizations may influence workers.

Work experiences related to commitment include social involvement, organizational dependence, personal importance to the organization, pay equity, and group norms regarding hard work (Porter, Crampon and Smith 1976).

Another research was conducted by Gould-Williams, Julian on HR practices, organizational climate, and employee outcomes: evaluating social exchange relationships in the local government. The findings suggest that, consistent with social exchange theory, positive exchanges lead to enhanced worker attitude and behaviour, with negative exchanges leading to increased work-related stress, reduced motivation, and a greater propensity to quit. Negative exchanges, however, did not result in reduced discretionary behaviour. Disaggregating the exchange practices revealed equitable rewards and organizational morale had consistent effects on worker attitudes and behaviours, with team working, employee involvement, and trust in managers having significant effects on employee motivation.

A research was conducted by Dan Hogan and Karen Roth (1984) titled, "Positive Organizational Climate: The Key to Quality Circles". The changes necessary for creating a quality school can best be made in a positive organizational climate because any real change requires the active involvement of people in the organization, who will not participate unless they are highly satisfied with their work environment.

6.2.8 Interviews of Managers on Organizational Commitment

The interviews conducted (as described below) with four senior officials of an organization reflect certain important perceptions on the dynamics of organizational commitment.

Interview with Vice President

- What are your general views on organizational commitment?

Organizational commitment is towards all stakeholders like the shareholders, customers, employees, government, and the society. An organization which delivers its commitment to the stakeholders is the one which will march forward and make name for itself and the product or services that it offers. It will create a reputation in any segment of the society and every one will be willing to be a part of such a committed organization.

- How should organizational commitment be encouraged?

There has to be a written policy on organizations' commitment for recruitment, promotion, training, and development. This can evolve from the vision statement of the organization. The value which the organization promotes, a positive work culture, having performance measurement for all functions, rewarding adequately based on performance; enrolling professionals to head all functions so that they will display how the organization will be benefited by delivering its commitment. Frequent interaction with all stakeholders will ensure that the organization will work towards developing and delivering its commitment.

- How does organizational climate influence commitment to work?

Enjoying any work is the most essential aspect of performance. Organizational climate is paramount to ensuring performance. By complying with the organization's commitment to the stakeholders which normally happens only with a good work culture and climate, will definitely influence the commitment to work.

- What climate exists in your organization and how does it influence your work commitment?

We have a very positive work culture where we recognize, understand various cultures of employees coming together for a common purpose, and we look towards inclusiveness of those cultures while we provide the best climate to learn, understand, and grow. We ensure that everyone is treated equally as a professional and rewarded for his deliveries. We extend adequate training and development to individuals to enhance competencies so that he can perform the best.

We also adequately compensate them for their performance and we have created a learning organization to help each and every individual to realize his professional and personal growth. All these activities influence the work commitment from each and every employee.

Interview with General Manager - Food Court

- What are your general views on organizational commitment?

Organization is a group of individuals coming together to achieve a common goal. If this group is not committed towards its team members then the purpose of an organization formation is defeated. Commitment is like a relationship where an individual commits himself or herself to an assignment or to an organization.

- How should organizational commitment be encouraged?

Like all relationships even commitments achieved need to be worked upon, acknowledged, and rewarded. Appreciating the hard work of employees goes a long way in motivating them to be more committed. At the same time every employee has to reciprocate in a similar manner by encouraging the company with results.

It is said that: 'Commitment means that it is possible for a man to yield.'

By understanding the possibility of an individual and by strengthening his or her capability, through a process of education, training, and counselling, it becomes easier for one to meet his commitment and thereby increase the overall organizational commitment.

- How does organizational climate influence commitment to work?

In an environment where fair practices are followed and where each one is considered equal, effectiveness is bound to increase thereby calling for high levels of commitment

Interview with General Manager – IT

- What are your general views on organizational commitment?

Organizations' commitment to its employees and employees' commitment towards the company are related. This relationship would help the company achieve the set targets and achieve the desired goals.

Interview with Deputy General Manager – Operations

- What are your general views on organizational commitment?

It is a give and take relation. The company has played an important role in my commitment to work. For example, I have got 8 promotions in 4 years which has been a motivating factor.

- How should organizational commitment be encouraged?

Rewards are very important. Instead of recruiting a person from other organizations employees of the organization should be promoted.

A bigger picture should be shown to employees to encourage them. The career path should be discussed and should be made known to the employees.

- How does organizational climate influence commitment to work?

Money, promotion, authority, career path are factors related to organizational climate. These factors encourage commitment and employees are motivated to put in more efforts.

- What climate exists in your organization and how does it influence your work commitment?

The climate is positive. It is friendly and professional at the same time. It gives a reason to come for work. Climate has encouraged me to be committed to my work and organization.

> **Good to Know**
> Individual friendships and positive organizational experiences increase affective commitment. Individuals feel more responsible for various aspects of organizational functioning leading to increased normative commitment.

SUMMARY

- Employee engagement is nothing but employee's psychological connection with his job, superiors, subordinates, and the organization as a whole.
- The level of employee engagement of employees drives the business outcomes and helps to build a stronger workplace.
- The various aspects of employee engagement such as leadership, overall satisfaction, communication, and work environment indicate that improvement is needed in some areas like communication, training, PMS (performance management system), and recognition.
- The lack of employee engagement also causes lack of commitment.
- Managers sensitive to commitment in the organization want to know what causes it.
- Employees who are meaningfully engaged in their job feel committed towards fulfilling the organizational goals.
- This chapter has provided the concept and researches on employee engagement and organizational commitment.

EXERCISE FOR CLASSROOM PRACTICE

For better understanding of the subject matter of this chapter, please read and check each of the following statements whether True (T) or False (F) or Uncertain (U).

1. An engaged employee is a person who is fully involved in, and enthusiastic about, his or her work.
2. The well-documented correlate of job involvement is an organizational commitment.
3. Organizational commitment refers to an attitude that reflects the strength of the linkage between an employee and an organization.
4. When a worker is dissatisfied with the job, he or she may have negative emotions.
5. Normative commitment is defined as a feeling of obligation to continue employment and a moral obligation to the organization.
6. Affective commitment refers to an employee's emotional attachment to, identification with, and involvement in the organization.
7. Researchers have found a negative correlation between group cohesion and job satisfaction, organizational citizenship behaviour, and productivity.
8. Highly cohesive groups can enforce group norms far more effectively than less cohesive groups.
9. Friendship opportunities are associated with increase in job satisfaction and decrease in organizational commitment.
10. Characteristics of organizational structure such as formalization, functional dependence, and decentralization are negatively related to employee commitment.

Answers: All statements are **True** except that statement numbers 7, 9, and 10 are **False.**

REVIEW QUESTIONS FOR DISCUSSIONS/EXAMINATIONS

1. Discuss the concept and process of employee engagement in an organization.
2. What are the stages of employee engagement?
3. How do employers build an engaged workforce?
4. Describe studies on employee engagement.
5. Discuss the concept of organizational commitment.
6. Describe two researches on organizational commitment.
7. Explore the relationship between employee engagement and organizational commitment.
8. Address an issue of enhancing performance through employee engagement in an organization.
9. Discuss the statement: 'Highly engaged employees grow twice as fast as peer companies'.
10. Consider the hypothesis for a research study: 'Highly engaged employees tend to support organisational change initiatives and are more resilient in the face of change'.

FIELD RESEARCH REPORT

This is a research assignment section for students for their internal marking by the teacher during the semester. This assignment is for understanding practical applications of the subject.

An action research project: Identify a group of minimum 15 executives and 15 non-executives across an organization preferably where you are placed for an internship. Conduct interviews with them by using a set of closed/open-ended questionnaire to signify the issues and concerns pertaining to the employee engagement practices and organizational commitment. Prepare a report of about 15 pages reflecting an action plan for better work practices.

REFERENCES

Allen, N.J. and J.P. Meyer (1990). 'The Measurement and Antecedents of Affective, Continuance and Normative Commitment to the Organization'. *Journal of Occupational Psychology,* 63, 1–18.

Angle, H. and J. Para (1981). 'An Empirical Assessment of Organizational Commitment and Organizational Effectiveness.' *Administrative Science Quarterly,* 26, 1–14.

Armstrong, M. (2006). *A Handbook of Human Resource Management Practice* (10th edition). Jean Cussons Typesetting, Diss, Norfolk.

Blau, G.J. (1986). 'Job Involvement and Organizational Commitment as Interactive Predictors of Tardiness and Absenteeism.' *Journal of Management,* 12 (4): 577–584.

Buchanan, B.II. (1974). 'Building Organizational Commitment: The Socialization of Managers in Work Organizations.' *Administrative Science Quarterly, 19,* 533–546.

Collins, Badu Agyemang (2014). Employee work engagement and organizational commitment: a comparative study of private and public sector organizations in Ghana. Retrieved on 8th May 2014. http://www.academia.edu/5271218/

Derek Stockley (2005). Employee Engagement Definition. http://derekstockley.com.au/definitions.html

Ellingwood, S. (2001). 'The Collective Advantage.' *Gallup Management Journal,* 1 (3).

Farrell, D., & Stamm, C. L. (1988). 'Meta-analysis of the correlates of employee absence.' *Human Relations,* 41, 211–227.

Greene, C.N. (1989). 'Cohesion and Productivity in Work Groups'. *Small Group Behavior,* 20, 70–86.

Greene, Charles N. (1978). 'Identification modes of professionals: Relationship with formalization role strain and alienation.' *Academy of Management Journal,* 21 (3): 486-92.

Hogan, Dan and Roth, Karen (1984). Positive Organizational Climate: The Key to Quality Circles. Guides - Non-Classroom Reports Research.

Holbeche, Linda (2013). Employee engagement as key to recovery: the management challenge. retrieved on 9 June 2013. http://www.mbsportal.bl.uk/taster/subjareas/hrmemplyrelat/britishlibrary/engagement13.aspx

Huselid, M. and Day, N. (1991). 'Organizational Commitment, Job Involvement, and Turnover: A Substantive and Methodological Analysis.' *Journal of Applied Psychology,* 76 (3), 380-391.

Hussami, A.L.M. and R.N. (2008). 'A Study of Nurses' Job Satisfaction.' *European Journal of Scientific Research.* 22 (2), 286–295.

Ingram, Thomas N., Keun S. Lee and George H. Lucas (1991), 'Commitment and Involvement: Assessing a Sales force Typology.' Journal of the Academy of Marketing Science, 19 (3), 187-197.

Kaila, H.L. (2007). *Organizational Behavior & HRM* (2nd edition). Delhi: AITBS Publishers.

Kanter, R.M. (1968). 'Commitment and Social Organization: A Study of Commitment Mechanisms in Utopian Communities.' *American Sociological Review, 33,* 499–517.

Kanungo, R.N. (1982). 'Measurement of Job and Work Involvement.' *Journal of Applied Psychology,* 67: 341–349.

Landy, J. Frank and Conte, M. Jeffrey (2005). *An Introduction to Industrial Psychology and Organizational Psychology.* Tata McGraw-Hill.

Lawler, Edward E.; Hall, Douglas T. (1970). 'Relationship of Job Characteristics to Job Involvement, Satisfaction, and Intrinsic Motivation.' *Journal of Applied Psychology,* 54(4), 305-312.

Losh, S. (2001). *Group Processes: Guide to the Material: Six Cohesiveness II.* Florida State University.

Melcrum (2007). Employee Engagement: A Review of the Most Current Research. Career Development International.

Meyer, J., S. Paunonen, I. Gellatly, R. Goffin and D. Jackson (1989). 'Organizational Commitment and Job Performance: It's the Nature of the Commitment that Counts.' In: Kaila, H.L. (2005). *Human Resource Management.* (Vol. 2). Delhi: Kalpaz Publications.

Meyer, J.P. and N.J. Allen (1991). 'A Three-component Conceptualization of Organizational Commitment.' *Human Resource Management Review, 1,* 61–89.

Meyer, J.P., N.J. Allen and C.A. Smith (1993). 'Commitment to Organizations and Occupations: Extension and Test of a Three-component Conceptualization.' *Journal of Applied Psychology, 78,* 538–551.

Meyer, J.P., N.J. Allen and R. Gellatly (1990). 'Affective & Continuance Commitment to the Organization: Evaluation of Measures and Analysis of Concurrent and Time Lagged Relations.' *Journal of Applied Psychology, 75,* 710–720.

Mowday, R.T., L.W. Porter and R.M. Steers (1982). *Employee-Organization Linkages: The Psychology of Commitment, Absenteeism and Turnover.* San Diego, CA: Academic Press.

Mowday, R.T., R.M. Steers and L.W. Porter (1979). 'The Measurement of Organizational Commitment.' *Journal of Vocational Behavior,* 14: 224–247.

O'Brien, T., D. Akroyd and B. Richards (1993). *Work Satisfaction and Organizational Commitment of Marketing Education Teachers.* Paper presented at the National Research Conference for Marketing Education, Galveston, TX.

Porter, L., R. Steers, R. Mowday and P. Boulian (1974). 'Organizational Commitment, Job Satisfaction, and Turnover Among Psychiatric Technicians.' *Journal of Applied Psychology,* 59, 603–609.

Porter, L., W. Crampon and F. Smith (1976). 'Organizational Commitment and Managerial Turnovers: A Longitudinal Study.' *Organizational Behavior and Human Performance,* 15, 87–98.

Porter, Lyman W., Richard M. Steers, Richard T. Mowday and Paul V. Boulian (1974). 'Organizational Commitment, Job Satisfaction, and Turnover among Psychiatric Technicians.' *Journal of Applied Psychology, 5,* 603–609.

Riordan, C.M. and W. Griffeth (1995). 'The Opportunity for Friendship in the Workplace: An Underexplored Construct.' *Journal of Business and Psychology,* 10(2): 141–154.

Robbins, S.P. and T.A. Judge (2008). *Organizational Behavior* (2nd Edition). Pearson Prentice Education. 89–103.

Shore L.M., L.A. Newton and G.C. Thornton (1990). 'Job and Organizational Attitudes in Relation to Employee Behavioural Intention.' *Journal of Organizational Behaviour,* 11, 57-67.

Steve Crabtree (2004). 'Are Negative Relationships Squelching Productivity in Your Company?' *The Gallup Management Journal,* 74, 152–156.

Thomas W. Lee and Terence R. Mitchell (1994). 'An Alternative Approach: The Unfolding Model of Voluntary Employee Turnover.' *The Academy of Management Review,* 19 (1), 51-89.

Wayne, F. Cascio (1995). *Managing Human Resources* (5th edition). Tata McGraw-Hill Publishing Company, New Delhi. 154–163.

Wech, B., K. Mossholder, R. Steel and N. Bennett (1998). 'Does Work Group Cohesiveness Affect Individual Performance and Organizational Commitment? A Cross-level Examination.' *Small Group Research, 29,* 472–495.

Wright, T.L. and D. Duncan (1986). 'Attraction to Group, Group Cohesiveness, and Individual Outcome: A Study of Training Groups.' *Small Group Behavior. 17,* 487-492.

APPENDIX: I

Questionnaire on Employee Engagement

Please answer the questionnaire by ticking the appropriate box. Each statement is to be rated on a five point rating scale: 5, 4, 3, 2, and 1, indicating how much you agree with the 'correctness' of the statements, where

5 – extremely satisfied/fully agree

4 – satisfied/agree

3 – neutral

2 – dissatisfied/disagree

1 – extremely dissatisfied/fully disagree

Kindly answer all the questions

Sr. No.		*5*	*4*	*3*	*2*	*1*
1.	How satisfied are you with Origin India as a place to work?					
2.	I will recommend Origin India as a great place to build a meaningful career.					
3.	Two years from now, I can still see myself working for Origin India.					
4.	This last year, I have had opportunities at work to learn and grow.					
5.	In the last six months, someone at work has talked to me about my progress.					
6.	I have a best friend at work.					
7.	My associates or fellow employees are committed to doing quality work.					
8.	The mission or purpose of my company makes me feel my job is important.					
9.	At work, my opinions seem to count.					
10.	There is someone at work who encourages my development.					
11.	My supervisor, or someone at work, seems to care about me as a person.					
12.	In the last seven days, I have received recognition or praise for doing good work.					
13.	At work, I have the opportunity to do what I do best every day.					
14.	I have the materials and equipment I need to do my work right.					
15.	I know what is expected of me at work.					
16.	I take pride in working at Origin India.					
17.	All departments (support groups and business units) in my organization work towards achieving a common goal.					
18.	I feel that I am well informed of the various happenings across Origin India.					
19.	I am satisfied with the forums and platforms available to discuss important topics relevant to the organization.					
20.	I believe that the leadership at Origin India will successfully manage emerging challenges.					
21.	I believe that the leadership at Origin India communicates effectively with the rest of the organization.					
22.	I believe that the culture at Origin India is open and transparent.					
23.	I am given the freedom to experiment and learn at my work.					
24.	At Origin India, we feel great responsibility for the quality of service we deliver to our customers.					
25.	I'm satisfied with the speed of decision making on various issues at my company.					

26.	I believe the existing systems and processes in Origin India enable better service to customers.						
27.	I am satisfied with the cooperation that I get from colleagues from other departments.						
28.	I believe the performance management system at Origin India clearly distinguishes good performers from poor performers.						
29.	I believe the appraisal process is taken seriously by managers at Origin India.						
30.	I am satisfied with the job rotation opportunities available at Origin India.						
31.	I see a clear growth path for myself within Origin India.						
32.	At Origin India, I have received adequate training necessary to do my job well.						
33.	I am confident that the issues arising out of this survey will be acted upon.						
34.	Please express your ideas freely on any of the subject regarding Origin India that you wish to convey to the management. What are the strengths and improvements you see being a part of Origin India?						

APPENDIX: II

Questionnaire on Organizational Commitment

Occupation: Gender:

Please tick the most appropriate alternative according to you, and your working habits:

1. I like doing challenging work that allows me to explore my talents.
   - Always • Sometimes • Never
2. I put in extra hours to complete my work.
   - Always • Sometimes • Never
3. I cannot sit idle doing nothing.
   - Always • Sometimes • Never
4. Constant job changes motivate me.
   - Always • Sometimes • Never
5. There is a constant dread of losing my job.
   - Always • Sometimes • Never
6. I make a list of things to do before starting work.
   - Always • Sometimes • Never
7. I can work at anytime and anywhere.
   - Always • Sometimes • Never
8. It is important for me to complete work on time than the quality of it.
   - Always • Sometimes • Never

9. I enjoy doing my work.
   - Always • Sometimes • Never
10. I always like taking risk and trying new things which will enhance my work.
   - Always • Sometimes • Never
11. I work on weekends and holidays.
   - Always • Sometimes • Never
12. I feel motivated to work in my organization.
   - Always • Sometimes • Never
13. I get lot of satisfaction from achieving my targets.
   - Always • Sometimes • Never
14. My current job helps me to develop my skills and knowledge.
   - Always • Sometimes • Never
15. I take a break from work when I feel bored.
   - Always • Sometimes • Never
16. I exceed my company's expectations of me.
   - Always • Sometimes • Never
17. I do not take my work seriously.
   - Always • Sometimes • Never
18. I feel emotionally attached to my organization.
   - Always • Sometimes • Never
19. I am willing to work as hard as necessary to get the job done.
   - Always • Sometimes • Never
20. I waste a lot of time doing nothing productive.
   - Always • Sometimes • Never

7

Organizational Culture and Performance

Learning Objectives

This chapter would help the readers:

- to understand the concept and definitions of organizational culture;
- to review the organizational culture and its impact on performance;
- to be familiar with the researches on organizational culture; and
- to reflect upon case study about organizational culture.

An Opening Story: Organizational Culture and Performance

Both organizational culture and performance are correlated. Good culture would promote performance, and bad culture would discourage performance. The following case proves this.

OHSAS 18001:2007 (occupational health safety assessment series) recommended that organizations must adopt a 'procedure' to involve employees so that they would identify and control the risk at workplaces. Taking this further, a Navratna oil company implemented this procedure. In order to develop organizational safety culture, the company involved all employees and workmen in certain locations for conducting and leading safe behaviours/ performance. The company trained all employees to observe and correct any at-risk behaviour (that would trigger an accident) being done by any colleague at the workplace. This procedure was practised by employees on a regular basis which generated an organizational culture of safe behaviours or performances, which resulted in reduction of accidents and injuries at the workplaces. This organizational safety culture was adopted by many companies which proved that organizational culture and employee performance are truly correlated.

7.1 INTRODUCTION

Culture is the basis of people's beliefs and practices that drive an organization's performance. Cultures across an organization have been researched in many ways so as to impact the employee identity and performance, organizational change and leadership (Alvesson 2013). Healthy culture behaviours include collaboration, appreciation, and supportive and accountable behaviours, as well as selflessness for the greater good of the organization. Dysfunctional culture includes barriers such as internal competition, lack of ability to adapt or change, hierarchical leadership, a critical mindset that staunches new ideas, lack of accountability, trust issues, and hidden agendas (Niurka Rivero, Beth Zemetra, and Cynde Herman 2014).

Previous researches have shown that organizational culture has a considerable influence on employees' socialization and performance. Therefore, it is important for an organization to study the relationship between these two variables. To check this relationship, a case study is gathered from 50 employees of HR department of one of the leading power trading company by using questionnaire and interview techniques. The organizational culture is measureable by the questionnaire which reveals strong or weak culture. On the other hand, for measuring performance, a self-developed questionnaire is used. There is a positive relation between the organization's culture and performance of employees. By and large, a stronger organization culture will lead to a higher performance level of an employee.

This chapter highlights the significance and explores the relationship between organizational culture (OC) and employee performance.

7.2 THE IMPORTANCE OF ORGANIZATIONAL CULTURE

The importance of understanding OC is growing in recent developments. Understanding one's own culture and the impact of culture on the actions of others is essential for effective global business interactions. The culture of an organization is something that can have an enormous impact on the way in which an organization operates, and its effectiveness.

Organizational culture is concerned with the level of performance achieved by each employee in an organization. One of the main objectives of an organization is to build a strong OC which helps to improve staff performance and create an environment where people can work efficiently. HR plays an important role in the culture of the organization as it has to understand and communicate with both the management and the employees. It is useful to assess a firm's OC and hence it is important to find out the relationship between OC and performance.

> **Good to Know**
> Organizational values have a strong influence on employee behaviour as well as performance.

There is no single definition of organizational culture. Organizational culture refers to a system of shared meaning held by members that distinguishes the organization from other organizations. This system of shared meaning is actually a set of key characteristics that the organization values (Robbins and Sanghi 2007). Schein (1990), in a more comprehensive fashion, defines culture as values and behaviours that are believed to lead to success and are thus taught to new members.

The more clearly an organization shares its values, the more strongly people can associate themselves with their organization's mission and feel a vital part of it. The value of an organization's culture derives from the guidance it gives to direct people's behaviour toward higher performance.

7.3 DETERMINANTS OF STRONG ORGANIZATIONAL CULTURE

Managers are increasingly interested in knowing the components of OC. The effects of OC vary depending on whether the company has a strong culture or a weak culture. A strong organization will focus on the environment it creates for its workers because that will help encourage a more efficient and productive company.

> **Good to Know**
> Focussing on building and sustaining a strong organizational culture shows employees that they are considered an important part of the company.

Strong company culture can be defined as a set of norms and values that are widely shared and strongly held throughout the organization. A high degree of organization performance is related to an organization, which has a strong culture with well integrated and effective set of values, beliefs, and behaviours. Successful organizations have a focus on the performance of their employees. Here employees are rewarded based purely on their performance on a set criteria. Their performance goals and targets are clearly defined and communicated to them in a formal way.

Weak culture refers to an organization that either does not possess a clearly identifiable set of values and beliefs, or else possesses them but fails to get them widely shared by employees. A culture is weak or fragmented to the extent that those widely different values and beliefs are held which lead to employee feelings of separateness from the organization. Low performance culture can derail a company's strategy thereby negatively affecting performance. It is generally accepted that strong corporate cultures are 'good' while weak cultures are 'bad' for an organization. Therefore, each organization would need to create strong and adaptive culture to achieve positive effect on performance level.

> **Good to Know**
> It is vital to recognize that a strong relationship exists between organizational culture and employee performance.

If strong culture helps building high performance company, the past performance and successes influence people behaviours which, with time, become part of the culture. The literature on OC and performance revealed that companies that know how to develop their cultures in an effective way most probably have the benefit of advancement in performance and the quality of work life among the employees. Measuring OC to find its relationship with performance, the opposition between strong and weak OC is widely spread. For example, Gordon et al. (1992) and Lim (1995) have found that the stronger the OC, the better the performance of the organization and also claim to have found a link between strong cultures and high levels of corporate performance.

Many studies of OC are focussed on other factors also, for example, a study conducted by Marcoulides and Heck (1993) measured OC using several latent variables (organizational structure, organizational values, task organization, climate, and individual values and beliefs) and organizational performance was measured using capital, market and financial indicators. The results of this study showed that all of the latent variables used to measure OC had some effect on performance with workers' attitudes and task organization activities being the most significant variables.

More recently study done by Ogbonna and Harris (2002) analysed the relationship between OC and performance by including the leadership style as a third variable in the model. To measure performance, companies used variables such as customer satisfaction, sales growth, market share, competitive advantage and sales volume. For OC they used measures such as competitive culture, innovative culture, bureaucratic culture, and community culture. The results showed that all four measures of OC were associated in some way with organization performance.

7.4 CORRELATION BETWEEN ORGANIZATIONAL CULTURE AND EMPLOYEE PERFORMANCE

Performance is defined as the extent to which an individual is carrying out an assignment or task. It refers to the degree of accomplishment of the task that makes up an employee's job. Therefore, culture or shared values within the organization may be related to increased performance.

> **Good to Know**
>
> Culture plays a vital role in improving performance and it is essential to study these two variables in order to find out their relationship.

There was a survey conducted by Kotter and Heskett (1992) which showed strong relationship between these two variables. They used data gathered from 207 firms over a five-year period and used various measures of culture and long-term economic performance data. Their objective was to examine the relationship between strong cultures and long-term performance subsequent investigations showed that firms with cultures suited to their market environment have better performance than those that are less fitted to their environment.

Companies endeavour to develop the right OC where employees focus on building a strong culture for a better performance. The culture has to be valuable, which means that it must allow the company to behave in a manner that will lead to higher profits, lower costs, and other results that improve the financial performance of the firm. Their aim is to encourage employees to be more responsible and act and think like owners. Also to encourage formation of teams, as a strong culture is one in which they work together effectively and share values. The overall purpose is to identify the OC, define relationship of OC with employee performance, and provide recommendations for future improvement in work.

7.5 A RESEARCH CASE STUDY

The objective of this study is to reflect that OC and employee job performance are related, that is, if a positive relationship is found between the two variables, then the organization must target on strengthening their 'culture' to check whether this will be the factor for improving employees job performance and thereby achieving company goals (H.L. Kaila 2007).

Description of Organization: The organization on which the current study was carried is a leading power trading company catalysing development of the Indian electricity market. In the organization the number of employees working is approximately 3800. The company's operations include wind, hydroelectric and thermal power generation, as well as power distribution and transmission in various locations like Mumbai, Jharkhand, West Bengal, Karnataka, and many other places. With vast technical, managerial, and financial capabilities, it provides a range of services to its customers. The organization provides a healthy workplace and friendly environment for its employees and it really motivates them in sharpening their skills. Therefore, it is actively pursuing growth and expansion plans to the meet the ever increasing power requirements.

Sample of the Study: In the present survey, the questionnaires were filled up by 50 employees of the Human Resources Department both at managerial and non-managerial level. Among the 50 respondents, 14 were female and the rest were male. The ages of the respondents varied from 26 years to 49 years. Some of the employees were managers and a few were marketing directors.

Measurement Used in Study: This study has been initiated to examine the relationship between culture and employee job performance. The necessary data to fulfil the research objective were obtained from the survey. In order to find the connection between the two variables the survey included two parts:

Measurement of Organization Culture: The questionnaire titled 'Organization Culture Questionnaire' (see Appendix A) developed by Dr. G. Revathi was used for the present study. Previously it was used for Sarva Shikksha Abhiyaan (SSA) state project set up in Tamil Nadu to understand the organization culture of SSA. Twenty-five items were used to assess the OC on a 5-point Likert scale. Respondents were simply asked to indicate their agreement with the above items on a scale ranging from 'strongly disagree' to 'strongly agree'. If the subject's score is between 25–70 then it's a weak culture and if between 71–125 then it's a strong culture.

Measurement of Performance: Self-developed questionnaire titled 'Employee Job Performance' was used (see Appendix B). Thirty-four items were used to assess the OC on a 5-point Likert scale. Respondents were simply asked to indicate their agreement with the above items on a scale ranging from 'strongly agree' to 'strongly disagree'. If the subject's score is between 34–90 it reflects high on performance and if between 91–170 then low on performance.

Procedure of Data Collection: The researcher distributed the questionnaire to the employees. Each participant in the survey was informed that the participation was voluntary. All the respondents were asked to return the questionnaire directly to the researcher. After calculating the scores, employees were interviewed on the basis of the results obtained.

Research Techniques Used: The survey research design was adopted in this study. Every research focusses on collecting data accurately and economically therefore, the method of data collection used consists of a number of structured questionnaires that were administered to the respondents which included interview of a few employees. In the present investigation, the random sampling technique has been employed for sampling where each and every member of the population has an equal chance of being included in the sample. The statistical technique used in the present research is correlation. This method has been used where there is an attempt to search the relationship between two variables or to find out the extent to which the two variables are related to each other.

Analysis of Data: The present study was done in order to study the relationship between OC and employee performance among employees aged 26-49 years using the correlation method. Since result of the study showed that there is a positive relationship between the two variables, the high scores on OC revealed a strong culture and therefore employees' level of performance will be high.

To measure OC of a company, a questionnaire on OC was administered to a sample of 50 employees and to measure performance, the Employees Performance Questionnaire also administered to the same sample. After that the correlation was calculated using the Pearson's Correlation Coefficient.

In the beginning, the sample was given the OC questionnaire, for which out of 50 the percentage of employees showing stronger and weak culture was also calculated. The following range was used for the interpretation:

25–70 - Weak culture

71–125 - Strong culture

From the above mentioned range it is clearly visible that 66% of the employees reported strong culture and 34% reported weak culture (refer Table 7.1).

Survey Results: The results of the research project are derived from the collection and evaluation of all the data collected. The survey was administered to a sample of 50 employees and data has been analysed. Based on analysed data, the findings are:

- The findings of the present study revealed that there a positive relationship between OC and employee performance.
- On an OC scale, most of the employees responded between the range of (71–125) and some responded between the ranges of (25–70). Therefore, 66% of the employees reported strong culture and 34% reported weak culture.
- A large number of respondents lies between the range of (34–90) and very few lie between the ranges of 91–170. Therefore, 84% respondents showed high performance level and 16% showed low performance level on performance scale.
- This study further reveals that there is a positive relationship between OC and employee performance. Correlation coefficient (*r*) for the two variables are:

- Organization culture
- Employee performance

$$r = +.71$$

The correlation coefficient was calculated using Pearson's correlation coefficient formula which is given below:

$$R = \Sigma(X\text{-}X^{-})\ (Y\text{-}Y^{-})/\sqrt{}(SSx)\ (SSy), \text{ where } X = OC \text{ and } Y = \text{Performance}$$

Further, from the statements mentioned on the OC questionnaire, it can be concluded that each of the specific aspects of improvement such as more freedom at work, higher receptivity to feedback, more open communication, less bureaucracy and more flexibility in the organization, adequacy and appropriateness of training, and pleasantness of the work environment, have also received a high percentage of endorsement. Many respondents agree that their attitude towards work and/or the organization has become more positive. A very small percentage of the respondents did not agree that their attitude towards work and/or the organization had become more positive: around half of them agreed that this was because they did not find their work interesting; around one-third felt that they did not have the knowledge and/or the skills to do their jobs properly; less than half agreed that their job/role was not clear. More than three-fourths of the respondents agreed that they felt comfortable working in the organization. On queries about organizational leadership there is a high percentage of positive responses. A majority of the respondents agree that they can talk freely and openly about issues or problems in the organization to their colleagues as well as their superiors, and they also agree that the organization is willing to listen to feedback from employees, as well as clarify any doubts that employees might have about their roles or the new systems. Almost three-fourths of the respondents agree that they are allowed to make decisions regarding their work, new ideas are encouraged by management at all levels of the organization, the organization forgives mistakes and allows people to learn from them, and the organization is flexible enough to respond to changes quickly. More than three-fourths of the respondents agree that people in the organization are aware of the organization's vision or purpose. Almost one-third of the respondents described the organization's culture as collaborative. Lastly, respondents suggested focussing on an effective culture to align with the business strategy to ensure the organization meets its long-term goals.

These results definitely show a strong or a positive OC of a company. A strong OC could be one where the majority of the participants hold the same basic beliefs and values to the organization. This finding was consistent with pervious researches. Thus, results show that various aspects of OC of the company are strongly held by the employees.

The employees were also given Employee Performance Questionnaire for which out of 50 the percentage of employees showing high and low level of performance was calculated. The questionnaire has two scales:

34–90 - (High performance)

91–170 - (Low performance)

From the above-mentioned scale it is clearly visible that most of the employees lie between the range of 35–90 and a few lie between the range of 91–170. Therefore, 84% respondents showed high performance whereas 16% showed low performance (Table 7.1). Building a high performance OC is more important now than ever before. In high performing OC, employees have a sense of personal responsibility for understanding and staying with current external trends in the environment.

Table 7.1 Score Range of OC and Empoyee Performance Questionnaire

Organization Culture		*Employee Performance*	
Score Range	Percentage of Sample	Score Range	Percentage of Sample
25–70	34%	34–90	84%
71–125	66%	91–170	16%

Further, from the statements mentioned on the Employee Performance Questionnaire it can be seen that majority of the respondents, agree that goals will enable to improve performance, clarity of goal will help in planning work better, resource planning to achieve goal needs to be improved, a regular review of goals will enable one to take early corrective action. A very small percentage of respondents agrees that resolution can be reached only by proper understanding of the other parties' position and judgments can be made by segregating relevant information from irrelevant information. About almost three-fourths of the respondents agree that goals are dependent on the goals of other members of their team, they are able to understand the relationship between their goals and activities. Also, 90% of the respondents agree that attending various sessions related to their area of interest improved their performance, setting goals will enable them to achieve a better work life balance and they would like to acquire new knowledge and skills that contribute to individual and organizational growth. Lastly, for both induction and skill training, employees gave 'fair' ratings which means there is a need for better training programmes. But the overall result reveals that employees have achieved high level of performance.

The Pearson's correlation coefficient has been used to assess relationship between the existing OC and the employee performance scales. Table 7.2 shows there was a strong, significant positive relationship between the organization culture and the employee performance. The correlation coefficient value was $r = +.71$.

Table 7.2 Correlation Coefficient Between OC and Employee Performance

Two Variables	*Correlation Coefficient (R)*
Organization Culture (X) Employee Performance (Y)	0.7136

Organizational culture and performance have a mutually reciprocating relationship. If strong culture helps building high performance company, the past performance and successes shape and influence people's behaviours which with time become part of the culture. High scores on both OC and employee performance scales indicate a linear relationship between the two variables. Therefore, if one variable increases the other will also increase. The findings of this research are supported by Gordon et al. (1992) and Lim's (1995) study stating that the stronger the OC, the better the performance of the organization.

Culture enables people to see the goal alignment and motivates them to higher levels of performance, as shared values make people feel good about the organization and commit their capability and potential sincerely for the company. A strong culture acts like an intrinsic motivator. Empowerment, decisiveness, learning attitude, and team working are some of the attributes of a strong OC. Culture at this level is the real driver for superior performance and a definite source of competitive advantage that is very difficult for competitors to emulate. For example, Microsoft believes it is very important for the entire organization to have the company's values align with its overall performance, including employee retention. Recently, the company did a few changes in the value system and is looking at a few more like feedback from peers and stakeholders.

7.5.1 Interview Data Support Relationship between Organization Culture and Performance

The interview session was held after evaluating the results of the current study and it was found that responses of the employees are in line with the current study and also support the researches mentioned earlier. The researcher conducted face-to-face interview with few employees and it helped to gather in-depth information about the relationship between OC and performance.

During the interview the interviewees were questioned about their understanding of OC, importance of culture at work place, some **characteristics that have made people successful in the organization, whether their performance is evaluated periodically,** *how strongly does OC affect performance of an employee, and about what changes they want in the organization for future improvement.* Most of the employees stated that they feel OC is simply the culture of an organization and having a set culture for any organization will help to define employee expectations. According to them importance of any company is based on a set value system and matching the culture and values of the organization to each candidate's personal values is important to achieve success. Many things contribute to be successful at work, that is, good environment, sharing same beliefs and values, having trust, how employees interact and the training and skills development they receive, which they need both on the job and to keep themselves marketable for future jobs. Also, their performance is evaluated annually which helps them to know where they stand and make initiatives for better results, this will also help to increase the salary. Very importantly, for future growth a strong organization should focus on the environment it creates for its workers because that will help encourage a more efficient and productive company. Further, they said that developing the right OC is not just the responsibility of the human resource department; the top management of every company should be proactively involved in the process because OC has a major impact on employee morale and productivity.

Recommendations

Since the organization is perceived to be effective, and since most of the respondents have positive feelings about it, the management should take care to maintain the current way of working. A strong and positive OC will help make everyone more efficient and successful. Right from the mail room worker to the CEO, a strong culture helps everyone. In addition, on the basis of some of the responses from the respondents, the following recommendations are made:

- An individual should be allowed to internalize himself first with the organization's culture and values to know whether he can cope with them or not this because every individual had a different culture that he works with.
- In strong cultures, the values that shape the organization's culture can be uncovered by observing how employees interact and the choices they make as well as by inquiring about their beliefs and perceptions regarding what is correct and appropriate behaviour.
- Since respondents gave 'fair' rating to training programmes held in the company, the focus on training should continue. More days should be allotted for training, and the schedules should be intimated in advance.
- Employees must absorb the OC at the maximum strength and the top management should provide precise guidelines and directions to motivate the employees for achieving the company's objectives. This will help in better performance at the workplace.

7.6 CASES OF A POWER AND A COMMUNICATION (MOBILE PHONE) COMPANY

This case has explored the nature of relationship between organizational culture and motivation. It was hypothesized that there will be a positive correlation between strong OC and motivational needs whereas there will be a negative correlation between weak organizational culture and motivational needs. The sample size consisted of 50 employees belonging to two different organizations – a power and a mobile phone company. In each organization 25 employees were tested, that is, 13 males and 12 females, respectively. The tools utilized were two close-ended questionnaires—Organizational Culture Assessment Instrument (OCAI) and McClelland's Motivation (M) questionnaire. *Statistical analysis of Pearson's Product Moment correlation* (*r*) [*consisting of Strong Organizational Culture and Motivational Needs*] *of Males in Tata Power* showed a high positive correlation between Organizational Culture (OCAI-Clan Culture Type) and Motivational needs [n-Ach] ($r = 0.73, p < 0.01$); moderate positive correlation between Organizational Culture (OCAI-Clan Culture Type) and Motivational needs [n-Affil] ($r = 0.58, p < 0.05$), and moderate positive correlation between Organizational Culture (OCAI-Clan Culture Type) and Motivational needs [n-Pow] ($r = 0.60, p < 0.05$). The '*r*' of *Females in Tata Power* showed a moderate positive correlation between Organizational Culture (OCAI-Clan Culture Type) and Motivational needs [n-Ach] (r = 0.65, $p <$ 0.05), high positive correlation between Organizational Culture (OCAI-Clan Culture Type) and Motivational needs [n-Affil] (r = 0.80, $p < 0.01$), and moderate positive correlation between Organizational Culture (OCAI-Clan Culture Type) and Motivational needs [n-Pow] (r = 0.68, $p < 0.05$). In case of *'r' [consisting of Weak Organizational Culture and Motivational Needs] of Males in* Mobile Phone Company, it showed high negative correlation between Organizational Culture (OCAI-Market Culture Type) and Motivational needs [n-Ach] (r = – 0.74, $p < 0.05$), high negative correlation between Organizational Culture (OCAI-Market Culture Type) and Motivational needs [n-Affil] (r = – 0.76, $p < 0.05$), and high negative correlation between Organizational Culture (OCAI-Market Culture Type) and Motivational needs [n-Pow] (r = – 0.80, $p < 0.05$). The '*r*' of *Females in Airtel DTH* showed high negative correlation between Organizational Culture (OCAI-Market Culture Type) and Motivational needs [n-Ach] (r = – 0.71, $p <$ 0.05), moderate negative correlation between Organizational Culture (OCAI-Market Culture Type) and Motivational needs [n-Affil] (r = – 0.69, p < 0.05), and moderate negative correlation between Organizational Culture (OCAI-Market Culture Type) and Motivational needs [n-Pow] (r = –0.68, $p < 0.05$). The present Correlational Study (H.L. Kaila 2007) was conducted to assist the organizations to recognize their prevailing OS and to successfully deal with their organizational changes by recognizing employees' motivational needs which will ultimately increase employees' job satisfaction, production, organizational growth and development, and decrease attrition rate in the future.

The above case study results can be explained by saying that the power company, through its visions, has rendered productive services in all frontiers to the Indian community from several decades and successfully continues to do so through its excellent OC and climate approaches. The company has clear-cut vision, mission, values like integrity, trust, care, collaboration, agility, respect, excellence, and agreement which forces the employees to adhere to the code of conduct that is followed very diligently by most of its employees that makes the organization a class apart from the rest. The results of this power company employees' shows positive relationship between strong organizational culture (clan culture type) and motivational needs (n-Ach, n-Affil, n-Pow) which is due to their adoption of the Tata Business Excellence Model (TBEM). There are various initiatives conducted at the company like learning initiatives, developmental initiatives, induction programmes, and the like which are responsible for the healthy OC that results into increased satisfaction of all motivational needs of employees.

In the case of a mobile phone company, it is an Indian direct broadcast satellite service provider which has the legacy of leadership. The company also has a laid down vision, mission, brand promise, brand scorecard, brand essence, values like alive, inclusive, and respectful which are responsible for its survival in cut-throat market competition. The results of the mobile phone company employees show a negative relationship between weak organizational culture (market culture type) and motivational needs (n-Ach, n-Affil, n-Pow) which is due to the employees orientation in preferring to desire for an organizational change, that is, from market culture type (high competition, success, individualism leading to decrease of prevailing employee relationships with each other, and so on) to opting for adhocracy and clan market culture types along with dominant prevailing market culture type, that can further increase the motivational needs of the employees, high job satisfaction, and high performance.

Thus, the strong and weak organizational culture types can accordingly affect the employees' motivational needs. Through the administration of OCAI (organizational culture assessment instrument) and motivation (M) questionnaires the organizations can accordingly deal with their organizational changes, by recognizing employees' motivational needs, which will ultimately increase employees' job satisfaction, production, organizational growth and development and decrease, attrition rate in the future.

SUMMARY

- Organizational culture has a significant contribution towards employees socialization and performance processes.
- Organizational culture across the world has been studied in diverse ways as to influence performance, identity, leadership, and organizational change.
- Particularly, the relationship between organizational culture and performance has been in focus on a regular basis by the companies which is strongly depicted by earlier researches.
- Companies that know how to develop their strong organizational culture in an effective way will most probably have the benefit of increased performance and the quality of work life among the employees.
- This chapter revealed the importance of organizational culture, correlation between organizational culture and employee performance, the determinants of strong organizational culture, and research case studies of two companies.

EXERCISE FOR CLASSROOM PRACTICE

For better understanding of the subject matter of this chapter, please read and check each of the following statements whether True (T) or False (F) or Uncertain (U).

1. Organizational culture has an impact on the employee performance, organizational change, and leadership.
2. Organizational culture is measureable by the organizational hierarchy and structure.
3. One of the main objectives of an organization is to build a strong organizational culture and create an environment where people can work efficiently.

4. Human resource department plays an important role in the culture of the organization as it has to understand and communicate with both the management and the employees.
5. Organizational culture refers to a system of shared values and beliefs held by members that distinguishes the organization from other organizations.
6. The significance of an organization's culture derives from the guidance it gives to direct people's behaviour toward higher salary and promotion.
7. Performance is defined as the extent to which an individual is carrying out a task and the degree of accomplishment of the task that makes up an employee's job.
8. Companies endeavour to develop the right organizational culture where employees focus on building a strong culture for a better performance.
9. Strong cultures can be defined as a set of norms and values that are widely shared and strongly held throughout the organization.
10. Weak culture refers to an organization that either does not possess a clearly identifiable set of values and beliefs, or else possesses them but fails to get them widely shared by employees.
11. Studies reveal that the stronger the OC, the lower the performance of the organization.
12. To measure performance, companies used variables such as customer satisfaction, sales growth, market share, competitive advantage, and sales volume.

Answers: All statements are **True** except that statement numbers 2, 6, and 11 are **False.**

REVIEW QUESTIONS FOR DISCUSSIONS/EXAMINATIONS

1. Describe the concept and definitions of organizational culture?
2. Discuss a few researches on organizational culture in the Indian context?
3. Critically review the relationship between organizational culture and performance of employees.
4. Discuss a case study on organizational culture and its implications.
5. Address diverse ways in which organizational culture can be understood to impact employee work life.
6. Reflect upon the relationship between organizational culture and leadership.
7. Explore issues related to multiple levels of culture and its influence on employee performance.
8. Describe how a culture can be a constraint in organizational change.
9. How can an employee's identity be affected by the organizational culture?
10. Compare and contrast between the organizational cultures of two organizations.

FIELD RESEARCH REPORT

This is a research assignment section for students for their internal marking by the teacher during the semester. This assignment is for understanding practical application of the subject.

An action research project: Identify a group of minimum 15 executives and 15 non-executives across an organization preferably where you are placed for an internship. Conduct interviews with them by using a set of closed/open-ended questionnaire to signify the issues and concerns pertaining to the organizational culture and employee performance. Prepare a report of about 15 pages reflecting an action plan for better work practices.

REFERENCES

Alvesson Mats (2013). *Understanding Organizational Culture.* London: SAGE Publications Ltd.

Gordon, G.G. and N. DiTomaso (1992). 'Predicting Corporate Performance from Organizational Culture.' *Journal of Management Studies,* 29, 783–798.

Kaila H.L. (2007). *Organizational Behavior & HRM.* (2nd edition). Delhi: AITBS Publishers.

Kotter, John P., James L. Heskett (1992). *Corporate Culture and Performance.* New York: Free Press.

Lim, B. (1995). 'Examining the Organizational Culture and Organizational Performance Link.' *Leadership and Organization Development Journal,* 16 (5), 16–21.

Marcoulides, G. and R. Heck (1993). 'Organizational Culture and Performance: Proposing and Testing a Model.' *Organization Science,* 4(2), 209–225.

Niurka Rivero, Beth Zemetra and Cynde Herman (2014). Intersection of Leadership, Organizational Culture, and Clinical Performance. Pediatric and Congenital Cardiology, Cardiac Surgery and Intensive Care, 2014, pp 3391-3408.

Ogbonna, E. and L. Harris (2002). 'Managing Organizational Culture: Insights from the Hospitality Industry.' *Human Resource Management Journal,* 12(1), 22–53.

Robbins, S.P. and S. Sanghi (2007). *Organizational Behavior.* New Delhi: Pearson Education.

Schein, E.H. (1990). 'Organizational Culture.' *American Psychologist,* 43 (2), 109–119.

APPENDIX: I

Organization Culture Questionnaire

Name :

Designation :

Gender : M\F

Please encircle the appropriate column:

Strongly disagree	Disagree	Neither	Agree	Strongly agree
1	2	3	4	5

Please go through the following explanations for clarity on the statements:

1. The organization has become less bureaucratic and more flexible.
   (You are not required to sign your attendance at your office at a particular time each day; you have the freedom to report to office even after visiting a school.)
2. How would you describe your organization's culture? Competitive/Collaborative
   (Competitive – there is rivalry/jealousy/competition amongst the employees; Collaborative – people are willing to help and cooperate with one another.)

1.	In the recent past, there have been some improvements in the organization.	1	2	3	4	5
2.	People have more freedom in their work.	1	2	3	4	5
3.	The organization has become more receptive to feedback.	1	2	3	4	5
4.	There is more open communication within the organization.	1	2	3	4	5
5.	Roles and jobs are now quite clear.	1	2	3	4	5
6.	The organization has become less bureaucratic and more flexible.	1	2	3	4	5
7.	The organization is providing adequate and appropriate training.	1	2	3	4	5
8.	The work environment is pleasant.	1	2	3	4	5
9.	In the recent past, your attitude towards your work and/or the organization has become more positive.	1	2	3	4	5
10.	You now have the knowledge and/or skills to do your job properly.	1	2	3	4	5
11.	Your job/role is now clearer than before.	1	2	3	4	5
12.	You are happy with your own leadership abilities.	1	2	3	4	5
13.	You trust the management of your organization.	1	2	3	4	5
14.	You can talk freely and openly to your colleagues, about issues or problems in the organization.	1	2	3	4	5
15.	You can talk freely and openly to your superiors, about issues or problems in the organization.	1	2	3	4	5
16.	You feel you are spending your time more usefully than before.	1	2	3	4	5
17.	You feel comfortable working here.	1	2	3	4	5
18.	The organization is willing to listen to feedback from employees.	1	2	3	4	5
19.	New ideas from employees are encouraged by management.	1	2	3	4	5
20.	People are allowed to ask questions or clarify doubts (about their roles, the new systems and other issues).	1	2	3	4	5
21.	The organization forgives mistakes and allows people to learn from them.	1	2	3	4	5
22.	You are allowed to make decisions concerning your work.	1	2	3	4	5
23.	The organization is flexible enough to respond to changes quickly.	1	2	3	4	5
24.	People in the organization are aware of the organization's vision/ purpose.	1	2	3	4	5
25.	New ideas from employees are encouraged by the management.	1	2	3	4	5
26.	How would you describe your organization's culture? (Please tick the appropriate option.)	1	2	3	4	5
27.	What are your suggestions for improving your organization still further?	1	2	3	4	5

APPENDIX: II

Employees Performance Questionnaire

Name :

Designation :

Gender : M\F

Please encircle the appropriate column:

Strongly disagree	Disagree	Neither	Agree	Strongly agree
1	2	3	4	5

1.	A clear definition of my goals will enable me to improve my performance.	1	2	3	4	5
2.	My job role has changed substantially over the last 3 years.	1	2	3	4	5
3.	I begin each year with a clear understanding of my goals for the current year.	1	2	3	4	5
4.	Clarity of goal will help me in planning my work better.	1	2	3	4	5
5.	Resource planning to achieve my goal needs to be improved.	1	2	3	4	5
6.	A regular review of my goals will enable me to take early corrective action.	1	2	3	4	5
7.	My goals have been documented and measurable.	1	2	3	4	5
8.	My goals depend on the goals of other members of my team.	1	2	3	4	5
9.	I am able to understand the relationship between my goals and my activities.	1	2	3	4	5
10.	Setting goals will enable me to achieve a better work life balance.	1	2	3	4	5
11.	Proper maintenance and arrangement of the records improve the presentation of my performance.	1	2	3	4	5
12.	At the end of each quarter the updated records are checked and managed for future reference and clarification.	1	2	3	4	5
13.	According to the department norms, I have sorted out my routine activities for better performance.	1	2	3	4	5
14.	Agenda for every project is set and used to review the action performed to reach the goal.	1	2	3	4	5
15.	I regularly review my achievement in the current performance with a pre-set standard.	1	2	3	4	5
16.	Clear understanding of my responsibilities in a team enables me to achieve the shared aims.	1	2	3	4	5
17.	Maintaining unity in our teamwork improves efficiency and able to finish the task within a period.	1	2	3	4	5
18.	Equal sharing of the information in a team and unit, help to improve group cooperation.	1	2	3	4	5
19.	I firmly believe that one can improve oneself by involving in on-job activities and active participation.	1	2	3	4	5

20.	I constantly improve myself by attending various sessions related to my area of interest.	1	2	3	4	5
21.	I would like to acquire new knowledge and skills that contribute to individual and organizational growth.	1	2	3	4	5
22.	Adapting to changing circumstances is the key for my success.	1	2	3	4	5
23.	I am ready to accept change as a part of my achievement and flexible in dealing with diverse situation.	1	2	3	4	5
24.	I constantly improve my ability to manage the changing circumstance readily.	1	2	3	4	5
25.	Applying creative or out of box thinking allows me to modernize and improve the existing process.	1	2	3	4	5
26.	I try to find innovative solution in unique situation, which will improve productivity.	1	2	3	4	5
27.	Proceeding further with creativity will lead to achieve my career path.	1	2	3	4	5
28.	All our activities are focussed on the field of customer orientation.	1	2	3	4	5
29.	My centre of attraction is to assess and balance the interest of different customers and respond to the changing demand.	1	2	3	4	5
30.	We understand each customer is unique and handle each one of them in different ways.	1	2	3	4	5
31.	I firmly believe that clear understanding of the situation will allow me to reach a settlement.	1	2	3	4	5
32.	Resolution reached only by proper understanding of other parties'.	1	2	3	4	5
33.	Judgments can be made by segregating relevant information from irrelevant information.	1	2	3	4	5
34.	My participation in the closing stage of shared decision-making.	1	2	3	4	5

35. How do you rate the organization for the following?

Rating of organization	Very good	Good	Fair	Very poor	Poor
Induction training					
Skill training					
Other (mention)					

8

Motivation and Job Satisfaction

Learning Objectives

This chapter would help the readers:

- to understand the concepts of motivation and job satisfaction;
- to familiarize with the theories of motivation and job satisfaction;
- to figure out job satisfaction in relation to job stress and organizational commitment;
- to be familiar with measuring motivation and job satisfaction; and
- to reflect upon researches on motivation and job satisfaction.

An Opening Story: Job Satisfaction Survey

As motivation and job satisfaction are highly correlated, the companies are now increasingly inclined to conduct periodic job satisfaction surveys in order to find out their employees' satisfaction level with regard to various factors associated with the job.

A multinational corporate launched a comprehensive job satisfaction survey across the company plants in India with an objective to find out areas of low satisfaction so that it could devise strategies to enhance satisfaction of employees on their respective jobs. This survey was conducted company-wide as an organizational intervention programme by an outside consultant.

The survey revealed very significant findings in terms of the employee satisfaction level with the factors as below:

• Achievement	56%
• Recognition for accomplishment	45%
• Challenging work	70%
• Growth and development	56%
• Pay	75%
• Autonomy	68%
• Hours of work	85%
• Interpersonal relationships	82%

From these broad indices, the company received sufficient feedback from employees as to their level of satisfaction on their job measures. The company then discussed the data with different departmental heads and employee representatives in order to take appropriate steps to improve these satisfaction levels which, in turn, would possibly enhance employee motivation, commitment, and performance levels in the company.

8.1 INTRODUCTION

Motivation is defined as a set of forces, needs, and drives within people that will create and maintain voluntary action and energy directed toward the achievement of personal, social, or organizational goals.

According to Pinder (1998), job motivation can be generally defined as a set of energetic forces that originates both within as well as beyond the individual, to initiate work related behaviour, and to determine its form, intensity, direction, and duration.

What motivates people and what demotivates people depends upon two different sets of factors. Similarly, what satisfies people and what dissatisfies them depends upon two diverse bunches of factors. By dealing with sources of demotivation, a manager would not succeed in motivating employees; he must understand the sources that would motivate people. Similarly, a manager must know what factors satisfy and what factors dissatisfy employees. He/she must work on both sets of factors separately to remove dissatisfaction and achieve satisfaction for employees for fulfilling organizational goals.

According to Stephen P. Robbins (1988), job satisfaction is defined as a positive feeling about one's job resulting from an evaluation of its characteristics. Job satisfaction is influenced by the way employees are treated by the organization. Employees who are satisfied with the job stay within, and those not satisfied leave the organization (Khan and Parveen 2014).

Good to Know

Every HR/functional manager is bothered about enhancing employee motivation and satisfaction to maximizing achievement of organizational goals.

This chapter would provide detailed insights about different theoretical and practical aspects of employee motivation and satisfaction in industrial settings.

8.1.1 Types of Motivation

If managers wish to motivate their employees, it is very important for them to know various types of motivation in order to understand the motivational factors for employees.

8.1.2 Intrinsic and Extrinsic Motivation

People are more likely to be intrinsically motivated if they:

- Identify their success with internal factors (for example, the amount of effort they put in).
- Feel that they are effective in reaching desired goals.

Extrinsic motivation comes from outside of the performer, for example, the crowd cheers the performer; it makes the performer want to win and beat the other competitors, thereby motivating the performer. In work environments, money may provide a more powerful extrinsic factor than the intrinsic motivation provided by an enjoyable workplace (Herzberg 1966).

Both intrinsic and extrinsic motivations are pertinent and need to be dealt with by supervisors, immediate managers, and HoDs for motivating employees. It is more important to know and discuss how employees perceive these factors rather than just providing intrinsic and extrinsic motivations. There is always a scope to re-look and re-work on these intrinsic and extrinsic motivations after employee review so that the entire process of motivation becomes relevant both for employees and the employer for achieving business success.

> **Good to Know**
> Both intrinsic and extrinsic factors are equally important for employee motivation.

8.2 THEORIES OF JOB MOTIVATION

As job motivation is a vast subject, these theories provide diverse frameworks to comprehend the variety of factors that would be relevant to consider for motivation of employees.

(a) Need Hierarchy Theory

Abraham Maslow's hierarchy of human needs theory (1943, 1954) is the most widely discussed theory of motivation which summarized the assumptions that

- human beings have wants and desires which influence their behaviour; only unsatisfied needs can influence behaviour, satisfied needs cannot.
- since needs are many, they are arranged in order of importance, from the basic to the complex;
- the person advances to the next level of needs only after the lower level need is at least minimally satisfied; and
- the further the progress up the hierarchy, the more individuality, humanness, and psychological health a person will show.

The hierarchy of needs (as in figure below), listed from basic (lowest, earliest) to most complex (highest, latest) are as follows:

- Physiological
- Safety and security
- Social
- Esteem
- Self-actualization

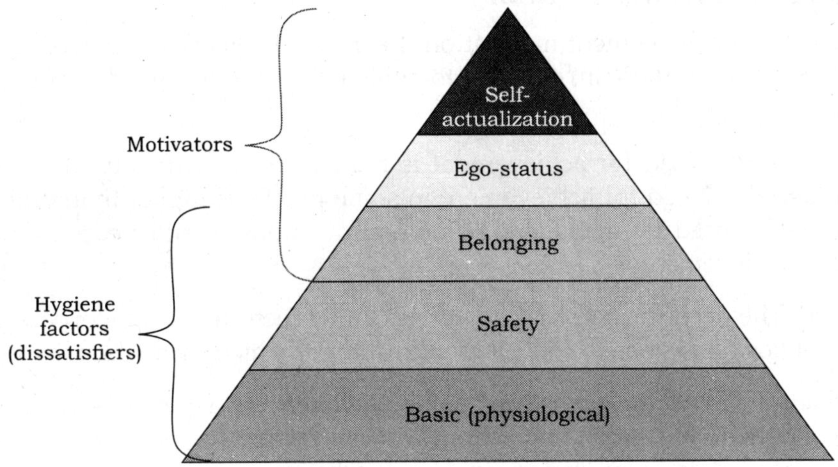

Motivation: Maslow's Hierarchy of needs & Herzerg's motivation-Hygiene theory

(b) Herzberg's Two-factor Theory

Professor Frederick Herzberg's two-factor theory (1966) concludes that certain factors (intrinsic/extrinsic motivation in the workplace) result in job satisfaction, but if absent, lead to dissatisfaction.

He distinguished between:

- motivators (for example, challenging work, recognition, responsibility) which give positive satisfaction; and
- hygiene factors; (for example, status, job security, salary, and fringe benefits) that do not motivate if present, but, if absent, result in demotivation.

The term hygiene factors is used because, like hygiene, its presence will not make you healthier, but absence can cause health deterioration. The theory is sometimes called the Motivator-Hygiene theory.

Good to Know

Motivator-Hygiene theory maintains that what makes people happy or satisfied is different from what makes people unhappy. So by reducing the factors of unhappiness or dissatisfaction does not make people happy.

(c) Alderfer's ERG Theory

Alderfer Clayton (2007), expanding on Maslow's hierarchy of needs, created the ERG theory (existence, relatedness, and growth). Physiological and safety, the lower order needs, are placed in the existence category, while love and self-esteem needs are placed in the relatedness category. The growth category contains our self-actualization and self-esteem needs.

(d) Need Achievement Theory

McClelland's (1965) achievement motivation theory envisions that a person has a need for three things, but differs in degrees to which the various needs influence their behaviour.

Need for achievement: Need for achievement is related to the difficulty of tasks people choose to undertake. Need for achievement in some people is higher than others which can be very well sensed by managers. Some organizations recruit people who have a high need for achievement.

Need for power: The need for personal power as can be seen that, most corporate leaders seek high level positions so as to control the direction in which their company is moving.

Need for affiliation: Need for affiliation is characterized by a person's need to feel a sense of involvement and belonging within a social group. People with high need for affiliation are needed as team leaders and for marketing positions.

(e) Goal-setting Theory

Goal-setting theory is based on the notion that individuals sometimes have a drive to reach a clearly defined end state.

Douglas Vermeeren (2013) states that unless individuals can clearly identify their motivating factor or their significant and meaningful reasons why they wish to attain the goal, they will never have the drive to attain it. Hence people need to set their professional/life goals to achieve.

8.3 MEASURING MOTIVATION IN ORGANIZATIONS

Motivating people and measuring motivation both are a tough job for managers and immediate supervisors as people differ in their job motivation and performance.

> **Good to Know**
> Managers and supervisors attempt all means to motivate employees yet they fail many times.

An employee's performance typically is influenced by a host of factors such as motivation, ability, and the work environment. Some deficiencies can be addressed by providing training or altering the environment (Cummins 1990).

Motivation is important because of its significance as a determinant of performance and its intangible nature.

MAO-B TEST (motivational analysis of organizations-behaviour) is a measurement tool.

Six primary needs or motives that are relevant for understanding the behaviour of people in organizations have been defined (Pareek 1997). These are as follows:

Achievement: Characterized by concern for excellence, competition with the standards of excellence set for others or by oneself, the setting of challenging goals for oneself.

Affiliation: Characterized by a concern for establishing and maintaining close, personal relationships, by value on friendships, and a tendency to express one's emotions.

Influence: Characterized by a concern to make an impact on others, a desire to make people do what one thinks is right, and an urge to change matters and people.

Control: Characterized by a concern for orderliness, a desire to remain informed, and an urge to monitor and take corrective action when needed.

Extension: Characterized by a concern for others, interest in superordinate goals, and an urge to be relevant and useful to larger groups including society.

Dependence: Characterized by a desire of help from others in one's own self-development, checking with significant others.

The six motives of achievement, affiliation, influence, control, extension, and dependence have been used in studying the behaviour of people in organizations.

Table 8.1 summarizes the approach and avoidance dimensions of six motives.

Table 8.1 Dimensions of Motives

Motive	*Approach {Hope of}*	*Avoidance {Fear of}*
Achievement	Success	Failure
Expert influence	Impact	Impotence
Control	Order	Chaos
Extension	Relevance	Irrelevance
Dependence	Growth	Loneliness
Affiliation	Inclusion	Exclusion

The behaviour of a manager or employee can thus be analysed not only in terms of the six primary motives but also from the perspective of positive approach or negative avoidance reflected by hope or fear, respectively.

An employee's effectiveness may result from the existence or absence of a particular motivation or from the extent of the approach or avoidance dimension of a particular motivation.

MAO-B contains 60 items, five for each dimension {approach and avoidance} of each of the six previously described motives: achievement, affiliation, influence, control, extension, and dependence.

Good to Know

MAO-B scores can be used to examine the motivational trends among employees across departments.

MAO-B can be administered in agroup. The participants should be told that there are no right or wrong answers since the test provides a profile of motivational aspect of role behaviour.

If the test is used for HRD purposes, the result can be used to help individuals and the group in order to increase the effectiveness in their respective roles.

8.4 JOB SATISFACTION

A satisfied employee is likely to be a loyal employee who is more likely to stand by the management in times of crises and is an asset to the organization. The success of an organization depends upon how satisfied its employees are. Hoppock (1935) defined job satisfaction as any combination of psychological, physiological, and environmental circumstances that causes a person to say truthfully, 'I am satisfied with my job'. Hence, it is the verbal expression of employee's evaluation of his work.

Abdullah, Ahsan, Alam, and Fie (2009) conducted a study to investigate the relationship between job stress and job satisfaction among university staff in Malaysia. They hypothesized a negative relationship between job stress and job satisfaction. They used multiple regression analysis and obtained results that were in line with the hypothesis at the 0.01 significance level.

Gole and Shahu (2008) studied the relationship between job stress, job satisfaction, and performance in managers of private manufacturing firms. The findings suggest that higher stress levels are related to lower performance whereas higher job satisfaction indicates higher performance.

Brewer and McMahan-Landers (2005) examined the relationship between job stress and job satisfaction among industrial and technical teacher educators. Correlational analysis revealed a strong inverse relationship between the constructs, with stressors related to lack of organizational support being more strongly associated with job satisfaction than stressors related to the job itself were. There also were significant differences ($p < 0.05$) in correlations between job satisfaction and frequency of stressors and correlations between job satisfaction and intensity of stressors, suggesting that frequency of stressors had a greater impact on participants' job satisfaction than did intensity of stressors.

Agrawal, Chandraiah, Manoharan, and Marimuthu (2003) planned a study to investigate the effect of age on occupational stress and job satisfaction among managers. The findings of the study reveal higher levels of job stress and less job satisfaction among managers younger in age as compared to older managers. The study also found that age was found to be negatively correlated with occupational stress and positively with job satisfaction.

8.5 THEORIES OF JOB SATISFACTION

Several approaches to job satisfaction (Judge, Locke, and Durham 1997) have been periodically reviewed by scholars in the published literature that provide adequate amount of framework based on researches to comprehend the nature of job satisfaction.

(a) *The Comparison Theory:* According to this theory, the magnitude of job satisfaction is a function of the size of the discrepancy between the individual's standards and what he/she believes he/she is receiving.

(b) *Aspiration Achievement or Expectation:* Aspiration can be set by the minimum needs of the individuals and/or by his current level of achievement of needs, linked in a significant way to the achievement level.

(c) *Instrumentality Theory:* Each individual has a set of judgements about how much he values certain outcomes such as pay, promotion, good working conditions, and other such outcomes. His job satisfaction results from the summation of the outcomes or instrumentalities obtained multiplied by the valences of these outcomes.

(d) *Equity Based Models:* Lawler's Facet Satisfaction Model: Satisfaction is a function of the extent to which the perceived amount of job rewards one receives matches the perceived deserved awards.

(e) *Locke's Value Theory:* Satisfaction is a function of the extent to which one's job is perceived as fulfilling important values. Thus, the discrepancy between preferred levels of job factors (pay, autonomy, and so on) and the actual level determines the level of satisfaction.

(f) *Social Influence Theory of Job Satisfaction:* People look around, see others like themselves who are satisfied or dissatisfied with these, and then influenced by these observations, they decide their level of satisfaction.

(g) *Herzberg's Two Factor Theory:* Herzberg's theory proposes that job satisfaction is derived from two sets of factors: first are the content factors of the work itself and he called them 'motivators' (intrinsic factors), such as responsibility, recognition, the nature of the work itself, achievement and advancement, are responsible for presence or absence of job satisfaction. Second is the the context factors or hygiene factors. These include pay, interpersonal relationship with co-workers, and working conditions. These factors do not promote satisfaction but reduce dissatisfaction.

8.6 FACTORS CONTRIBUTING TO JOB SATISFACTION

In a survey, Jeannette Taylor (2013) observed certain job characteristics impact the relationship between motivation and job satisfaction. Another survey reported certain job and organizational factors that are associated with or predict job satisfaction and would increase job satisfaction and staff motivation to perform (Houston and Waumsley 2003). These factors are:

- Achievement
- Recognition for accomplishment
- Challenging work
- Increased responsibility
- Growth and development
- Pay
- Autonomy
- Hours of work
- Interpersonal relationship
- Coworker satisfaction.

Good to Know

Many organizations opt for job satisfaction surveys in order to identify the factors that facilitate or constrain employees' job-satisfaction and to take directions for better organizational performance.

HoDs and HR managers must refer to the above factors to understand the perception and levels of job satisfaction among employees. All these factors have a bearing on each other; hence an inadequacy of one factor may affect the other. As these factors also impact the individual performance, managers need to take cognizance of each of these aspects of job satisfaction.

8.6.1 Job Stress and Job Satisfaction

A research (H.L. Kaila 2007) was conducted to study the relationship between job satisfaction and job stress levels in employees. It was hypothesized that there will be a negative correlation between the job satisfaction level and the job stress level of employees.

In the study, the researcher collected data of 30 respondents from an organization across various departments. The job satisfaction level of the employees was assessed using the job satisfaction survey (JSS), and the stress levels of the employees were measured using the chronic work related stress evaluation instrument.

Table 8.2 is the summary of the total score and the mean score of the participants on the job satisfaction survey and the chronic work related stress evaluation. The total score of the participants on the job satisfaction survey was 4139 and the mean score was 137.97, while the total score of the participants on the chronic work related stress evaluation was 1,721 and the mean score was 57.37. Figure 8.1 is a graphical representation of the mean scores of the participants on the two scales.

Table 8.2 Scores on the Job Satisfaction Scale and the Chronic Work Related Stress Evaluation

	Job Satisfaction Survey	*Chronic Work Related Stress Evaluation*
Total Score	4,139	1,721
Mean Score	137.97	57.37

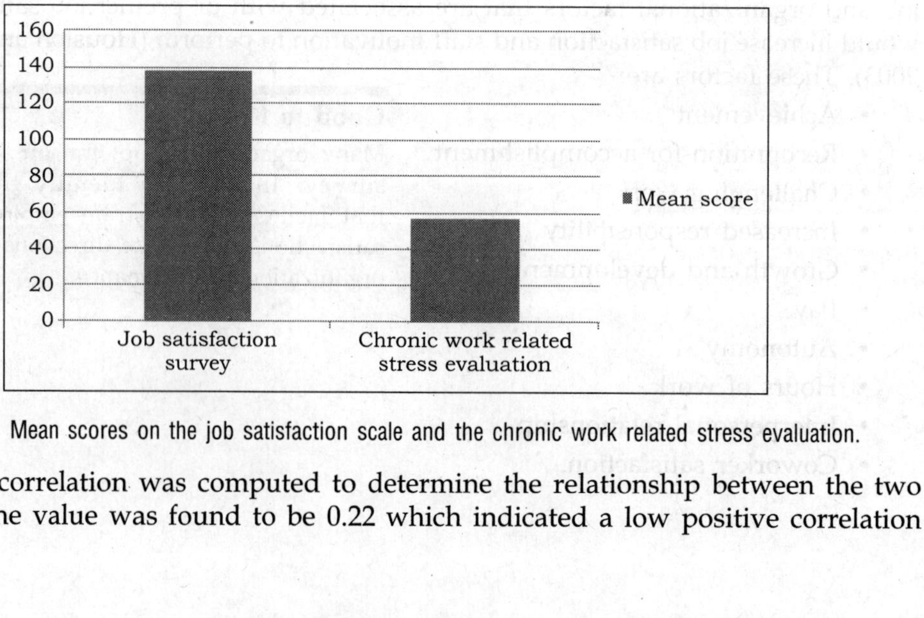

Fig. 8.1 Mean scores on the job satisfaction scale and the chronic work related stress evaluation.

Pearson correlation was computed to determine the relationship between the two variables. The value was found to be 0.22 which indicated a low positive correlation between job satisfaction and job stress. The obtained value was not significant at 0.05 level of significance.

The findings of this research show that even though there is job stress, the employees are still satisfied with their jobs. One reason for this could be that the job stress levels are in the moderate range, which encourages the employees to perform better or to the best of their ability which in fact increases their satisfaction with their jobs.

Another factor could be that in spite of the job stress, the rewards, compensation, and the benefits they receive for their work are good which motivates and satisfies them, hence there is high job satisfaction. Employees expect organizations to follow the market to remain pay-competitive.

8.6.2 Job Satisfaction and Organizational Commitment

Organizations tend to determine whether feelings of job satisfaction would lead to organizational commitment by employees. It is very important to study whether employees are satisfied, because it is intuitively believed that workers who are more satisfied will likely exhibit more positive feelings, thoughts, and actions toward their job. Similarly, studying about whether employees are committed to the organization that they work for is important.

By definition, organizational commitment refers to an attitude that reflects the strength of the linkage between an employee and an organization (Stephen P. Robbins, 1988). The level of commitment has implications as to whether a person would stay with an organization. Commitment can be identified as three different types: affective, continuance, and normative. Organizational commitment can be ranked as high, moderate, or low. Thus, managers are interested in maximizing their workers' level of commitment.

It is important to study the relationship between job satisfaction and organizational commitment because this will help managers to understand how an employee's job satisfaction will affect his or her level of commitment in the organization. Generally, it is expected that employees are more likely to stay with their organization and be highly committed when they can see a strong linkage between the organization and their work.

When employees experience low job satisfaction and organizational commitment, it can be very costly especially in case of the IT-industry which has an extremely high turnover rate. This may also be a result of low pay (for lower level positions) and little opportunity for advancement. Absenteeism may also be a costly issue because it can result in reduced productivity when lowly committed employees do not see any link between the tasks they do and the organization's profitability. To solve the problems of high turnover and absenteeism, it is important to analyse and determine the factors that would affect commitment. In recent times, employees switch jobs so frequently and with such ease at every possible opportunity for gaining personal benefits. A major question that the recruitment personnel in various organizations face at the recruitment process is whether the employee being recruited will benefit the organization in the long run and will he/she remain with the organization for a longer period of time than what the current trend shows. Another common dilemma for the HR managers is to hold back the potential employees in the organization and prevent them from leaving it (Gilmer and Luthans 2000). To succeed in this, what ideally should be done is to not just offer these employees high material incentives but also try and create a sense of commitment by them to the organization, so that the employee remains and works with the organization by choice and not force and identifies himself with the organization.

There was a survey conducted by Vermeeren (2013) in order to examine the relationship between organizational commitment, job satisfaction, and turnover intention of missionaries. Around 468 missionaries were surveyed and they found that 70% of the samples were dissatisfied with their job and thus the level of organizational commitment was also low and, in return, the probability of turnover was very high.

At times, employees may not leave an organization even when they are dissatisfied or do not feel committed to the organization. Greater importance should be given to studying the two variables. When workers are dissatisfied, this may create grievances, which can lead to a lower level of organizational commitment is but may increase productivity. With an improvement in productivity, organizations will operate better and have higher growth, which is an important goal for most organizations. Thus, a manager should investigate their employees' level of satisfaction, which can signal whether there is commitment from their workers (K. Aswathappa 2008).

Analysing the relationship between job satisfaction and organizational commitment is particularly crucial nowadays, as people often do not work at the same organization or job throughout their lifetime. It is also sometimes hard to find suitable people for certain positions. So once an ideal candidate is chosen, organizations would like to make a great effort to retain those employees. If two employees exhibit different levels of job satisfaction and that job satisfaction can be proven to lead to organizational commitment, the employer will likely hire the employee with the higher level of job satisfaction (Cascio Wayne 1995). This is because the employer can expect the more satisfied individual to stay with the organization. Another reason as to why satisfaction will lead to commitment is that a higher level of job satisfaction may lead to a better family life and a reduction in stress. The reason is because an employee's feelings of jobs satisfaction may affect his or her emotions. This feeling will affect the worker's behaviours inside and outside the organization.

When a worker is dissatisfied with his or her job, he/she may have negative emotions. The consequence is that she or he may start to think about quitting. The decision process will begin with the individual identifying and evaluating alternatives, about whether to quit or to stay on in their job (Robbins and Sanghi 2008). The sequence of decisions will change the employee's commitment level. Managers would be most interested in knowing about the relationship between job satisfaction and organizational commitment, because it would become clear as to how important and worthy it would be to retain their most satisfied employees. In turn, having this knowledge would motivate managers to satisfy their employees. This would ultimately benefit the organization, as it is expected that these same employees will be highly committed. When employees are committed, their personal goals may go in line with those of the organization that they work for.

The relationship between job satisfaction and organizational commitment has been studied from various other aspects also. For example, a research was conducted in 2008 by RN and Mahmoud AL-Hussami (Professors, Faculty of Nursing, University of Jordan) in order to study the job satisfaction of nurses in relationship to organizational commitment, perceived organizational support, transactional leadership, transformational leadership, and level of education. This study investigated two distinct paths to job satisfaction—organizational commitment and perceived organizational support. Results indicated that there was a strong correlation between the dependent variables and the independent variables. Of the five independent variables, organizational support was most strongly related to job satisfaction. The researcher chose randomly four nursing homes from a total of 53 Medicare certified nursing homes located in Miami-Dade county. This study provides new support to previous research about the importance of nurses' commitment and satisfaction for organizational effectiveness and performance.

Apart from this, the relationship between job satisfaction and organizational commitment has also been studied in relation to the psychological climatic dimensions (autonomy, cohesion, trust, pressure, support, recognition, fairness, innovation). This study was carried out by Bob Delaney and Gary Johns in 2001 of New York State University. The results of the study clearly demonstrated that psychological climate as a perceptual multidimensional phenomenon can render toward better understanding of a person's evaluating reaction and functioning in an organization.

The job attitude and organizational commitment also vary from culture to culture. Whether employees from different cultures were committed to their organizations in similar ways was the objective of the research carried out by Y. Cheng and M.S. Stockdale in 2003. This study compared the organizational commitment of Chinese employees to the commitment of Canadian and South Korean workers. Although results revealed that the three types of commitment – normative, continuance, and affective – are present in all three cultures, results also showed that there are some differences among the three countries in how important each type of commitment is.

> **Good to Know**
> Satisfied employees tend to be more loyal to their organization.

If job satisfaction and organizational commitment are related, organizations would need to increase one variable (job satisfaction) to achieve the positive effect of the other (organizational commitment). For example, a company could reward workers with job advancement opportunities or change a facet of the job in a desirable way, which will increase job satisfaction and ultimately lead to a higher level of organizational loyalty and commitment.

Generally, when people are satisfied with their jobs, they will have a positive attitude about their jobs and the organization. In their minds, other jobs would not be better than the current one. Therefore, it is unlikely that they will change their jobs. Employees prefer to stay in their company and work hard for a return. If employees feel that the company treats them fairly or well, the workers will feel that they are responsible to keep working hard for their companies. Also, in order to maintain their current satisfied jobs, employees will perform well and work effectively, which is beneficial for the company. Therefore, in order to increase the employees' level of commitment, the manager can try to increase their level of job satisfaction. Factors like working conditions, pay, security, and the like, which surround the job, if perceived positive can prevent feelings of dissatisfaction and negative reactions. Positive attitudes are related more directly with work performance and are referred to as motivators. Organizations which give an opportunity to their employees for personal growth, recognition, promotion, responsibility, and a sense of achievement will have the least turnover and absenteeism rate. For an organization to expect commitment from their respective employees, the managers or the supervisors must pull up their socks for this purpose. A study by John W. Newstrom and Keith Davis (2001) has revealed that commitment tends to be higher when employees believe their supervisors are competent, have their best interest in mind, and treat them with dignity and respect. When an employee feels that a manger has the legitimate authority to establish goals, the employee will feel more committed to the goals than if he/she perceives the manager to lack authority. Management has to keep its promise to be committed to employees if it expects the employees to be committed to the organization. Also, if employees' peers believe in the goals and provide encouragement, the employee will be more committed to the organization.

8.7 ORGANIZATIONAL CLIMATE AND JOB SATISFACTION

Organizational climate is a collective view of people within the organization as to the nature of the environment they work in. It is a combined perception of individuals. It useful in differentiating organizations according to their procedures and practices.

Job satisfaction is the sense of fulfilment and pride felt by people who enjoy their work and do it well. The previous researches reflected that the organizational climate has positive effects on job satisfaction.

An objective of this research case (H.L. Kaila 2007) was to explore the correlation between organizational climate satisfaction and job satisfaction, that is, higher the organizational climate satisfaction, higher the job satisfaction, and vice versa.

Organizational climate is a set of descriptive characteristics of an organization that are relatively enduring over a period of time. These characteristics influence the behaviour of people that belong to it, thereby affecting job satisfaction of the employees.

Job satisfaction can be described as one's feelings or state of mind regarding the nature of the work. It can be influenced by a variety of factors such as the quality of the academics' relationships with their supervisors, the quality of the physical environment in which they work in, and the degree of fulfilment in their work which are all part of organizational climate.

In this research, two questionnaires were used, one for the organizational climate satisfaction and other for determining job satisfaction. A self-made questionnaire was used to determine organizational climate satisfaction while a job satisfaction inventory was used to measure the levels of job satisfaction. Both the questionnaires (see appendix) were administered to 60 subjects to determine their level of organizational climate satisfaction and job satisfaction.

For this research a questionnaire was carefully structured which included all the dimensions of organizational climate like compensation, decision making, performance evaluation, supervision, training and development, communication, team work and other parameters which, in turn, affect job satisfaction. Job satisfaction describes how contented an individual is with his or her job. The happier people are within their job, the more satisfied they are said to be.

Pearson's correlation coefficient was used to determine the correlation between the two. The correlation between organizational climate satisfaction and job satisfaction is 0.87. Thus, the hypothesis, that is, higher the organizational climate satisfaction, higher the job satisfaction has been supported by the above correlation.

Organizational climate has a major influence on human performance and satisfaction. Individuals in the organization have certain expectations and fulfilment of these expectations depends upon their perception as to how the organizational climate suits the satisfaction of their needs. If they perceive that organization climate can fulfill their expectancies, the satisfaction is higher, or vice versa.

It was observed through this case that that there is a positive correlation between organizational climate satisfaction and job satisfaction. The correlation coefficient is 0.87. Thus, it can be said that higher the organizational climate satisfaction, higher is the job satisfaction of an employee, or vice versa.

SUMMARY

- Motivation and job satisfaction are two significant components of the work processes that are experienced by employees as a result of personal joy and contentment while doing their work.
- An employee's performance typically is influenced by his motivation and job satisfaction.
- Both motivation and job satisfaction can be measured by an organizational intervention to achieve regular improvements in performance.
- Motives are relevant for understanding the behaviour of people in organizations.
- Job stress, organizational commitment, and job satisfaction are inter-correlated.
- This chapter has broadly provided understanding about the concepts, theories and measurement of motivation, and job satisfaction, types of motivation, and factors contributing to job satisfaction.

EXERCISE FOR CLASSROOM PRACTICE

For better understanding of the subject matter of this chapter, please read and check each of the following statements whether True (T) or False (F) or Uncertain (U).

1. People are more likely to be intrinsically motivated if they identify their success with external factors.
2. Both intrinsic and extrinsic motivation are pertinent and to be dealt with by supervisors.
3. Two-factor theory concludes that certain factors (intrinsic/extrinsic motivation in the workplace) result in job satisfaction, but if absent, leads to dissatisfaction.
4. Need for affiliation is characterized by a person's need to feel a sense of involvement and belonging within a social group.
5. Goal-setting theory is based on the notion that individuals sometimes have a drive to reach clearly defined goals.
6. Measuring motivation is a challenging job for managers as people differ in their job motivation and performance.
7. MAO-B means motivational analysis of organization's beliefs.
8. An employee's performance typically is influenced by motivation, ability, and the work environment.
9. Need for influence is characterized by a concern to make an impact on others and a desire to make people do what one thinks is right.
10. Need for control is characterized by a concern for orderliness and an urge to monitor and take corrective action when needed.
11. Research shows a significantly positive relationship between job stress and job satisfaction.
12. Herzberg's theory proposes that job satisfaction is derived from two sets of factors, i.e., the content of the work and context factors.

Answers: All statements are **True** except that statement numbers 1, 7, and 11 are **False.**

REVIEW QUESTIONS FOR DISCUSSIONS/EXAMINATIONS

1. Discuss the concepts of motivation.
2. Describe the concept of job satisfaction.
3. Describe the types of motivation with illustrations.
4. Illustrate job satisfaction in relation to job stress and organizational commitment.
5. Discuss various theories of job satisfaction with regard to Indian organizations.
6. Critically reflect upon various theories of job motivation.
7. Address issues with regard to measuring motivation in organizations.
8. Explain relevant factors contributing to job satisfaction in your organization.
9. Discuss the relationship between organizational climate and job satisfaction.

FIELD RESEARCH REPORT

This is a research assignment section for students for their internal marking by the teacher during the semester. This assignment is for understanding practical application of the subject.

An action research project: Identify a group of minimum 15 executives and 15 non-executives across an organization preferably where you are placed for an internship. Conduct interviews with them by using a set of closed/open-ended questionnaire to signify the issues and concerns pertaining to the employee job satisfaction and motivational strategies of your company. Prepare a report of about 15 pages reflecting an action plan for better work practices.

REFERENCES

Abdullah, Z., N. Ahsan, S.S. Alam and D.Y.G. Fie (2009). 'A Study of Job Stress and Job Satisfaction Among University Staff in Malaysia: Empirical Study.' *European Journal of Social Sciences*, 8(1), 121–131.

Agrawal, S.C., K. Chandraiah, N. Manoharan and P. Marimuthu (2003). 'Occupational Stress and Job Satisfaction among Managers.' *Indian Journal of Occupational and Environmental Medicine*, 7(2), 6–11.

Alderfer P. Clayton (2007). ERG Theory (Existence, Relatedness, and Growth). Envision Software. http://www.envisionsoftware.com/articles/ERG_Theory.html (retrieved on 6th February 2015).

Aswathappa, K. (2008). *Human Resource Management* (6th edition). New Delhi: Tata McGraw-Hill Publishing Company.

Brewer, E. and McMahan-Landers, J. (2005). The Relationship between Job Stress and Job Satisfaction Among Industrial and Technical Teacher Educators.

Brewer, E.W. & McMahan-Landers, J. (2003). 'Job Satisfaction Among Industrial and Technical Teacher Educators.' *Journal of Industrial Teacher Education*, 40(2), 65–85.

Cheng, Y. & Stockdale, M.S. 2003. 'The Validity of the Three-component Model of Organizational Commitment in a Chinese Context.' *Journal of Vocational Behaviour*, 62: 456–489.

Cummins, R.C. (1990), 'Job Stress and the Buffering Effort of Supervisory Support', *Group and Organizational Studies*, 15 (1), 92–104.

Douglas Vermeeren (2013). Is Goal Setting Holding You Back? http://www.myarticlearchive.com/author/vermeeren.htm (retrieved on 14 January 2013).

Gilmer, B.A. and F. Luthans (2000). *Industrial Psychology* (5th edition). New York. McGraw Hill.

Herzberg, F. (1966). *Work and Nature of Man*. Cleveland: World Publishing.

Hoppock R. (1935). *Job Satisfaction*. NY: Harper.

Houston, D.M. and J.A. Waumsley (2003). *Attitudes to Flexible Working and Family Life*. Bristol. Published for the Joseph Rowntree Foundation by The Policy Press.

Hussami, A.L.M. and R.N. (2008). 'A Study of Nurses' Job Satisfaction.' *European Journal of Scientific Research*. 22 (2), 286–295.

Judge, T.A., E.A. Locke and C.C. Durham (1997). 'The Dispositional Causes of Job Satisfaction: A Core Evaluations Approach.' *Research in Organizational Behavior*, 19, 151–188.

Kaila, H.L. (2007). *Organizational Behavior & HRM* (2nd edition). Delhi: AITBS Publishers.

Khan, N.A. and S. Parveen (2014). 'Measuring Job Satisfaction: Evidence from Indian Banking Industry.' *Management Guru: Journal of Management Research*, 2 (3), 134–149.

Maslow Abraham Harold (1954). Motivation and Personality (1st edition). NY: Harper.

Maslow, A.H. (1943). 'A Theory of Motivation.' *Psychological Review*, 50, 370–396.

Mason, L.J. (2001). Retaining Key Personnel. Plus: Top 10 Retention Tips. Stress Education Center. Retrieved February 27, 2005, from http:www.dstress.com

McClelland, D.C. (1965). 'Toward a Theory of Motive Acquisition.' *American Psychologist*, 20, 321-333.

Newstrom, John W.; Davis, Keith (2001). *Organizational Behavior: Human Behavior at Work*. McGraw-Hill College, Boston, MA.

Pareek, U. (1997). *Training Instruments for Human Resource Development*. New Delhi: Tata McGraw-Hill.

Pinder Craig C. (1998). *Work Motivation in Organizational Behavior*. New Jersey: Prentice Hall.

Rashmi Shahu & S.V. Gole (2008). 'Effects of Job Stress and Job Satisfaction on Performance: An Empirical Study.' *International Journal of Management*, 2 (3), 237-248.

Robbins S.P. and Sanghi S. (2008). *Organizational Behaviour*, (11th edition). Tata McGraw-Hill Education, India.

Stephen P Robbins (1988). *Organization Theory: Structures, Designs and Applications* (3rd edition). Pearson Education India.

Taylor Jeannette (2013). Public service motivation, relational job design, and job satisfaction in local government. http://onlinelibrary.wiley.com/doi/10.1111/j.1467-9299.2012.02108.x/abstract

Wayne, F. Cascio (1995). *Managing Human Resources*. (5th edition). New Delhi: Tata McGraw-Hill Publishing Company.

APPENDIX

Job Satisfaction Inventory

Instructions: Please circle the appropriate response after each item. 1—strongly disagree 2—no opinion, 3—strongly agree.

1.	I like my current job.	1	2	3
2.	I am clear about my career direction.	1	2	3
3.	It is easy for me to set goals for myself.	1	2	3
4.	I usually attain the goals I set.	1	2	3
5.	I have no fears about changing jobs.	1	2	3
6.	I think of myself as a successful person.	1	2	3
7.	I have high self-esteem.	1	2	3

8.	Once I decide to make a change in my life, I usually move ahead and do so without making excuses or procrastinating.	1	2	3
9.	I view change as a healthy occurrence.	1	2	3
10.	The work environment in my current job meets all of my needs.	1	2	3
11.	I know exactly which career field I want to enter (or in which I want to stay).	1	2	3
12.	I understand what motivates me to work, and I make job choices based on those factors.	1	2	3
13.	I understand the inner needs that I feel a job should fulfil.	1	2	3
14.	My inner needs are fulfilled through my work.	1	2	3
15.	I know the signs that tell me when it is time for me to change jobs or careers.	1	2	3
16.	I enjoy nearly all of the tasks performed in my job.	1	2	3
17.	My job allows me to satisfy my personal values and fulfil my personal goals as I do the work.	1	2	3

Scoring Key: 40 and above: High level of satisfaction
27–39: Moderate level of satisfaction
17–26: Low level of satisfaction

Organizational Climate Satisfaction Questionnaire

Instructions: Please circle the appropriate response after each item. 1—strongly disagree 2—no opinion, 3—strongly agree.

1.	Mistakes are treated with understanding and we are helped to learn from them.	1	2	3
2.	We have a good performance appraisal system to measure individual performance and potential.	1	2	3
3.	Many learning opportunities are provided in our organization.	1	2	3
4.	Our company offers good career growth opportunities.	1	2	3
5.	In difficult times I get support and help from my colleagues.	1	2	3
6.	Our compensation structure is fair and promotes high performance.	1	2	3
7.	Employees do not hesitate to discuss personal problems with their supervisors/ managers.	1	2	3
8.	Team work is recognized and rewarded in our company.	1	2	3
9.	Within departments we have effective team work.	1	2	3
10.	We are encouraged to evaluate and improve systems and procedures regularly.	1	2	3
11.	I enjoy my work and the challenges it provides.	1	2	3
12.	I am fully aware of what's expected of me in my work.	1	2	3
13.	We get clarification and feedback promptly from our superiors.	1	2	3
14.	Management appreciates and recognizes small improvements.	1	2	3
15.	Our management gives priority to quality.	1	2	3
16.	Our company gives priority to safety.	1	2	3

17.	We are encouraged to experiment with new methods and take risks.	1	2	3
18.	Our communication modes are effective and reach all employees.	1	2	3
19.	Important decisions are made taking into account a wide variety of perspectives.	1	2	3
20.	We have clear goals for each department/team.	1	2	3
21.	I have challenging work, goals, and objectives.	1	2	3
22.	We receive training necessary for the changing needs.	1	2	3
23.	We have a stress-free work environment.	1	2	3
24.	Our organization cares for its people.	1	2	3
25.	People are motivated because of their sense of contribution and personal vision.	1	2	3
26.	We can freely differ with and question our supervisors and managers.	1	2	3
27.	There is good co-ordination and co-operation among various departments in the company.	1	2	3
28.	We receive sincere recognition and appreciation for the good work done.	1	2	3
29.	Superiors take the active interest in getting to know the employees.	1	2	3
30.	I am satisfied with the present work environment.	1	2	3
31.	I enjoy my work and the challenges it provides.	1	2	3
32.	I am fully aware of what's expected of me in my work.	1	2	3
33.	We get clarification and feedback promptly from our superiors.	1	2	3
34.	Management appreciates and recognizes small improvements.	1	2	3
35.	Our management gives priority to quality.	1	2	3

Scoring Key: 35-58: Low level satisfaction
59-77: Moderate level satisfaction
78-105: High level satisfaction

9

Work-life Balance

Learning Objectives

This chapter would help the readers:

- to acquaint with the concept of work-life balance in organizations;
- to understand various domains of work-life balance;
- to be familiar with the research perspective on work-life balance;
- to reflect upon the case study about work-life balance.

An Opening Story: A Case on Work-life Balance

Work-life balancing has become an important aspect for both employees as well as employers. In one such case, a lady employee who was highly bothered about her personal life issues. A mature manager played a very significant role to support and mentor her to resolve her personal life issues that she became a very satisfied person to perform much better. She was recently separated and going through legal hassles of divorce. Her personal life became a mess and she underwent severe depression. In the beginning, she did not report this to her manager as this was an emotional issue.

Due to sharp observation skills, her manager noticed that she was only keeping herself to the work and was not friendly with anyone in the office which did not appear very normal. After a few meetings at work when she became little comfortable, he asked her to open up her feelings if there was any serious issue. She told him that she has been deceived by her husband and was in a very disturbed state of mind as within a few days of her marriage, her husband told her that she is not the one he was looking for and started torturing her so that she was compelled to go back to her parents home. The manager disclosed that a similar incident happened to his sister. Then she believed that he could understand her problem. The manager took up the role of her mentor and supported her to prioritize between her career and personal issues. His regular counselling for about six months helped her to come out of the emotional imbalance. She then became a happy person and a very performing employee. Nowadays, almost all progressive companies have work-life balancing (WLB) strategies in place such as flexible work time, crèches, counselling and mentoring, transport and housing facilities, and many others to support employees in order to maximize their potential.

9.1 INTRODUCTION

Zedeck and Mosier (1990) and O'Driscoll (1996) noted that there are typically five main models to explain the relationship between work and life outside work. The segmentation model hypothesizes that work and non-work are two distinct domains of life that are quite distinct and have no influence on each other; on the other hand, Spillover's model hypothesizes that one world can influence the other in either a positive or negative way. A compensation model proposes that what may be lacking in one sphere, in terms of demands or satisfaction can be made up in the other; the Instrumental model suggests that activities in one sphere facilitate success in the other and the conflict model proposes that with high levels of demand in all spheres of life, some difficult choices have to be made and possibly some significant overload occurs on an individual.

Clark (2000) defined work-life balance as satisfaction and good functioning at work and at home with a minimum of role conflict. Guest and Conway (2000) gave a more subjective definition of work-life balance as a person's perceived balance between work and the rest of life.

Work-life balance (WLB) has always been a concern for those interested in the quality of working life and its relation to broader quality of life. Work-life balance reflects the extent to which an individual is equally engaged in and equally satisfied with his or her work role and family role (Greenhaus and Singh 2003).

According to Martin Stairs, Martin Galpin, Nicky Page, and Alex Linley (2006), the employees have multiple life roles within and outside work. In order to feel truly engaged, they need to be supported to achieve an acceptable balance in order that they are able to meet the multiple demands placed on them. Laura Stack (2013) observed that in order to find a WLB, it requires to walk a tightrope.

Parul Agarwal (2014) observed that it is primarily the responsibility of an individual to balance work and life and initiate steps to reduce stress and burnout. Work-life programmes have the potential to significantly improve employee morale, reduce absenteeism, and retain organizational knowledge particularly during the difficult economic times. In fact, in India, WLB is aligned to social context, and except for a few big corporates, not much effective programmes and practices are in place that enable employees to strike WLB. It's not just women, men too struggle for this (Business Manager 2015).

9.2 WORK-LIFE BALANCE

O'Driscoll (1996) observed that work and life satisfaction have manifold effects in terms of well-being, mental and physical health, and individual performance in organizations.

A typical example can be found in the work of Mauno and Kinnunen (1999) who report a Finnish study of 215 dual earning couples in which they explored the impact of a range of work stressors on marital satisfaction. One of the stressors was work-family conflict.

According to Sylvia Hewlett, president of the Center for Work-Life Policy, if a woman takes time off to care for children or an older parent, employers tend to see these people as less than fully committed.

In cases where employers made some changes to make it easier for women to work shorter or more flexible hours, female workers reported a number of positive aspects about their jobs and other segments of life. Women worked shorter hours, with 44% of women contracted to work fewer than 35 hours per week compared with 18% of men. Female workers were also happier with their WLB and felt they got more support to work flexible hours than their male counterparts. A total of 58% of women surveyed said they were happy with their WLB, compared to 52% of men.

> **Good to Know**
> Work life balance is the boundary that you create between your profession, career, or business and every other segment that makes up your life. Aside from your career, these segments include your family, personal growth, spirituality, fitness and health, and community and friendships.

Once you begin to establish healthy boundaries between your work life and your personal life, you begin to feel more fulfilment and personal satisfaction (Kaila 2005).

According to Nancy R. Lockwood (2007), one of the top trends that leads to focus on employee engagement includes the WLB. Nancy also mentions WLB policies and practices as one of the key retention factors. The positive correlation between the two, leads to the conclusion that if an employee is highly engaged, he/she will have a balance between work and life. One of the major factors for an employee to be engaged is WLB. This study made us understand the relationship between employee engagement and WLB.

Effective WLB policies (Frone, Russell, and Cooper 1992) are valuable to organizations for a number of reasons, including:

- reduced staff turnover rates
- becoming a good employer or an employer of choice
- increased return on investment in training as employees stay longer
- reduced absenteeism and sick leave
- improved morale or satisfaction
- greater staff loyalty and commitment
- improved productivity

Susan Cartwright and Nicola Holmes (2006) discussed the balance and the organizational need to recognize the meaning and emotional aspects of work.

> **Good to Know**
> Individuals are increasingly seeking a job which enables them to achieve a satisfactory work-life balance.

For many employees today (both male/female) their lives are becoming more consumed with a host of family and other personal responsibilities and interests. Therefore, in an effort to retain employees, it is increasingly important for organizations to recognize that their employees feel satisfied to WLB.

9.2.1 Major Parameters of Work-life Balance

Four parameters of WLB have been identified based on the research literature. The first includes average working hours that each generation puts in. Second, the problems or compromises which are specific to each generation are essentially hindrances to WLB. Third, emphasis is given on different coping strategies each generation has as the problems managing WLB are different for all the three generations. Considering there are numerous studies that deal with WLB and stress, the fourth parameter of coping with stress is also included and the organization's role is to reduce stress and promote.

(a) Average working hours

It was seen from the analysis that generation *X* (21–30 yrs) and *Y* (31–40 yrs) put in around 6–7 hrs and baby boomers (51–60 yrs) on an average put 8–10 hrs of work every day. The reason for this can be attributed to the competitive work environment.

However, it was seen that Generation X managed their work time by effective planning. They focussed on deadlines in advance and worked accordingly. For baby boomers, long hours can be contributed to sudden emergencies and their decision-making authority in such situations. For generation *X* and *Y*, their work was partly routine and predictable in which they could decide their working hours in advance.

The implications for the organization can be huge. In general, generation *X* and *Y* employees do not work less or have less work but they want to control when and where they work.

Regarding additional work, it can be seen that generation X and *Y* do not readily take work at home, instead they prefer staying back longer and completing the task at hand.

(b) Problems and Compromises

Baby boomers quoted that they often miss on important family events because of their busy travelling schedules. Although they said they would make it a point to attend close family weddings, for them work is a priority 98% of the times.

Generation X quoted that when there is excess workload they would not attend weekend parties or socialize with friends. They would at times not be a part of social family outings, but they like 'making up' for it when their work gets easy. However, they do not seem to like the word 'compromise' and want the best of both the worlds. Family remains a priority for them most of the times. It has been seen from research that the issue of WLB has been stimulated by writers advocating the arrival of Generation X (Tulgan 1996), a cohort of workers who give greater priority to seeking a balance between work and the rest of life.

Generation *Y* also said they at times have to sacrifice weekend outings. However, this situation is not common for them. They try to work harder on the week days, stay longer hours, and come to work early rather than working on weekends. Generation *Y* noted that they do not like to take work home unless it is very important and urgent.

The participants from generation X and Y noted that many a times WLB programmes are doomed if management asks employees to cancel or reschedule vacations and personal time off because there is so much work to do. At the same time, if management is perceived to be working 80 hours a week, always stressed out, and not taking care of their health, employees get the same message that they can't take time off or take advantage of programmes that could help them.

(c) Coping Strategies

Participants belonging to the age group of 41–60 yrs preferred taking a yearly off for a week and quoted that they liked spending time with the family by taking them for a holiday. It was seen from the responses that their family had adapted to their busy working schedule. People after the age of 50 usually belonged to high-end posts in their respective organizations. They have to travel probably throughout the year for meetings and conferences and thus their calendar for family vacation is booked way in advance. People within this age bracket also felt having worked closer home, reduces their travelling time and increases their chances of being at home early.

On the other hand participants between age group of 21–30 yrs and 31–40 yrs took short trips all round the year to be with their family. Respondents in these age groups quoted that they planned for their weekend getaways at least once a month. They also reported that they spent time with their spouses by travelling together for work. Also people belonging to these generations made it a point to have lunch together every fortnight if their respective spouses had offices in proximal areas.

For them time management is a key to achieving WLB. Generation *X* and Generation *Y* often make use of technology for communication when their schedules seem busy. It is as simple as sending messages or sending e-mails to let a person know that you are remembered. This finding is similar to the findings of research done by Wentworth (2002). He pointed that electronically enhanced work environment which includes e-mails, fax machines; cell phones give people never-out-of-touch feeling.

Participants of Generation *Y* noted that their own work culture supports the concept of WLB for all its employees. This means that it is being driven by senior management and is incorporated into the culture at all levels. The CEO and everyone in management sets the example and allows employees to take personal time off, spend time with friends and family, and attend workshops.

(d) Strategies to Reduce Stress

For generation *Y*, seeking support from friends and peers helped them take off their work stress rather than taking it back home. Also, they liked exercising, practising yoga, and pursuing a hobby like playing a musical instrument or playing outdoor sports to take their mind off the work and thus keeping themselves happy which eventually can be linked to a better family life. Generation *X* mentioned that when stressed or de-motivated they prefer to take a day off. During long working hours, taking a break and taking quick walks outside office helped them to concentrate better.

Respondents of all the three generations noted that their organizations helped them achieve WLB to an extent by introducing some of the services such as:

- Flexible working hours
- Telecommuting
- 7 days paternal leave
- Company sponsored family holiday plans (once a year)
- Health care expenses
- Leaves (paid and unpaid family care leaves, maternity phase-back, and so on)
- Employee assistance programmes

Seventy-five per cent of employees believe that the personal effectiveness programmes like self-help trainings of 'discover self workshop' and effective interpersonal skill building trainings helped them personally as well as professionally. Happiness with one self reflects positively in family and work life and leads to increased productivity as well. The three generations agreed that the organizational culture played a great role in managing their work and home effectively. A good bond with supervisors helps Generation *X* and *Y* to a great extent. This finding is consistent with Goff, Mount, and Jaminson (1990) wherein they found close supervision was closely related to WLB.

The following recommendations are considered for increasing an organization's role in promoting WLB:

> **Good to Know**
> Organizations are implementing wellness programmes or pay for their employees' gym membership as part of a benefits package.

- Organizations must have WLB programmes because there is high return on investment, for appropriate recruitment of candidates, and retention of employees. Companies should invite fitness trainers or yoga instructors into the office to take sessions.
- Organizations should undertake initiatives to improve employees' healthy eating habits. Like in the West, companies should also set up plays centre/crèche in the organization itself. This will go a long way in promoting WLB.
- According to a study by Messmer (2006), flexible scheduling is the benefit valued most by employees. However, increased flexibility, if implemented without conditions and used for facilitating business ends without provision for worker consent, could compromise instead of enhancing WLB.
- Sometimes in order to achieve WLB, organizations can reduce the amount of work given to each employee. To accomplish this, employers can hire new people, reduce time spent in job-related travel, allow for job sharing, or re-evaluate the work itself.

A one-size-fits-all approach cannot be adopted by the organization. Organizations should have tailor-made benefit packages for WLB keeping in mind the priority of a cohort. A holiday plan will appeal to a person who has family; for singletons insurance benefits may be more suited. The concept of benefit packages for different kinds of people is popular in one West, in India it still needs to be implemented more forcefully.

This is very important to keep employees happy which, in turn, would result in an effective and efficient working environment.

9.3 WORK-LIFE BALANCE IN MUMBAI

The perceptions of WLB are examined across various firms in Mumbai (H.L. Kaila 2005). The sample comprised 73 full-time employed males and females working in different companies such as banks, colleges, and private sector companies such as finance and CA firms, service industry and others. The data collection was done by administering the standardized WLB among the sample group aged between 22–60 yrs and who were married with/without kids and unmarried. These candidates averagely worked for 5–6 days a week.

The analysis of each WLB question has been given below in the respective were graphs:

On the basis of the questionnaire items (see appendix), the respondents were first asked to give a confirmation whether they are being able to balance their work life and personal life. Thus the results obtained indicated that 35 females (85%) and 24 male candidates (83%) are successful in obtaining a balanced work and personal life. The remaining respondents 6 females (15%) and 5 males (17%) stated an imbalanced work and personal life.

The respondents were also asked about their comfort on working hours. A large chunk of 29 female respondents (72%) indicated that their working hours were comfortable to the work and 11 female respondents (28%) indicated that their working hours were more stringent as compared to their work. The situation was slightly different for the male respondents with 25 (75%) reporting comfort with working hours and 8 (25%) reporting hectic work hours with respect to their work.

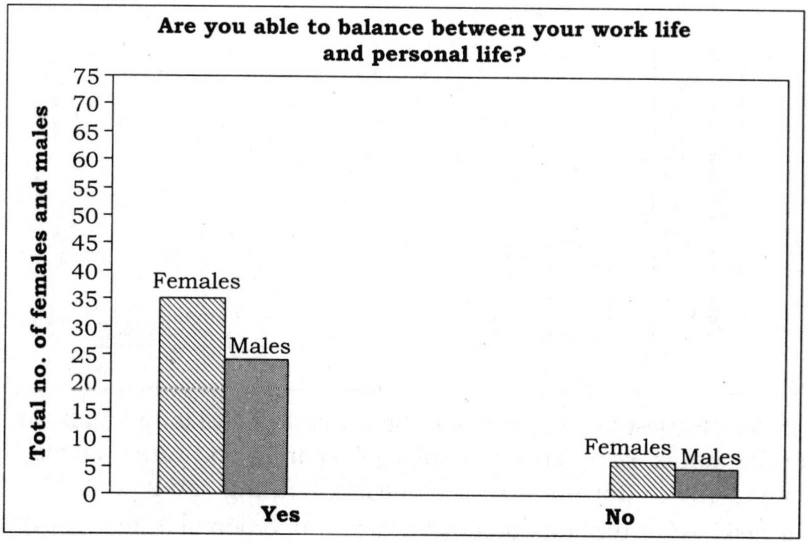

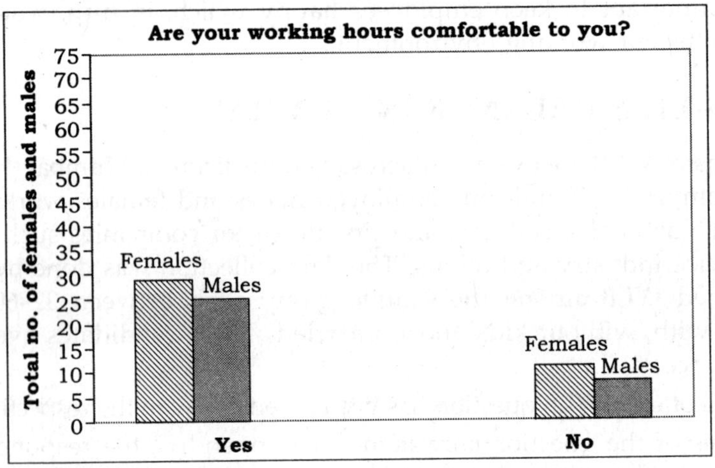

Further in the sample of the study, 20 male (80%) and 20 female respondents (83%) claimed that they receive support from their family members towards their career life. And a minimal of 4 female (17%) and 5 male respondents (20%) indicated a negative support from their family members towards their career life. The obtained results highlight the changing trend of importance offered to the career life of men and women.

Good to Know

"My husband does so much around the house. We are definitely 50/50 on all things home-related." – Jessie Randall, award winning designer of Loeffler Randall (Walls 2013).

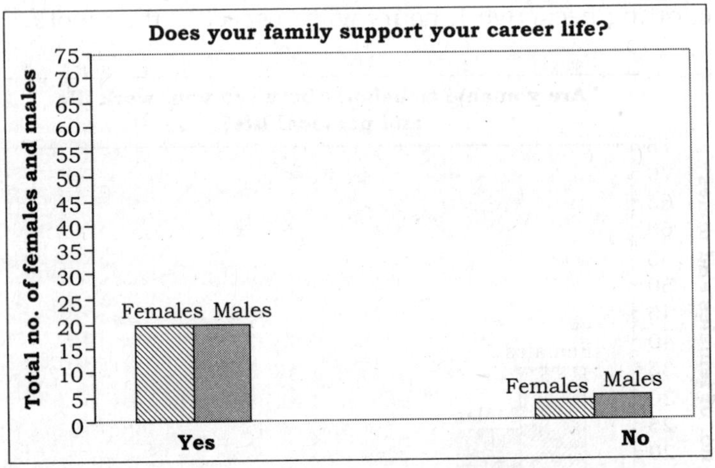

The next set of questions targeted on the interest of the individuals on areas such as flexible working hours, part/term time jobs, job sharing and career breaks, and source of information and advice (for example care, health, housing and so on).

Thus, the obtained results indicated that a large proportion of 32 female (84%) and 28 male respondents (80%) were interested in participating in flexible working hours and 6 females (6%) and 7 males (10%) claimed they were satisfied with the pattern of working hours.

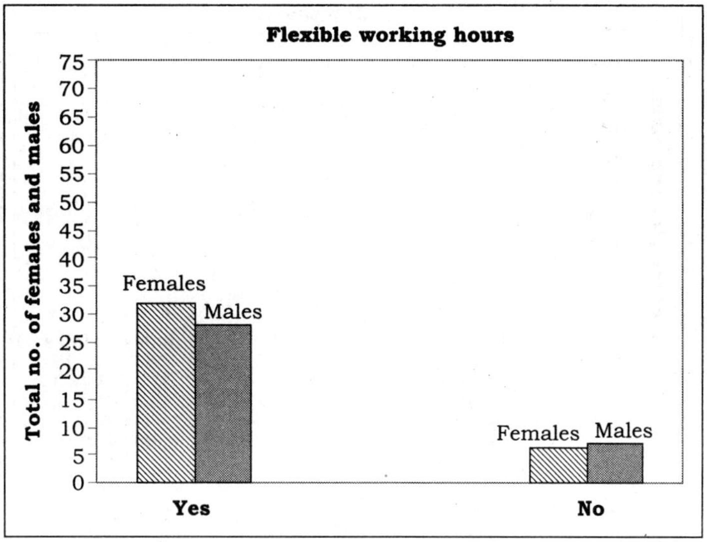

Small portion of 14 females (35%) and 7 males (21%) showed interest in working part time or on term time, with the rest showing disinterest on it.

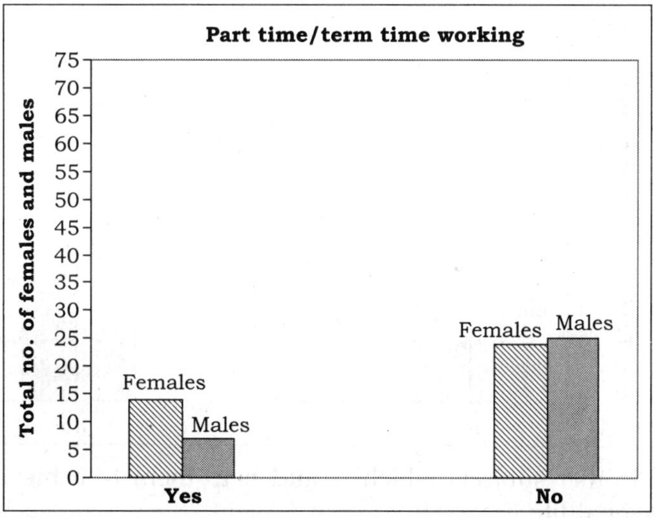

Interest on job sharing was shown by 17 females (46%) and 13 males (39%) with 20 males (61%) and 20 (54%) females showing a disinterest towards job sharing, respectively.

A considerable number of 13 females (35%) and 14 males (42%) were interested in career break while 24 females (65%) and 14 males (50%) indicated a continuation of their respective career. Thus, one may infer that this sample also reported high levels of job satisfaction and job dedication.

A high number of respondents, that is, 34 females (92%) and 28 males (85%) showed great interest in gaining knowledge on various information and advice such as health

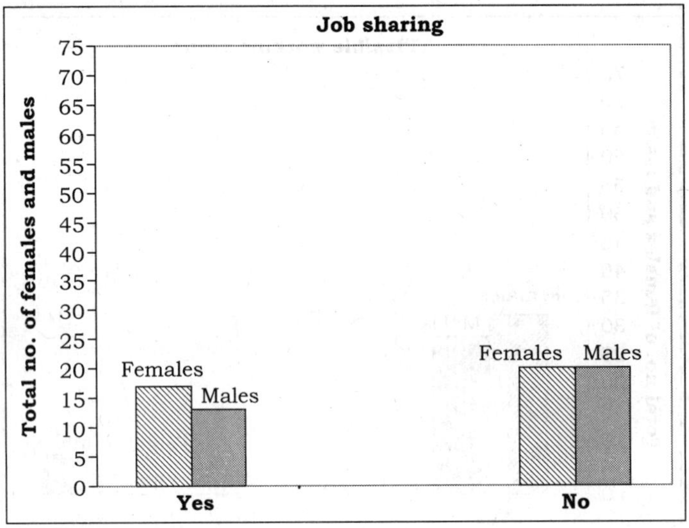

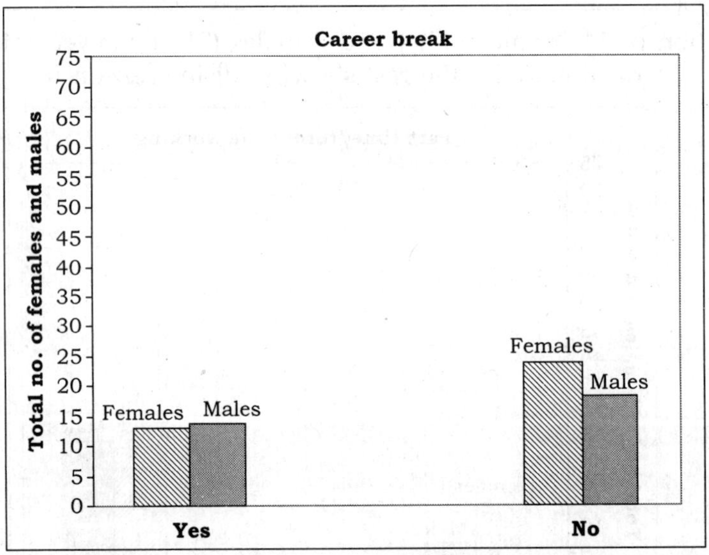

care, housing and other subjects which would help them to achieve a better balance on work and personal life.

The sample was also interested in other sources such as flexible pay, sports and such others.

The above findings on work life domains present interesting results of Mumbai metro which can be compared further with other metros in India or globally for gaining insights into WLB.

Good to Know

Work-life balance is increasingly becoming a significant concern for employers in order to help employees combat their stress and maximize utilization of their potentials.

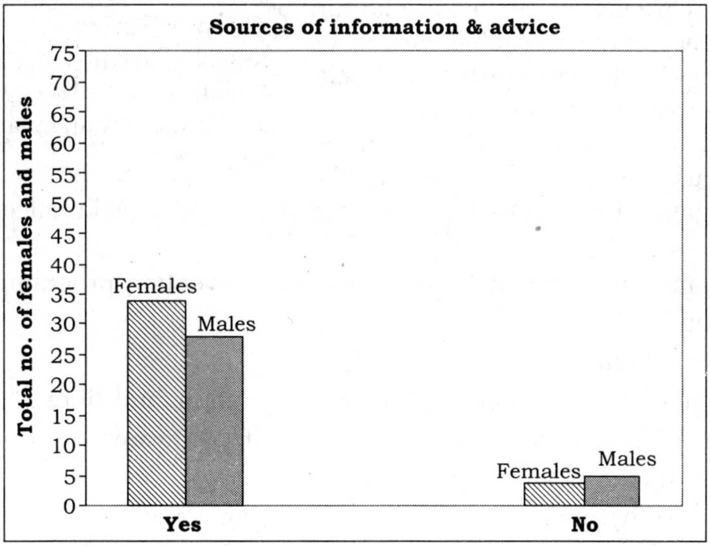

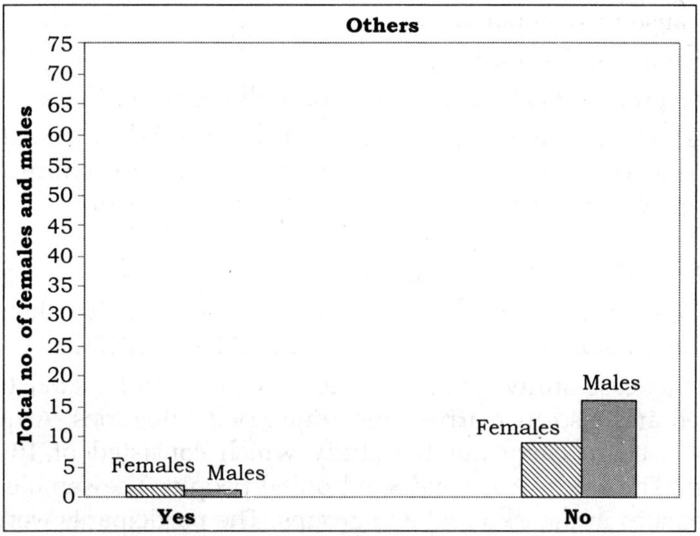

9.3.1 Stress Reduction Techniques

With businesses going large-scale and competition becoming extreme, there is mounting pressure on employees to deliver more and better than before. As a result the stress faced by workers is substantial. Managers experience stress wherein they are forced to indulge in tasks irrelevant to their job description. The sheer volume of work can be an overwhelming experience at times.

Role stress can have serious consequences. It can develop into a nightmare of running faster and faster to stay in the same place, feeling undervalued, feeling unable to say 'no' to any demand. The signs of stress can include sleeplessness, aches and pains, and sometimes physical symptoms of anxiety about going to work. What is more, people who are chronically stressed are no fun to work with. They may be irritable, miserable, lacking in energy and commitment, and self-absorbed. They may find it hard to concentrate on any one task and cannot be relied on to do their share. Thus, it is important to help the managers recognize the reasons for their role stress and to take adequate actions at the right time.

> **Good to Know**
> Stresses arising out of work life imbalance can be very difficult to even recognize and manage for many employees.

Many companies have opted for certain stress prevention programmes such as:

- meditation
- relaxation programmes
- change diet (less fat), more fresh fruits, vegetables, and fibre
- self-permission to experience emotions, cry if you want
- physical exercise or fitness programmes
- building healthy personal relationships, having someone to talk to
- controlling displaced aggressions; desire to yell at the kids and kick the dog at home because of stress at work
- re-appraise life and priorities
- consulting professionally a qualified counsellor or psychiatrist

Stress management training programmes teach workers about the nature and sources of stress, the effects of stress on health, and personal skills to reduce stress. This plan has the advantage of being inexpensive and easy to implement.

9.3.2 A Research Case Study

Good WLB is defined as a situation in which workers feel that they are capable of balancing their work and non-work commitments (Moore 2007).

The aim of this case study (H.L. Kaila 2007) was to understand the WLB among men and women and also in married and unmarried categories. A questionnaire (as appended) was used to carry out the study which consisted of 10 questions with multiple choices. The study was conducted on 80 people. The sample consisted of 40 males and 40 females in the different age groups. The participants were from different organizations like Hinduja Hospital, Air check monitoring, and the like. The sample of 80 participants was divided into 20 male married, 20 female married, 20 male unmarried, and 20 female unmarried.

The respondents were made to answer the questionnaire on the spot and doubts if any were clarified at the time the questionnaire was administered, participants were debriefed and told that the true nature of the study was to study the WLB among men and women, married and unmarried both.

Table 9.1 shows raw score under unmarried category for men and women. It can be seen that the raw score obtained for unmarried male category was 662 whereas for unmarried female category it was 672. From the table we can see that there is not much difference in the raw score but still unmarried female score is higher than the male score. This shows that women are better at balancing work and life than men.

Table 9.1 Raw Scores of 40 S's under Unmarried Category for Men and Women

Unmarried Category

	Female		
S's No.	*Raw Score*	χ *(X-M)*	χ_1^2
1.	36	2.4	5.76
2.	30	–3.6	12.96
3.	34	0.4	0.16
4.	42	8.4	70.56
5.	35	1.4	1.96
6.	26	–7.6	57.76
7.	44	10.4	108.16
8.	32	–1.6	2.56
9.	31	–2.6	6.76
10.	30	–3.6	12.96
11.	36	2.4	5.76
12.	39	5.4	29.16
13.	32	–1.6	2.56
14.	33	–0.6	0.36
15.	36	2.4	5.76
16.	34	0.4	0.16
17.	34	0.4	0.16
18.	30	–3.6	12.96
19.	28	–5.6	31.36
20.	30	–3.6	12.96
Σ	672	0	380.8

	Male		
S's No.	*Raw Score*	χ *(X-M)*	χ_1^2
1.	32	–1.1	–1.21
2.	24	-9.1	82.81
3.	32	–1.1	1.21
4.	32	–1.1	1.21
5.	25	–8.1	65.61
6.	32	–1.1	1.21
7.	39	5.9	34.81
8.	33	–0.1	0.01
9.	34	0.9	0.81
10.	32	–1.1	1.21
11.	36	2.9	8.41
12.	39	5.9	34.81
13.	32	–1.1	1.21
14.	32	–1.1	1.21
15.	39	5.9	34.81
16.	32	–1.1	1.21
17.	33	–0.1	0.01
18.	36	2.9	8.41
19.	34	0.9	0.81
20.	34	0.9	0.81
Σ	662	0	281.8

Table 9.2 shows the raw score under married category for men and women. Looking at the table it can be seen that the raw score for married men was 715 whereas raw score for married women it was 794. This again shows that married women are better at balancing work and life than men.

Looking at Summary Table 9.3 of total sample and mean for men and women it can be seen that mean score for unmarried men was 33.1 And for unmarried women was 33.6 and the mean was found to be 35.75 for married men and 39.7 For married women.

Table 9.2 Raw Scores of 40S's Under Married Category for Men and Women

Married Category

	Female		
	Raw Score	$\chi(X\text{-}M)$	χ_1^2
1.	43	3.3	10.89
2.	39	–0.7	0.49
3.	25	–14.70	216.09
4.	35	–4.7	22.09
5.	34	–5.7	32.49
6.	38	–1.7	2.89
7.	42	2.3	5.29
8.	41	1.3	1.69
9.	36	–3.7	13.69
10.	42	2.3	5.29
11.	40	0.3	0.09
12.	42	2.3	5.29
13.	40	0.30	0.09
14.	39	–0.70	0.49
15.	44	4.30	18.49
16.	40	0.30	0.09
17.	42	2.30	5.29
18.	48	8.30	68.89
19.	45	5.30	28.09
20.	39	–0.70	0.49
Total	794	0	438.2

	Male		
	Raw Score	$\chi(X\text{-}M)$	χ_1^2
1.	32	–3.75	14.0625
2.	36	0.25	0.0625
3.	30	–5.75	33.0625
4.	31	–4.75	22.5625
5.	39	3.25	10.5625
6.	39	3.25	10.5625
7.	36	0.25	0.0625
8.	38	2.25	5.0625
9.	40	4.25	18.0625
10.	42	6.25	39.0625
11.	30	–5.75	33.0625
12.	30	–5.75	33.0625
13.	39	3.25	10.5625
14.	30	–5.75	33.0625
15.	42	6.25	39.0625
16.	38	2.25	5.0625
17.	35	–0.75	0.5625
18.	39	3.25	10.5625
19.	32	–3.75	14.0625
20.	37	1.25	1.5625
Total	715	0	333.75

Table 9.3 Summary Table of Total Sample and Mean for Men and Women in both Unmarried and Married Category

		N	*Mean*
Male	Married	20	35.75
	Unmarried	20	33.1
Female	Married	20	39.7
	Unmarried	20	33.6

Independent t-test was administered to study the WLB among men and women in married and unmarried category. The degree of freedom was 38. The results showed that the obtained *t* value for unmarried male and female *t* value was 0.37 which is not significant and for married men and women *t* value was 2.76 which is significant at 0.01 levels (Table 9.4). Figure 9.1 shows WLB among men and women in married and unmarried categories. This again shows that women have scored higher than men in both married and unmarried category.

Table 9.4 Independent Sample t-test for both Married and Unmarried Categories

		t Value	*df*	*Level of Significance*
Unmarried	Male	0.37	38	Not significant
	Female			
Married	Male	2.76	38	0.01
	Female			

Legend: *t*-Computed value of *t*-test; *df*-degree of freedom

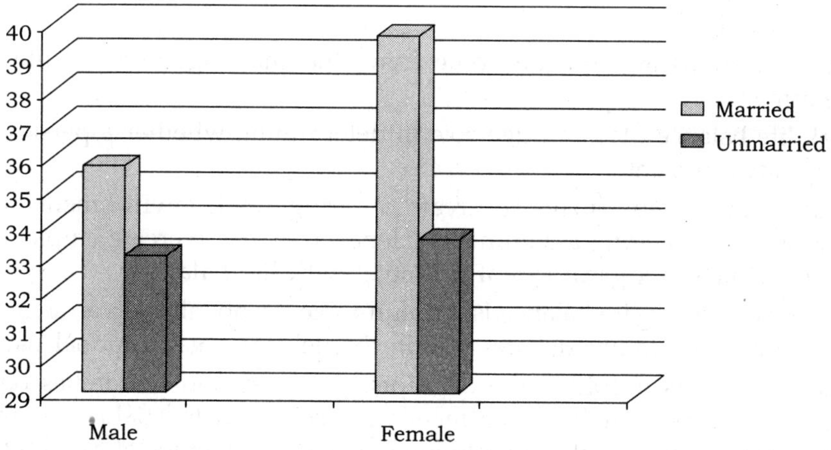

Fig. 9.1 Work life balance among men and women in married and unmarried categories.

The reason for the results obtained could be that the women are increasingly becoming a part of the active workforce and are not just handling work successfully but are also running their homes commendably. A major reason for this difference is probably the upbringing. In every traditional Indian household, women are taught from childhood itself that they will be handling family responsibilities when they grow up. The upbringing also helps them learn about managing things in a better manner. In addition to this, with modern education and opportunities, women have actually become capable of handling all that and much more. This exposure and experience makes them better managers at work too. This is probably because women are emotionally and mentally stronger than men, as proven by various other studies. This helps them handle pressure and stress in a better way and with greater agility. Moreover, it also helps them stand firm in the face of adversities and this is exactly what gives them an edge. Another reason for women's ability to manage work and life is the way they set up their priorities. Men have been considered the bread earners of the family for ages. So, they tend to be concerned only about their work and career, to a large extent. Women, on the other hand, know that family and home are equally important. So, they try to ensure that they are able to balance work and life in such a manner that both get equal importance and quality time. There are many women, who at the peak of their careers, quit their jobs to take care of their families or children and joined the workforce again when things had settled. These women are almost as successful as men who started their career at the same time. This also shows that giving the much needed time and importance to family does not necessarily impact career growth.

SUMMARY

- Work-life balance has always been a concern for those interested in the quality of working life.
- In organizations and on the home front, the challenge of work-life balance is escalating.
- Work-life balance plays a huge role in determining whether a person will reach career advancement.
- Organizations today strive to create a caring work environment and culture along with challenging assignments. Hence, they try to create employee friendly policies which to a great extent promote work life balance.
- The study of work-life balance is a useful topic for opening up a range of familiar and a few less familiar debates within the field of organizational psychology.
- This chapter has unfolded the concepts, domains, and researches on work-life balance as a great challenge to meet with boldly in the field of organizational psychology, and has also highlighted major parameters of work-life balance, stress reduction techniques, and work-life balance in Mumbai metro.

EXERCISE FOR CLASSROOM PRACTICE

For better understanding of the subject matter of this chapter, please read and check each of the following statements whether True (T) or False (F) or Uncertain (U).

1. Work-life balance is defined as satisfaction and good functioning at work and at home with a minimum of role conflict.
2. Effective work-life balance policies are valuable to organizations for a number of reasons.
3. The organization's role is to increase stress and promote work-life balance.
4. Organizations undertake initiatives to improve employees' healthy eating habits.

5. There is a changing trend of importance offered to the career life of men and women.
6. Organizations have increasingly showed great interest in employee health care which would help them to achieve a better balance on work and personal life.
7. Role stress has positive impact in work-life balance.
8. Married women are better at balancing work and life than men, is a myth.
9. Consulting a professionally qualified counsellor or a psychiatrist would help in work-life balance.
10. Flexible working hours, part time jobs, job sharing, and career breaks are some good techniques that organizations have used for work-life balance.

Answers: All statements are **True** except that statement numbers 3, 7, and 8 are **False.**

REVIEW QUESTIONS FOR DISCUSSIONS/EXAMINATIONS

1. Discuss the concept of work-life balance.
2. Describe two researches on work-life balance along with its implications.
3. Illustrate various parameters of work-life balance.
4. Critically discuss the applications of work-life balance in Indian organizations?
5. Develop a stress reduction programme for your high-stressed employees.
6. Address the strategies for coping with work-life balance relevant in your organization.
7. Develop some case studies of your employees on successful work-life balance.
8. Differentiate between men and women on work-life balance approaches.
9. Describe how an outdated but pervasive ideals and rigid behavioural rules constrain work-life balance.
10. Comment on the statement – 'Women do not need to choose between work and life; they choose both and live both fully'.

FIELD RESEARCH REPORT

This is a research assignment section for students for their internal marking by the teacher during the semester. This assignment is for understanding practical applications of the subject.

An action research project: Identify a group of minimum 15 executives and 15 non-executives across an organization preferably where you are placed for an internship. Conduct interviews with them by using a set of closed/open-ended questionnaire to signify the issues and concerns pertaining to the work-life balance strategies of your company. Also highlight successful work-life balance practices. Prepare a report of about 15 pages reflecting an action plan for better work practices.

REFERENCES

Work-life Balance: Myth or Reality. *Business Manager* (2015). 17 (7), 3, 20.

Cartwright, S.H. (2006). 'The Meaning of Work: The Challenge of Regaining Employee Engagement and Reducing Cynicism.' *Human Resource Management Review* 16, 199–208.

Clark, S.C. (2000). 'Work/Family Border Theory: A New Theory of Work/Life Balance.' *Human Relations*, 53, (6) 747–770.

Frone, M.R. Russell, M. and Cooper, M.L. (1992). 'Antecedents and Outcomes of Work Family Conflict: Testing a Model of the Work-Family Interface.' *Journal of Applied Psychology*, 77, 65-78.

Greenhaus, J. and R. Singh (2003). *Work-Family Linkages, a Sloan Work and Family Encyclopedia Entry*. Chestnut Hill, MA: Boston College.

Guest, D. and N. Conway (2000). *The Psychological Contract in the Public Sector*. London: CIPD.

In Carolyn Hayes, ed. (2002). *Innovations in Interdisciplinary Teaching*. Westport, CT: The Oryx Press, 16-37.

Kaila H.L. (2005). *Women, Work and Family*. New Delhi: Rawat Publications.

Kaila H.L. (2007). *Organizational Behavior & HRM* (2nd edition). Delhi: AITBS Publishers.

Laura Stack (2013). Walking the Tightrope: Find a Work-Life Balance. Retrieved on June 10, 2013. http://www.success.com/articles/2335-walking-the-tightrope-work-life-balance

Lockwood, N.R. (2007). 'Leveraging Employee Engagement for Competitive Advantage: HR's Strategic Role.' *SHRM Research Quarterly*, 2, 11.

Mauno, S. and U. Kinnunen (1999). 'The Effects of Job Stressors on Marital Satisfaction in Finnish Dual-Earner Couples.' *Journal of Organizational Behavior*, 20 (6) 879–895.

Messmer Max (2006). 'Four Keys to Improved Staff Retention.' *Strategic Finance*, October 2006, 1-7.

Moore, F. (2007). 'Work Life Balance: Contrasting Managers and Workers in an MNC.' *Journal of Employee Relations*, 29 (4) 385–399.

O'Driscoll, M. (1996). 'The Interface Between Job and Off-Job Roles: Enhancement and Conflict.' In C. Cooper and I. Robertson (eds). *International Review of Industrial and Organizational Psychology*, Volume 11. Chichester: John Wiley.

Parul Agarwal (2014). 'A Study of Work Life Balance with Special Reference to Indian Call Center Employees.' *International Journal of Engineering and Management Research*, 4 (1), 157–164.

Stairs, M.G. (2006). 'Retention on a Knife Edge: The Role of Employee Engagement in Talent Management.' *Selection and Development Review*, 22 (4), 19-24.

Tulgan, B. (1996). *Managing Generation X*. Oxford: Capstone.

Walls Anne, (2013). 'Walking the Balance Beam-Finding Equilibrium with Work, Family and Life.' *SPAN*, May/June 2013, 5–8.

Wentworth, Jay and James R. Davis. "Enhancing Interdisciplinarity Through Team Teaching."

Zedeck, S. and K. Mosier (1990). 'Work in the Family and Employing Organization.' *American Psychologist,* 45, 240–251.

APPENDIX

Work-life Balance Questionnaire

*Name:*__________________ *Age:* _________

Designation: _____________ *Gender:* ___________ *Qualification:* _______________

The purpose of this instrument is to survey work-life balance of the employee in an organization. There are no right or wrong answers. Please read each question in the enclosed list. Based on your experience tick the answers.

1. How many hours a week do you spend at work and travelling to work?
   (a) 50–59 (b) Less than 39
   (c) More than 70 (d) 40–49
   (e) 60–69
2. How often do you think or worry about work (when you are not actually at work or travelling to work)?
   (a) Most days (b) I don't
   (c) Rarely (d) Most of time
   (e) Once a week
3. How do you feel about the amount of time you spend at work, travelling to work, or thinking about work?
   (a) Very unhappy (b) Very happy
   (c) Happy (d) Unhappy
   (e) Ok
4. How often do you take a lunch break lasting more than 30 minutes?
   (a) Most days (b) Once a week
   (c) Every day (d) Lunch is for wimps
   (e) If it is free
5. Do you ever miss out on quality time with your family or your friends because of pressure of work?
   (a) Not very often (b) Often
   (c) No, family comes first (d) No time for friends
   (e) All the time
6. Does work ever have a negative effect on your personal life?
   (a) Not very often (b) Often
   (c) No, its only a job (d) No personal life
   (e) All the time

7. When was the last time you did something for yourself rather than for someone else?
   (a) This week (b) A few weeks ago
   (c) Every day (d) Can't remember
   (e) Over a year ago
8. Do you ever feel anxious or upset because of what is happening at work?
   (a) Not very often (b) Often
   (c) No, its only a job (d) No time to be anxious
   (e) All the time
9. When was the last time you lost your temper at work?
   (a) Can't remember (b) Yesterday/today
   (c) More than a week (d) Always angry
   (e) More than a month
10. Do you ever feel tired or depressed because of work?
    (a) Not very often (b) Often
    (c) No, its only a job (d) Too tired to be depressed
    (e) All the time
11. Scoring key of the questionnaire
    1. a3 b5 c1 d2 e4
    2. a2 b5 c4 d1 e3
    3. a1 b5 c4 d2 e3
    4. a4 b3 c5 d1 e2
    5. a4 b3 c5 d1 e2
    6. a4 b3 c5 d1 e2
    7. a4 b3 c5 d1 e2
    8. a4 b3 c5 d1 e2
    9. a5 b2 c3 d1 e4
    10. a4 b3 c5 d1 e2

The higher is the score, better is the work-life balance.
Scores of 40–50 show that you have a fair work-life balance.
Scores of 20–39 show that you need to look at your work-life balance in some areas.
Scores of 1–19 show that you need help in sorting out your work-life balance.

10

Safety at Workplace

Learning Objectives

This chapter would help the readers:

- to understand the legislation of occupational health and safety;
- to know the framework and process of behaviour based safety (BBS);
- to acquaint with the researches on behaviour based safety;
- to be familiar with an application of BBS in organizations; and
- to reflect upon case study about BBS.

An Opening Story: Review on Occupational Safety

Companies are increasingly inclined to reviewing their occupational health safety administration systems. The main reason for this is that in organizations the safety systems and procedures are in place but they are not reflected in safe behaviours of their employees. In one such recent review meeting at Maharatna Company, the top officials of the major oil and gas organization made a very challenging proposition to the contractor who was assigned the contract to revamp and/or reinforce their safety systems. They asked the contractor to implement not only the behaviour based safety (BBS) system but also build an organizational structure to sustain the safety effort on the part of every employee and the workmen which would focus and achieve zero unsafe behaviour. This project would be reviewed every month by the BBS steering team including the chief managing director, executive director, and the general managers of HSE and training departments. The emphasis was to create such a safety system that can be replicated to all locations of the company in India. The company asked the contractor to conduct a safety perception survey to find out gaps/weaknesses in the existing safety systems. The company reiterated to create IT enabled behaviour safety data system that would generate monthly report of safe and unsafe behaviours. In each location, the BBS observers would be trained to observe and correct unsafe behaviour of the employees and workmen. This case highlights that the top managements today are concerned and demanding for an organizational change towards developing a strong sense of safe behaviour in every person of the company in order to create an injury-free workplace.

10.1 INTRODUCTION

'Safety first' is only a slogan in Indian industry; it does not appear in practice. Most employers and top managements have faulty perception that safety is majorly a cost to the company. This perception is a constraint to consider safety as a value to save lives at workplace. Every day, 6300 people die as a result of occupational accidents or work-related diseases – more than 2.3 million deaths per year (International Labour Organization 2013). Even after having all the safety systems in place, it's difficult to achieve injury-free culture. Indian corporates are far behind in ensuring women safety at work (Business Manager 2015).

It is important for workers and safety personnel to prevent and minimize the consequences of catastrophic releases of toxic, reactive, flammable, or explosive chemical substances, which result in toxic or explosive hazards (Dikshith 2013).

Three clauses of OHSAS 18001:2007 document emphasize behavioural aspects of safety in Occupational Health & Safety (OH&S) Management Systems that organizations shall establish, implement, and maintain a procedure(s) for: the participation of workers by their appropriate involvement in hazard identification, risk assessments, and determination of controls; for hazard identification and risk assessment that shall take into account: human behaviour, capabilities, and other human factors; and to make persons working under its control aware of the OH&S consequences, actual or potential, of their work activities, their behaviour, and the OH&S benefits of improved personal performance.

Behaviour Based Safety (BBS) process has included the OHSAS 18001:2007 compliances on human factors in its training applications. BBS would help organizations implement OHSAS 18001:2007 clauses. BBS approach enables the participation and involvement of workers in hazard identification, risk assessments, and determination of controls; and BBS also makes workers aware of their unsafe as well as safe behaviours. BBS would help maintain an account of human behaviour in terms of percentages of unsafe and safe behaviours of workers on monthly basis (Kaila 2010).

Unsafe behaviours are at the core of any near misses, injury, fatalities (Fig. 10.1). If we control unsafe behaviours, we may not even have near misses (Reason 1990, 1997). Research experiences indicate that almost 50% of the unsafe behaviours are identified or noticeable at any plant at any given point of time; 25-30% of safety awareness is lacking among employees which gets reflected in their unsafe behaviours (Kaila 2010).

Engineering solutions have been achieved to a great extent in organizations but behavioural engineering in managing safety is a lot more challenging to learn and implement (Kaila 2007; Skinner 1974; Stewart 1991).

To reduce accidents, the managements have taken safety interventions such as risk assessment, suggestion scheme, training, safety committee, auditing, motivational programmes (quiz, award, incentives), SOPs, plant inspection, work permit system and such others. Most of these safety management systems have aimed at controlling unsafe conditions, whereas almost 100% of accidents are triggered by unsafe acts or behaviours (Kaila 2014; Marsh et al. 1998; Algera 1990; Pettinger 2001). Even unsafe conditions are nothing but the result of unsafe behaviours.

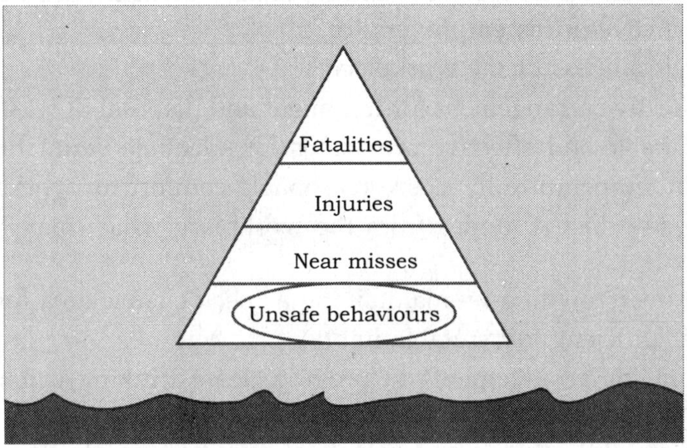

Fig. 10.1 BBS triangle.

10.2 OCCUPATIONAL HEALTH AND SAFETY (OHS) LEGISLATION

A safe and healthy work environment is the basic right of every worker. However, the global situation falls far short of this right. The International Labour Organization (ILO) estimates that more than 125 million workers are victims of occupational accidents and diseases every year.

India has had legislation on occupational health and safety for over 50 years. India was under British rule in the 19th and the early 20th century, hence the principal health and safety laws are based on the British Factories Act. The Factories Act, 1948 has been amended from time to time, and especially after the Bhopal Gas disaster which could have been prevented. This demanded a shift from dealing with disaster (or disease) to prevent its occurrence. The Factories (Amendment) Act came into force on 1 December 1987.

Various laws have come into force for the protection of safety and health of the workforce in India which are in line the international labour office (ILO) conventions. The organizations are bound to implement these laws to ensure safety and health of people at work. By and large, the Indian organizations care very much for these laws and implement, in addition the enforcement inspectorates also ensure the implementation in the respective states in India. For reference, some of these legislations are as follows:

- The Factories Act 1948, amended 1954, 1970, 1976, 1987
- The Mines Act, 1952
- The Dock Workers (Safety, Health, and Welfare) Act, 1986
- The Plantation Labour Act, 1951
- The Explosives Act, 1884
- The Petroleum Act, 1934
- The Insecticide Act, 1968

The Factories Act requires employers to:

- ensure cleanliness of the workplace;
- make effective arrangement for treatment and disposal of waste and effluent;
- make suitable and effective provisions for adequate ventilation;
- maintain temperature to secure reasonable comfort for workers;
- remove any dust or fumes from the workplace which may be injurious to workers;
- prevent overcrowding by maintaining a specific cubic area for each worker;
- provide sufficient and suitable light;
- make suitable arrangements to provide clean drinking water conveniently situated for all workers and;
- provide suitable latrines and urinals of specified standards.

The Factories Act requires employers to provide basic safety measures including:

- securely guarding all parts of dangerous machinery;
- precautions for working on machinery;
- emergency devices for cutting off power;
- maintain hoists and lifts;
- lifting machines, chains, ropes, and other lifting tackle must be maintained in good condition;
- test pressurized vessels regularly;
- ensure walking surfaces are of sound construction;
- provide protective equipment;
- measures to remove gas and dust before entering confined places;
- measures to prevent fires.

- The Indian Boilers Act, 1923
- The Indian Electricity Act, 1910
- The Dangerous Machines (Regulations) Act, 1983
- The Indian Atomic Energy Act, 1962
- The Radiological Protection Rules, 1971
- The Manufacture, Storage and Import of Hazardous Chemicals Rules, 1989

The factory occupier must disclose information about:

- dangers, health hazards, and measures to protect workers from substances or materials in manufacture, transportation, storage and so on, to the workers, the chief factory inspector, and the local authority;
- safety and policy;
- quantity and characteristics and disposal of substances and waste;
- emergency plans to workers and the local public;

- handling, using, transportation, storage and disposal of hazardous substances to workers and the local public.

The Factories Act also binds the employer to maintain up-to-date health records of workers, to appoint a person experienced in handling hazardous substances to supervise handling, and provide protective measures and regular medical examinations.

The Chief Factory Inspector of the Factory Inspectorate enforces the Factories Act. But a major problem is poor enforcement of the law. There are a few factory inspectors who are not even provided with adequate resources. The Factories Act also specifies worker participation in safety management and safety committee membership which are normally followed in organizations. It is assured through training that a worker on the shop floor knows about the hazards at the workplace.

10.3 OCCUPATIONAL SAFETY AND HEALTH INSTITUTIONS

There are three major institutions devoted to occupational health and safety which are set up by the Government of India under the Ministry of Labour:

- Central Labour Institute (CLI), Mumbai and Regional Labour Institutes (RLI) in Kolkata, Kanpur and Chennai under Ministry of Labour;
- National Safety Council (NSC), Navi Mumbai
- These institutes have strong systems for consultation with employers and trade unions for training, research, consultancy and the like.
- National Institute of Occupational Health, Ahmedabad and regional institutes in Kolkata and Bengaluru under the Indian Council of Medical Research (ICMR), Ministry of Health.
- The National Institute of Occupational Health (NIOH) has many facilities. It is quite active as a research institute.

10.3.1 BBS Concepts

Behaviour Based Safety (BBS) is intended to be an effective approach to prevent occupational injuries. It can be described as the psychology of prevention. However, in practice it only reaches its potential when everyone in the organization understands the BBS principles and practises the procedures.

> **Good to Know**
> Behaviour Based Safety is a process that helps employees identify and choose a safe behaviour over unsafe/at-risk one.

Professors Scott Geller and David Broadbent opined that BBS has helped employees understand why at-risk behaviours occur and it has empowered employees to substitute safe for at-risk work practices and help others do the same.

Wikipedia describes behavioural safety as an application of the science of behaviour change to real-world problems. BBS focusses on what people do, analyses why they do it, and then applies a research supported intervention strategy to improve what people do. At its very core, BBS is based on a larger scientific field called Organizational Behaviour Analysis.

It is more about changing the behaviour of front-line employees. It is about identifying the barriers to safe behaviour and designing and implementing a strategy for ensuring that work environment, practices, and policies support behaving safely.

> **Good to Know**
> Each employee can make a difference in organizational safety.

BBS emphasizes that each employee takes an ownership of their safe as well as unsafe behaviours. If they behave unsafely, they are not punished, instead they are repeatedly told to correct; and when they behave safely, they are encouraged. Both unsafe and safe behaviours are counted and displayed. BBS also discusses the unsafe conditions that influence unsafe behaviours.

BBS is a data-driven decision-making process. BBS believes that what gets measured gets done. Employees are the basic source of expertise of behavioural change (observe and correct). BBS begins by briefing sessions for all work areas and departments. BBS is teamwork; it is company-wide and people-driven. BBS purpose (Kaila 2007) is not to enforce safety rules, force change, gossip about others, reporting to the boss. Its purpose is to identify safe and at-risk behaviours, identify possibility for injury, communicate the risk and help to identify safer solutions. An implementation team or BBS steering committee monitors its progress. Essentially, BBS is not a management-driven tool for safety. It's an employee-driven approach with management support (Pearse, 1997).

According to Professor Geller, BBS follows DO-IT: Define, observe, intervene, and test.

Define - Critical unsafe behaviours

Observe - Target unsafe behaviours.

Intervene - To change the target of unsafe behaviour in desired direction (safe behaviours).

Test - Test and measure the impact of programme (improvements in safe behaviours).

BBS focusses on three aspects — the person, environment, and behaviour for creating total safety culture. The environment of safe behaviours is created by involving all persons at work.

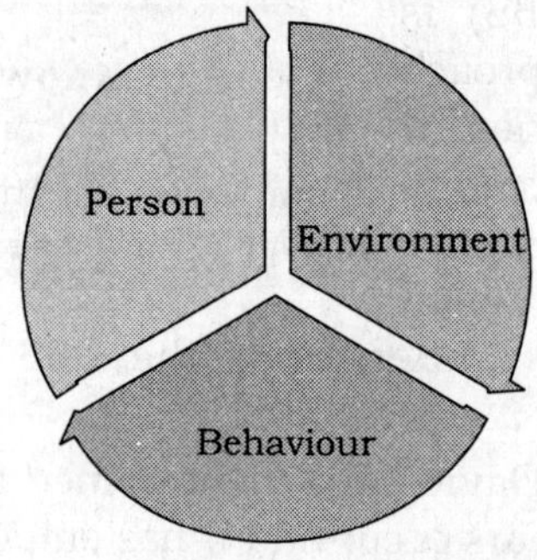

BBS is concerned with correcting unsafe behaviours for reduction of accidents and promoting safe behaviours for developing injury-free culture in their organizations (Algera 1990). BBS touches the root cause of accidents.

10.3.2 What Behavioural Safety Training Does?

BBS is one of the best and latest safety approaches. BBS is a process of repeatedly going to an employee and making random observations till he reaches safe behaviours and learns the concept of self-observation and observing others for safe performance.

Nine aspects that behavioural safety takes care of in order to prevent unsafe behaviours and promote safe behaviours are:

- Personal protective equipment (PPE)
- Housekeeping
- Using tools and equipment
- Body positioning/protecting
- Material handling
- Communication (verbal/non-verbal/written)
- Following safety procedures
- Visual focussing (attentiveness)
- Use of mobile phone at work

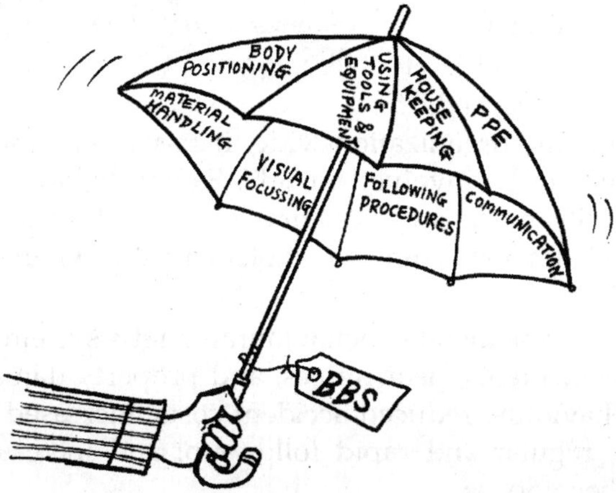

With the help of a checklist, BBS trained observers create data on the above nine critical behaviours to guide their observations. Each observer observes and provides feedback to his co-workers daily. This way safety becomes a daily reminder which in essence builds safety culture. We can almost check daily an increase or decrease in unsafe and safe behaviours by creating this data base.

10.4 BBS AND OHS CULTURE

Organizations that fail to take a scientific approach to safety's human-behaviour element are gambling with their futures and are ultimately only safe by accidents. BBS is concerned about correcting unsafe behaviours for reduction of accidents and promoting safe behaviours for developing injury-free culture in their organizations.

BBS trained observers create data by following behaviour, observation, and feedback process (BOFP). In an organization, if there are 50 trained observers, each day they create 50 checklists on the safe as well as unsafe behaviours of their fellow workmen. This way in a month, they generate almost 1500 checklists and provide feedback to these many workers in the organization. This way safety becomes a daily reminder which in essence builds safety culture.

Total Safety Culture (TSC) requires attention to the person (attitude, personality) and environment (management systems, organizational climate). BOFP helps creating TSC.

> **Good to Know**
> Safety is too vast a field to be left only to the safety department in the organizations. It requires an organization-wide intervention like BBS.

Safety professionals in industry are under-staffed and over-worked. If safety function is to become organization-wide, it has to be made a line function in companies. Everyone has to be involved in BBS. Safety departments in organizations are busy in training, audits, mock-drills, celebrations, reporting, accident investigations; they are neither trained nor have time to implement behavioural safety changes for every employee.

A well-planned and implemented behavioural safety system should lead to less number of accidents or incidents, near-misses, and property damage; improved levels of quantified safety behaviours; reduced accident costs; increased reporting of defects, near-misses, accidents; regular and rapid follow-up; and increased skills in positive reinforcement of safe behaviours.

BBS is by the people, of the people and for the people.

10.4.1 BBS Processes

The major process of BBS is BOFP. This process, followed by all observers, has many aspects as highlighted below:

- BBS is a process of repeatedly going to an employee and making random observations till he reaches safe behaviours and learns the concept of self-observation and observing others for safe performance.
- BBS is to collect observation data on specific safe and unsafe behaviours by department, date, month, and time.
- BBS trained observers monitor safety behaviours on regular basis.

- Behavioural change brings 'attitudinal change', not necessarily vice versa, so the focus is on behaviour observation and feedback process.
- Critical behaviours can be listed in checklist based on previous accident and injury records and also by brainstorming.
- Different observers will notice different safe and unsafe behaviours, which is why employees need to observe each other.
- Establish observation routines and continuously improve safety process.
- Feedback can be on-the-spot and graphical feedback, and also weekly/monthly briefings are given.
- Feedback is an interaction based on genuine concern; let us not doubt our own attitude in giving and receiving feedback, it provides insight into our own behaviours.
- Feedback is to be given one on one, immediate, specific behaviour to be reinforced, appreciate safe behaviour to set example.

  Some characteristics of a BBS observer are:
  - Concern for others.
  - Self-initiation for correcting the observee.
  - Developing mutual insight on safe behaviour.
  - Transforming the observee for self-observation on safe behaviour.

- Observers target observable safe and unsafe behaviours of co-workers.
- Individual name of an employee is not recorded in the BBS checklist.
- Observation and coaching may take some time to be accepted by co-workers.
- Observation and feedback skills improve with practice and by using checklist.
- Observation sampling should be undertaken randomly (not on fixed timings) throughout the week.
- Observational comments: wrong tool used, instead say which tool needs to be used and why.
- Observe both safe and at-risk behaviours and use detailed comments for problem solving, follow-up and so on.
- Observers may observe individually or in a team of two (new observer with veteran observer).
- Observers provide feedback on safe and unsafe behaviours to an observee as per completed checklist.

In Hindi language, BBS is all about *dekho* (see), and *bolo* (say) with sensitivity and concern.

- Observe and correct unsafe behaviours.
- Observers provide immediate feedback for correction of behaviours.
- Safety coaching fosters open communication about safety.
- Safety coaching serves as a constant reminder for workplace safety.
- Safety observer/coach in every department may use different critical behaviours (use of PPE, body positioning, use of tools) on checklist, and coaching process (problem solving, follow-up).
- In order to make BOFP easier, speak the language of the observee, adjust your level to the observee, lower your ego. One may be a manager as BBS observer

but during BOFP he is not a manager; he is playing the role of BBS observer so that BOFP functions as if it's peer to peer.

- Observers need to focus on behaviours rather the making an issue on unsafe conditions not corrected by the management. Observers need not expect certain changes overnight.

Every observer must go through the aspects listed above while following the process of observation and feedback.

10.5 BBS IMPLEMENTATION AND STEERING TEAM

BBS is all about involving people across departments in an organization as a bottom-up approach. In order to implement BBS at the workplace and create safety culture, the following action plan is desirable in launching BBS:

- Commitment from management;
- Training of employees across the plant;
- Select and train observers from BBS trained employees;
- Form a steering team/committee of 8–10 people from BBS-trained employees including all departments;
- Develop checklists;
- Selection of areas/deparments for BOFP;
- Develop schedule timetable;
- Documentation, analysis, and display;
- Review to determine BBS progress in the organization;
- Allocate time for BBS observations, meetings and the like.

BBS implementation problems include lack of workforce buy-in; unsafe behaviours not defined with precision; accident records/near misses injuries not analysed properly for targeting accident causing behaviours.

BBS implementation guidelines are as follows:

- BBS may start small and build which means that make a beginning in one department. Remember that there is no best approach. BBS can be customized.
- The implementation in the plant must begin as soon as BBS training gets over to keep up the zeal of trained observers.
- Observers have to work within their limitations—don't argue with the observee, don't stress others or yourself, keep revising your patience threshold level, concentrate on what percentage of change in safe/unsafe behaviours you achieve, keep revising your goal to achieve higher level of safe behaviours on a month-on-month basis.
- People are asked to volunteer to either become observers or be a part of steering team. These people carry out responsibilities/duties.
- BBS needs to be integrated as an organizational system. It's a new initiative, new emphasis, and new direction on safety.
- BBS's secret of success is that the safety control is in the hands of each employee, they feel empowered and responsible.
- BBS should have pre- and post-measures of safety awareness levels of employees in all departments through safety awareness survey in order to compare its effects before and after implementation.
- BBS's speed of success depends upon existing injury/accident rate and readiness to implement it.
- BBS's success depends upon a strong steering team, which clearly defines its roles and responsibilities.
- Behavioural safety management support and leadership of first line and senior managers can be measured quantitatively.
- Implementation team/steering committee routinely monitor the progress of BBS without which BBS project may collapse.
- In the long run, BBS is cost effective as it reduces accidents, which actually are costly.
- Initially, BBS can be implemented in one or two departments and then introduced to other departments.
- Normally, self-nominations are invited from amongst the BBS trained employees to be observers, and they are further trained practically on 2-days in-plant training.
- It requires a steering committee comprising a senior manager, a front-line manager and about 10 BBS trained safety observers.
- It's an employee movement on behavioural safety with support and commitment of management.
- Management allows observers time to conduct observation tours, conduct feedback sessions, and organize data analysis to display, without which BBS will fail.

- BBS is an active partnership between managers and shop-floor members of the steering committee.

- Managers in the steering committee should not take a passive role and dump BBS on operators; managers' role is very crucial such as appreciating BBS observers and analysing data and the like.
- Managers/HoDs must appreciate observer's performance as they show progress in percentage of safe behaviours.
- Researches indicate that BBS has reduced 40–75% accident rates within six months to one year of its implementation.

To begin implementing BBS at the shop-floor, let the BBS trained employees complete a checklist of BOFP daily. Continued BBS training. More the number of BBS trained employees, more the number of BBS checklists coming in. Hence, you will find increasing frequency of unsafe and safe behaviours being collected on a daily basis.

10.6 AN INDIAN EXPERIENCE ON BBS

In India, companies such as ITC, ESSAR, RIL, Vedanta, Colourtex, Reliance Energy, Ultratech, GAIL, Chambal Fertilizers, HPCL, NPC, ONGC, GE, BFL, FMC, PI Industries, M&M, BHEL, ICC, Excel, Vedanta, Bayer CropScience, Sanofi-Aventis, Foseco, IOCL, Larsen & Toubro, and many others have implemented BBS.

In the past 10 years, BBS has been launched in Indian locations in its diverse sectors. Every organization has introduced and customized BBS as per their cultural background. Some organizations first exposed their senior management to the BBS concept, process, and implementation; and then took it down to lower levels.

Some have started off with bottom-level employees and contract workers. Other organizations exposed their middle management and non-management employees together. At some places, organizations have introduced 'train the trainers' programme and then these in-house trainers have trained other employees in various departments. Practically, a one-day BBS workshop in organizations has helped the participants to know the concept, process and implementation. The next step would be to identify BBS observers and then train them thoroughly on the BOFD. Practically 20% of employees in each department would be trained as BBS observers. A one-day review after a month by the BBS master trainer helps refining the process. Enthusiastically, BBS starts giving results very quickly. Forming an in-house BBS core committee has been useful in coordinating BBS activity and progress.

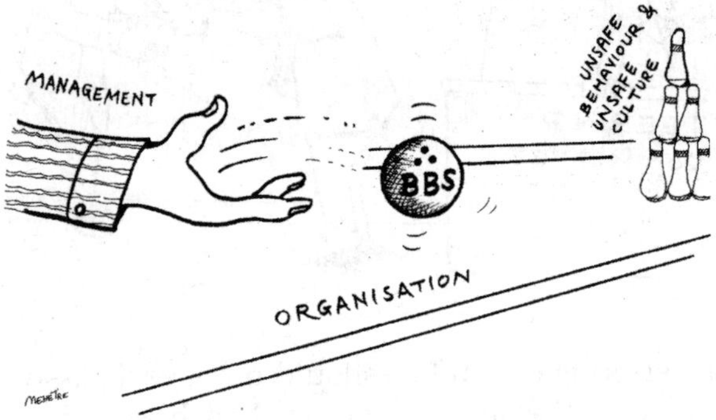

BBS has shown positive results in terms of reducing unsafe behaviours, promoting safe behaviours, and creating a safety culture in Indian organizations. BBS has provided better accident prevention practices than before. BBS exposure to employees has been an enriching and refreshing experience on understanding the fact that in order to prevent near misses at workplaces, we first need to tackle unsafe/at-risk behaviours through BBS approach. With the inclusion of behaviour aspects in the OHSAS 18001:2007 as safety compliances, Indian organizations have taken BBS seriously in its training applications.

10.7 PSYCHOSOCIAL ASPECTS OF SAFETY

In the safety research, the psychosocial aspects of safety have appeared prominently in India and abroad. The field of safety psychology has touched upon many aspects such as motivation for safety, use of PPE, safe worker profile, and facilitating and constraining factors for safety performance which are summarized here below:

(1) Conclusions and findings of an international Conference on 'Strategies on Occupational Accident Prevention' (1989) indicate that:

Most people active in controlling the risk are those who have the following perceptions:

(a) Their job is interesting and contributes to the final product,

(b) Their immediate supervisor responds positively to initiatives,

(c) The company provides a vision of positive future prospects, and

(d) Incentives system (wages and benefits) encourage initiatives.

(2) For improvement of safety performance, informational strategy (for example, accident investigation, safety inspections, and safety campaigns) need to be complemented by motivational strategies (for example, performance feedback).

- Instead of concentrating only on accidents, work and organizational behaviour need to be considered more comprehensively.
- Higher priority on work environment problems in all countries.

(3) Certain facilitating and constraining factors for safety performance have been identified in Indian industries as below:

- Health and safe working conditions are to be provided, failing which the employees are likely to perform unsafe acts.
- Work carried out by employees has to be appreciated both through monetary incentives and recognition, in the absence of which employees may overlook and develop low concern for safety rules and practices.
- The interpersonal relations between workers and supervisors need to be improved.
- Closed supervision is more likely to be viewed by the workers as a negative approach that may put a constraint on safe behaviour.
- Training and education provide an opportunity to the workers to develop safe ways of performing the job. The lack of safety education and training poses an impediment to safe performance.
- Finally, the support from top management in words and deeds is a must. The lack of cooperation and concern from senior level executives in the organization is perceived as an obstacle to safety promotion. Effective health and safety performance comes from the top; members of the board have both collective and individual responsibility for health and safety. Directors and boards need to examine their own behaviours, both individually and collectively (Health and Safety Executive 2013).

(4) Non-use of PPE: There are almost 50 types of PPE used in organizations for protection of employees. Some of these PPE are helmet, safety shoes, gloves, safety belt and so on. Factors that are identified for non-use of personal protective equipment (PPE) by workers are as follows.

- PPE are uncomfortable
- Lack of concern for own safety
- Lack of education and training
- Over-confidence
- Poor quality of PPE
- Wearing PPE decreases efficiency/productivity
- Resistance to use/indifferent
- Lack of proper enforcement
- Selling PPE for financial gains
- Improper PPE size/fittings
- Short supply/PPE not available
- Inappropriate/inefficient PPE

- Inadequate storage facility
- Lack of supervision
- Non-use of PPE by supervisor/management.

Some facts on PPE:

- 60% of eye injuries, 100% of face injuries, 80% of head injuries, 78% of foot injuries occurred to workers who were not wearing applicable PPE.
- Analysis of all fatal accidents in Sweden revealed that in 1/3rd of fatal accidents, chances of survival would have increased considerably if PPE had been used in all relevant situations.
- A study in 38 large organizations has shown that 53% of the organizations have no committees to monitor the quality of PPE, 65% of the industries make use of casual/contract labour, but 61% of them are not supplied with PPE.

(5) The profile of safe worker: It is important to understand the characteristics of a safe worker as follows:

Item No.	*Safe Worker is the one who-*	*% of response*
1.	Uses proper personal protective equipment..........	52
2.	Understands the job and hazards	40
3.	Obeys safety rules and regulations........	26
4.	Possesses good qualification, knowledge, ability, skill, and discipline.	25
5.	Is educated, trained and having safety habits	21
6.	Cooperated with his supervisor and others and follows the instructions of supervisor.	18
7.	Has safe working practice and safety awareness	17
8.	Is working carefully and in a better way not over-confidence.	13
9.	Is always alert and knows the safety functions.	12
10.	Works safety.	12
11.	Has balanced thinking	11
12.	Motivates others	11
13.	Uses proper tools in proper way	9
14.	Works for developing better working conditions.	7

The above-mentioned psychosocial factors for safety in organizations shall facilitate the managements in promoting occupational safety for their employees.

10.8 A RESEARCH CASE ON BBS

This research survey (H.L. Kaila 2007) on behavioural safety in India included a sample (Table 10.1) of 1751 executives and 713 workers in 64 multinational organizations during almost 200 BBS training workshops conducted across Indian organizations (such as petroleum, engineering, automobile, cement, power, chemical, pharmaceutical and others) in a period of 10 years between 1997 and 2007.

Table 10.1

Number & Type of Organizations	*Number of Employees*	
	Executives	*Workers*
12 Chemicals	321	130
05 Power/Energy	110	90
09 Gas/Petroleum	270	53
16 Heavy Engineering	260	63
02 Cement	90	102
03 Shipping	121	48
03 Automobile	72	36
05 Pharmaceutical	190	87
09 Others (Construction, Nuclear, Paper, Electrical)	317	104
Total: 64	1,751	713

The training exposure to all the survey participants was provided for a day which incorporated the BBS components such as concepts, processes, and implementation of behavioural safety. During BBS training interventions, the trained observers used a checklist of critical unsafe/safe behaviours (Fig. 10.1) to collect observation data from their respective workplaces with the help of BOFP.

Observers Checklist of Critical Behaviours

Observer ____________________ Date/Time __________

Department/Job____

Behaviour Categories	*Safe*	*At-Risk*	*Corrections*
PPE Using PPE, e.g., Helmet, Eye protection, Ear protection, Dust Mask, Gloves, Coveralls, Safety Belt, Fall arrestor, Safety Shoes, Apron, Others (specify)			
Housekeeping Work area maintained appropriately, general cleanliness, e.g., trash and scrap removed, spills cleaned, walkways unobstructed, materials and tools organized, etc.			
Using tools and equipment Using correct tools for the job, using tools properly, and tools in good condition...			
Body positioning/protecting Positioning/protecting body parts, e.g., avoiding line of fire, avoiding pinch points...			
Material handling e.g., body mechanics while lifting, pushing and pulling, use of assist devices such as chain blocks, slings...			

Communication Verbal and non-verbal (signals) that affect safety...			
Following procedures e.g., obtaining and complying with permits, following SOPs, lockout, tag-out procedures...			
Visual focussing (attentiveness)			
Use of mobile at work			

An analysis (Table 10.2) shows an average of 52.6% for their unsafe behaviours and an average of 47.4% for their safe behaviours in organizations.

Table 10.2 Unsafe and Safe Behaviours Employees Themselves Engage-in on Daily Basis

Organization Type	*Number of Employees*	*Number & % of Unsafe Behaviours*	*Number & % of Safe Behaviours*	*Total Number of Behaviours*
1. Chemicals	30	311 48%	330 52%	643
2. Petroleum	28	230 49%	239 51%	469
3. Cement	23	158 54%	135 46%	291
4. Automobile	31	219 47%	243 53%	462
5. Pharmaceutical	25	226 65%	124 35%	350
Total	137	Average 52.6%	Average 47.4%	

This analysis reflects that while every employee has engaged in safe behaviours, they have simultaneously engaged in unsafe behaviours more than 50% of the times at home, workplace, and on the road while going from residence to their office and back. Therefore, they need someone else to look after their safety which is emphasized by the principle of BBS that people need to take care of safety for each other, that is, peer-to-peer safety.

The employees from various organizations were further asked to report unsafe behaviours of their co-workers as perceived during the last one year.

Almost every worker has practised on average 3.5 unsafe behaviours at their workplace on a daily basis which can convert into an accident, near-miss, or it can be fatal depending upon the activity workers engage in (Table 10.3).

Table 10.3 Unsafe Behaviours of Co-workers Observed

Organization Type	*No. of Employees*	*No. of Unsafe Behaviours Perceived*	*Average Unsafe Behaviours*
Petroleum	21	106	5
Fertilizers	21	61	3
Automobile	17	104	6

Contd...

Contd...

Shipping	16	81	5
Pharmaceutical	19	83	4.5
Chemicals	26	105	4
Engineering	27	81	3
Power/Energy	19	68	4
Construction	34	113	3.3
Nuclear	30	97	3.2
Paper	30	79	2.6
Electrical	30	59	2.0
Chemicals	26	70	2.7
Cement	24	66	2.8
Petroleum	22	38	1.7
			Grand Average 3.5

BBS interventions indicate that targeting zero accidents does not really imply safe organization; we need to aim at zero unsafe behaviour at workplaces.

Field observations during BBS action research:

The field observations (from diverse workplaces during BBS training interventions in a period of 12 years between 1997 and 2009 across 64 multinational organizations in India including 1,751 executives and 713 workers) convey a bunch of practical experiences on the BBS process and implementation as given below.

(a) Each of the BBS training groups consisting of 25–30 people has confirmed almost 50% of safe and 50% of unsafe behaviours as being practised regularly at home, on the way, and at the plant. Hence, it is felt that almost everybody carries a set of unsafe behaviours which are an integral part of their lives. Thus, these individual unsafe behaviours are potent enough for accidents and pose a threat to safety. BBS education can be useful to employees at home, on the way, and at the plant.

(b) It is perceived that conversion of unsafe behaviours into safe behaviours requires four to five interactions between an observer and observee. It is like when we go to a doctor and report four or five symptoms, he gives medicine and asks you to come after 3/4 days, and then again sees you and like this he has 4/5 interactions with you before you feel well.

(c) BBS checklist should not be filled-in so mechanically that the observer neglects the main purpose of BBS which is primarily to identify and control at-risk behaviour so that the observee is saved from risk. BBS observer must save the person first if observed doing a very risky work, should not go on filling checklist mechanically. In this case, first save, then document.

(d) An observer need not find out the 'reason' on why a person is engaged in an unsafe behaviour or why an observee 'should' not behave safe, rather an observer has to actively care, observe, and give feedback showing his concern to an observee.

(e) 'Observation schedule' is very important for each observer so that he can cover all locations/shifts/observes each working hour during his observation tour.

(f) There are two types of observers: one who observes unsafe behaviour of an observee but does not document; the other is the one who meticulously documents all at-risk behaviours and gives a feedback.

(g) All observers may be given some reward or incentives, for example, individual recognition, group accolade and other incentives as they participate in bringing down at-risk behaviours and creating a safe environment.

(h) The feedback process between observer and observee follows stages such as informing observee about unsafe and safe behaviours, observee denies and feels shy about his unsafe behaviours, then he experiences alertness, slowly he attempts to change his unsafe behaviours to safe behaviours, internalizes such behaviours, stabilizing change, self-observation, and then may be ready to change others.

(i) The workers should not feel that management is dumping safety on them by launching BBS as it is a bottoms–up approach, they should not get a feeling that management is shirking away from their safety responsibilities towards workers.

(j) Suppose a company implemented BBS and after six months of its implementation, an accident happens. The BBS observers may suddenly feel that they have failed in their duty. The management may feel that they gave safety control in the hands of workers, it's their problem. At such a time, the observers need to glance through the percentage of unsafe behaviours across months in different units because unsafe behaviour is the root cause of any near-miss, injury, or accident.

10.8.1 OHS Conclusions

Organizations are challenged every day to produce a safety culture characterized by a continual drive toward the goal of maximum attainable safety, one in which errors and incidents are not only reported, but are evaluated transparently (Niurka Rivero, Beth Zemetra, and Cynde Herman 2014).

> **Good to Know**
>
> "If you observe anybody behaving unsafe, you need to save him immediately, beyond which you may not get time to save him. I failed to alert one person as I was about to tell him, before that he turned and fell" - A plant head.

Though OHSAS 18001:2007 has included three clauses as mentioned above that emphasize behavioural aspects of safety, the organizations have yet not followed it exactly as the OHSAS 18001:2007 does not provide any guidelines on how to implement these clauses. However the Indian multinational organizations have begun to consider the human behaviour aspects of workplace safety more as compared to yester years.

A series of unsafe behaviours takes place ahead of any near-misses, injury, fatalities and surprisingly, hundreds/thousands unsafe behaviours are noticeable at any workplace on a daily basis depending upon the size of the organization.

Showing zero accidents record and international certifications do not really ensure a safe organization unless we target zero unsafe behaviour at workplaces.

> **Good to Know**
> BBS interventions have demonstrated fall in unsafe behaviours and rise in safe behaviours. Also BBS training has reduced the number of unsafe conditions in the organization.

The managements have started believing that engineering controls alone do not provide adequate safety at workplace and wherever behavioural safety is practised, it has demonstrated a significant decrease in unsafe behaviours in order to ensure total safety at workplace.

BBS is all about involving people across departments in an organization as a bottoms–up approach (Locke et al. 1998). In order to implement BBS at the workplace and create a safety culture, the following steps are recommended:

1. Organize an awareness programme on BBS for management staff at all levels.
2. Conduct awareness training of employees across the plant.
3. Select observers and form steering committee from amongst BBS trained employees.
4. Carry out in-plant practical training of BBS observers and steering committee members on how to set up the observation process, how to develop the measure, making accuracy and consistency checks, steering committee functioning and so on.

SUMMARY

- Struggle to manage safety situation at workplaces continues. Safety audits are done, awards have been received, and documents are in place. Still organizations wonder what to do to ensure adequate safety of people. An injury hurts the organization because a factory inspector comes and investigates and asks so many questions.
- The Factories Act clearly stated that 80–90% of accidents are caused by unsafe human acts; hence the involvement of workers and supervisors is mandatory for all occupational health and safety initiatives in the organization.
- It is widely published to understand that the unsafe behaviours are at the core of any near-misses, injury, fatalities, and they are identifiable or noticeable at any plant at any given point of time.
- Three clauses of OHSAS 18001:2007 document emphasize behavioural aspects of safety in occupations.
- This chapter has provided a clear understanding of the concepts of OHS legislation, BBS and OHS culture, BBS processes, BBS implementation and steering team, an Indian experience on BBS application, psychosocial aspects of safety, and OHS conclusions.

EXERCISE FOR CLASSROOM PRACTICE

For better understanding of the subject matter of this chapter, please read and check each of the following statements whether True (T) or False (F) or Uncertain (U).

1. Every day, 6300 people die as a result of occupational accidents or work-related diseases – more than 2.3 million deaths per year.
2. There are three clauses of OHSAS 18001:2007 document that emphasize behavioural aspects of safety.
3. Near-misses are the root cause of any injury and fatalities.
4. Research experiences indicate that many unsafe behaviours are noticeable at any plant at any given point of time.
5. Even unsafe conditions are nothing but the result of unsafe behaviours.
6. BBS emphasizes that employees need to take an ownership of their safe as well as unsafe behaviors.
7. BBS is a management-driven tool for safety. It's not an employee-driven approach.
8. BBS is concerned with correcting unsafe behaviours for reduction of accidents and promoting safe behaviours for developing injury-free culture in their organizations.
9. Total Safety Culture (TSC) requires attention to the person (attitude, personality) and environment (management systems, organizational climate).
10. The major process of BBS is BOFP, that is, behaviour observation and feedback process.

Answers: All statements are **True** except that statement numbers 2, 3, and 7 are **False.**

REVIEW QUESTIONS FOR DISCUSSIONS/EXAMINATIONS

1. Describe the occupational health and safety scenario in India, especially women safety at work.
2. Discuss the concepts and processes of behaviour based safety.
3. Reflect upon the implementation of behaviour based safety in organizations.
4. Discuss the relationship between BBS and OHS cultures.
5. Reflect upon the functions of BBS implementation and steering teams.
6. Address issues related to the effectiveness of occupational health and safety (OHS) legislations in India.
7. Highlight an Indian experience on behaviour based safety implementation of a few organizations.
8. Discuss the psychosocial aspects of safety with examples from industry.
9. Develop a research case on BBS implementation of a company.
10. Critically evaluate the benefits and limitations of BBS in organizations.

FIELD RESEARCH REPORT

This is a research assignment section for students for their internal marking by the teacher during the semester. This assignment is for understanding practical applications of the subject.

An action research project: Identify a group of minimum 15 executives and 15 non-executives across an organization preferably where you are placed for an internship. Conduct interviews with them by using a set of closed/open-ended questionnaire to signify the issues and concerns pertaining to the occupational health and safety practices and initiatives of your company. Prepare a report of about 15 pages reflecting an action plan for better work practices.

REFERENCES

Algera, J. (1990). *Feedback Systems in Organizations, International Review of Industrial and Organizational Psychology,* 5, London: John Wiley and Sons.

Business Manager (2015). HR News. 17 (7), 62.

Dikshith, T.S.S. (2013). *Hazardous Chemicals: Safety Management and Global Regulations.* Bangalore: Bilekahalli.

Govt. of India (1987). The Factories (Amendment) Act 1987, New Delhi.

Health and Safety Executive (2013). Why leadership is important. Retrieved on June 30, 2013. http://www.hse.gov.uk/leadership/whyleadership.htm

International Labour Organization (2013). Safety and health at work. Retrieved on June 30, 2013. http://www.ilo.org/global/topics/safety-and-health-at-work/lang--en/index.htm

Kaila H.L. (2007). *Organizational Behavior & HRM* (2nd edition). Delhi: AITBS Publishers.

Kaila, H.L. (2010). *Industrial Safety and Human Behaviour.* New Delhi: AITBS Publishers.

Kaila, H.L. (2014). Are We Really Prepared for Zero Accident at Work? *Business Manager,* 16 (9), 14–20.

Marsh, T. et al. (1998). 'The Role of Management Commitment in Determining the Success of a Behavioral Intervention,' *Journal of the Institute of Occupational Safety and Health,* 2 (4).

Niurka Rivero, Beth Zemetra and Cynde Herman, (2014). Intersection of Leadership, Organizational Culture, and Clinical Performance. *Pediatric and Congenital Cardiology, Cardiac Surgery and Intensive Care,* 2014, pp. 3391–3408.

OHSAS 18001 Health & Safety Standard. http://www.ohsas-18001-occupational-health-and-safety.com/

Pearse, A. (1997). Cited in *Managing the Risks of Organizational Accidents,* Reason, J. Ashgate Publishing, 20.

Pettinger, Chuck B. (2001), People-Based Safety: The Optimal Approach to Behavior-Based Safety. Safety Performance Solutions, Inc.

Reason, J. (1990). *Human Error*, Cambridge: Cambridge University Press.

Reason, J. (1997). *Managing the Risks of Organizational Accidents.* Aldershot: Ashgate Publishing.

Skinner, B. (1974). *About Behaviorism.* London: Jonathan Cape.

Stewart, M.G. (1991). Dependence of Human Error Probabilities, in Ergonomics and Human Environments. Proceedings of the 27th Annual Conference of the Ergonomics Society of Australia, Coolum, Australia, 207–14.

11

Leadership and Group Dynamics

Learning Objectives

This chapter would help the readers:

- to understand the fundamental concepts of leadership;
- to acquaint with the theories and styles of leadership;
- to know the concept and importance of delegation;
- to make out the relationship between leadership style and team effectiveness; and
- to reflect upon case study about leadership style and leader–member interactions.

An Opening Story: Best Leadership Practices

Both effective and ineffective leadership practices have direct or indirect implications on the entire organizational functioning as well as individual teams and their members. Dynamic leaders inculcate a strong sense of mission and belongingness for each other among the team members through their logical and conflict-solving techniques.

A company well known for its best leadership practices is the Larsen & Toubro Limited which has proven successful management stories. The graduate engineers who joined at the first level at graduate engineer trainee rose up to the level of general managers, vice presidents, and executive directors. The HR director used to say that we see that a person joins and retires from our company; we take care and train the people so well. The company selected people with the best psychometric tools, trained and appraised them so well that they could lead their business. The HoDs who stayed with the company for long years adopted and emphasized professional and innovative approaches in their production, quality, safety, and other areas. The company leaders transformed their employees into new leaders and they expanded the company into diversified businesses such as power, steel, construction, shipping, IT. By adopting the best leadership practices in every field, the company brought out the best quality products and made profit in spite of the economic and political changes. Today the companies which have survived are those that have the best leaders with them. Some other names that have shown the best leadership in India are the company groups such as Bajaj, Reliance, Vedanta, Godrej, Aditya Birla, Tata, Mahindra, Essar, ITC, and so on.

11.1 INTRODUCTION

Leadership is function of personality, situation, and the period. From time to time, several leadership theories emerged in literature as well as in modern management learning. There is also a school of thought that there are core attributes to leadership that don't change across times. Also, role-modelling is considered the potent leadership development tool of socialization, acculturating members with desired set of values, behaviour and attitude. In fact, leadership in theory and in practice is different. In the practical industrial world, a leader is impacted by so many factors such as personal, professional, job outcomes and so on.

Competencies that will make a people a manager, a great leader are: able to generate trust, able to direct people, being a source of hope and inspiration, have a defined vision, can achieve results, able to drive change, can analyse future trends, can lead people to development and personal effectiveness. Leaders must be able to connect with people, have clarity in communication, and demonstrate honesty and integrity.

For leaders, resilience is a core attribute which helps them in their leadership journey. It is the ability to see situations as they emerge and deal with them with courage, positivity, and creativity. To be an effective manager, it is imperative to be a good leader. One cannot exist without the other. For a manager possessing people management and leadership skills are mandatory to prove as an effective people's person.

Most of us achieve the status of a leader but not the state. State is totally different from status. The main role of a leader is to continuously integrate the team and keep them together. For this, a leader needs to be several steps ahead of the team.

Leadership is one of the most studied areas in business or organizational psychology. The leadership styles and its effect on the degree of leader–member interaction and team/group effectiveness have been well investigated in psychological research around the world.

Leadership is a process of influencing others to understand and agree about what needs to be accomplished and how to do it and the process of facilitating individual and collective efforts to achieve shared goals. Leadership means involving, engaging, and empowering the organization's all members and groups, both formally and informally towards achieving business goals with excellence.

The need of most organizations is not just managers or just leaders but management leaders who will support the vision of top leadership in achieving the organization's mission.

This chapter provides insights into a variety of aspects on leadership and group dynamics through researches, discussion and case studies.

11.2 MEANING AND NATURE OF LEADERSHIP

Many meanings have been drawn on leadership as per behaviours of leaders, followers, and the context. Kumpher Karol et al. (1993) in their study presented a theoretical model of coalition team effectiveness hypothesizing that an empowering style of leadership increases member satisfaction and perceptions of team efficacy, which ultimately increases team effectiveness.

Behavioural approach suggests that effective leaders influence their fellow members through their behaviour. Jeffrey (2009) suggests that there is some relationship between leadership roles and team effectiveness.

> **Good to Know**
> Leaders have an influence on both members' attitude and work situation and they are also affected by the team members' attitude and working situations at the same time.

All the above-mentioned studies suggest that the leader's leadership style can affect the follower's performance and their beliefs towards the leaders and indeed affect the relationship. Therefore, the relationship between the team leader and his members is significant as it can affect the other outcome variables.

Robert and Achua (2010) focussed on several key dimensions for leadership behaviour as below:

- Coaching
- Effective communication
- Encouraging teamwork
- Establishing high standards and getting results
- Effective delegation
- Rewarding performance
- Developing and releasing employees
- Building consensus
- Supporting reasonable risk taking
- Forecast thinking
- Improving the organization
- Managing diversity
- Overall effectiveness.

All these aspects reveal the range of leader's actions and frame of reference in the organizations. However, these need to be understood in terms of the degree of these characteristics leaders possess in conjunction with relevance to his/her organization.

11.2.1 Why Leadership Skills are Important?

Leadership skills have been found to be of much significance because there is a strong impact of these skills on the employee's behaviour as well as organizational performance.

Graen and Ulh-Bien (1995) found that high quality leader-member exchanges produced less employee turnover, better job attitudes, plus higher overall performance, organizational climate, innovation, empowerment, career progress, and other positive organizational outcomes. Graen et al. (1995) clearly incorporate operationalization of relationship-based approach to leadership.

Effective leadership processes occur when leaders and followers are able to develop mature leaderships and thus gain access to many benefits these relationships bring.

The relationship between the leadership style and the degree of leader member exchange and team's effectiveness needs to be understood clearly. It is observed that the authoritarian dimension of the leadership style is negatively related to the degree of leader–member exchange with its team members and to the team effectiveness. On the contrary, the score on the participative style of leadership is positively related to the degree of leader–member exchange with its team members and with team effectiveness.

11.3 FUNCTIONS OF A LEADER

Teams are not managed, controlled, or supervised but rather they are led by their mutual vision of the organization's purpose and goals. Thus there are two most important functions of a team leader: nurturing supportive milieu, and communicating role clarity.

11.3.1 Nurturing Supportive Milieu

> **Good to Know**
> Teamwork is most likely to develop when leader builds a supportive and congenial environment.

Supportive measures include emphasizing and facilitating goal-setting and its achievement, setting high standards together, rewarding high performers, and training/developing average performers. Since these steps contribute to further cooperation, trust, and compatibility, supervisors need to be trained on these aspects in order to develop an organizational culture which is motivating for employees. This requires to be continuously followed up by the top-level management in terms of communication, organization, and distribution of work roles. Teams are given objectives and a time-frame but the way the work is done (method), the goals they are to achieve, are not given to them by the top management. In fact these are changed and adapted as the teams grow and get to know each other, which is an excellent way of developing a supportive environment.

11.3.2 Communicating Role Clarity and Ensuring Skills Utilization

Role clarity and communication among members of a group by the leader is the primary function and also skill utilization of members of the group without which the individuals feel confused and lost, hence feel less motivated to perform.

Members can work together as a team only after all the members of the group know the roles of all the others with whom they will be interacting. When this understanding is provided by the leader, members can act immediately as a team based on requirements of that situation, without waiting for someone to give an order.

Secondly, the team members work well when integration of skills and knowledge is done by the leader. This is done by constant meetings and even socializing with the members. Most intra-team conflicts occur when the team members are not aware of each others' responsibility. Role clarity and skills to work or take on another's role also helps in keeping the team going.

We must not forget the individual in a team. Leaders give a sense of oneness and self-esteem to an individual, which motivates an individual to contribute to the group goal.

Good to Know

One of the major functions of a leader is to create a feeling of belongingness is what really keeps the team going.

11.3.3 Leadership Styles

Leadership style refers to a set of approaches or behaviours that are used by the leader while interacting with his team members or employees in an organization. In this perspective, James MacGregor (1978) considered leaders persuading followers to achieve certain goals following a bunch of values and expectations that both leaders and followers would practice. However, Toteja (1999) observed that theoretically, leadership is understood but in reality, it is the least understood phenomena. We need to conceptualize this when we go through various leadership styles. The major leadership styles are presented as follows.

(a) Transactional and Transformational Leadership

Two popularly used styles of leadership are transactional and transformational. Downton, (1973) first coined the term transformational leadership which was formally developed by Bernard Bass (1990). He perceived this concept as providing a way to bridge the gap between group dynamics and leadership. Burns recognized that transformational leadership style does not stand alone in the leadership lexicon. Thus, he coined another leadership term—transactional leadership style.

Transactional leadership is based on a process of transaction between the leader and the followers to maintain stability rather any change or transformation (Lussier and Achua 2004). Transactional leaders would consistently persuade followers to meet the jointly agreed goals (Bryant, 2003). They use rewards and punishment to promote such performance (Barnett 2001; Gellis 2001; Jung and Avolio 1999).

Transformational leadership uses a process of empowerment for the follower to lead in future. Bass (1998) and Gellis (2001) defined transformational leadership as the leader's effect on the followers to nurture their personal abilities. These leaders have a positive influence on followers' motivation to meet the team goals (Barbuto 2005; Feinberg, Ostroff and Burke 2005; Jung and Avolio 1999; Spreitzer, Perttula and Xin 2005).

Bernard Bass (1990) views four interrelated components as essential for transformational leaders to influence followers:

Idealized Influence: Genuine trust and respect should be built among the leader and the followers. It is also characterized by high moral and ethical standards.

Inspirational Motivation: Leaders tend to behave in ways that encourage envisioning, motivating and inspiring followers by providing them with challenges and meaning for engaging in shared goals and undertakings.

Intellectual Stimulation: Transformational leaders help followers to question assumptions, reframe problems, and to generate more creative solutions to problems.

Individual Consideration: These leaders treat each follower as an individual and provide coaching, mentoring, and growth opportunities, along with fulfilling the needs of self-actualization, self-fulfilment, and self-worth.

These four components when combined have a stabilizing effect that yields performance beyond expectation – a key distinction from the transactional type of leadership (Gellis 2001; Hall, Johnson, Wysocki and Kepner 2002; Kelly 2003).

Burns distinguishes between transactional and transformational leadership. He makes this distinction by considering transactional (ordinary) leaders, who exchange tangible rewards for the work of followers, and transformational (extraordinary), adaptive leaders who engage with followers and raise consciousness about being innovative in solving problems (Barbuto 2005; Barnett, McCormick and Conners 2001; Gellis 2001).

Burns distinguished the two styles of leadership, considering that they lie on opposite extremes of the leadership continuum (Bass 1990; Yukl 1989). This view was supported by early empirical studies which suggested that the two leadership approaches could appear independently of one another (Avolio, Bass and Jung 1999). Burns also claimed that the transformational leadership is more effective than transactional leadership (Brown and Moshavi 2002).

Good to Know

The best kind of leadership is both, transformational and transactional.

However, Bernard Bass (1990) proposes that transformational leadership enhances the effectiveness of transactional leadership and does not replace it (Walsman, Bass, and Yammarino 1990). Transaction is a necessary and effective tool for all managers. Various researches also indicate that all leaders display both kinds of leaderships traits, however at different degrees (Bryant 2003; Judge and Piccolo 2004; Sanders, Hopkins and Geroy 2003; Yukl 1989). Yet another research by Carlson and Perrewe (1995) suggests that transformational leadership is sometimes used interchangeably with transactional leadership. Walsman, Bass, and Yammarino (1990) proposed that when a transformational leader encounters a win-lose negotiation, he/she tries to convert it into a win-win problem solving situation.

In the current organizational context where there is cultural diversity, high levels of interdependence and integration, there is need for a leadership style that goes beyond simple transactional approach to styles characterized by inspiration, stimulation, motivation, and charisma as in the transformational leadership (Feinberg, Ostroff and Burke, 2005).

Thus, considering various researches, it can be concluded that transactional and transformational leaderships are not at odds with one another but complement each other depending on the circumstances. However, when to make the transition between the leadership styles is only an act of education, learning, and experience.

(b) Authoritarian Leadership

Authoritarian leaders behave in an autocratic manner and give understandable instructions to their followers about what to do, how to do, and convey the deadline to follow for completing the work. Authoritarian leaders decide almost everything on their own and leave no room for followers for decision making, for target setting, or production norms, and the like. The autocratic management permits quick decision making as only one person decides for the whole group. In this case the leader has to be most knowledgeable. This style of leadership is best suited in a small enterprise or family-run units or department of a company which is highly specialized in nature such as designing, chemical testing laboratory, and other such organizations.

(c) Participative Leadership

Participative leaders practise democratic leadership which is considered a very effective leadership style. Democratic leaders involve all members of the group to participate in the decision-making process on almost all matters of group functioning. Group members experience satisfaction and feel motivated. All functional managers ought to practise this leadership style as it would directly add to production, marketing, safety, maintenance of plants.

(d) Delegative (Laissez-Faire) Leadership

Delegative leaders offer little or no guidance to group members. Members decide almost every matter concerning the group goals. This style would prevail when members are capable and qualified in their work areas. This style of leadership may face conflicts from members who would tend to influence and lead more than the members who are less influential in the group functioning or less capable.

11.4 LEADERSHIP THEORIES

The theories of leadership are categorized as classical theories and contingency theories. Early leadership theories focussed on what qualities distinguished leaders from followers, while subsequent theories looked at other variables, situational factors and skill levels.

11.4.1 Classical Theories

Great Man Theory: This theory assumes that leadership is innate and great leaders are born and not made. These theories often portray great leaders as heroic, and destined to rise to leadership when needed. This theory attributed the success of leaders to the possession of qualities such as courage, passion, energy, intuition, and foresight. For example, Hillary who failed to scale the Mount Everest first time, did not give up to scale the Everest next time, simply because he demonstrated all those qualities of perseverance and focusedness and such others as described in Great Man Theory. Hence, any leader when determined like a great man would achieve the unachievable.

Trait Theory: Trait theory states that leadership traits are just acquired, but people have these traits in their personality. Six traits on which leaders tend to differ from non-leaders are ambition and energy, desire to lead, honesty and integrity, self-confidence, intelligence, and job relevant knowledge. Mr A.M. Naik, the earlier CMD of Larsen & Toubro who joined the organization as graduate engineer, depicted all those personality traits/characteristics required to be a great leader which his colleagues at that time did not depict. He was the only one who rose up to the highest position in the company faster than his peers because of innate traits of a leader.

Behavioural Theories: This theory postulates that great leaders are made, not born. People can learn to become leaders through an effective training. Based on the behavioural theories, various management institutions developed executive leadership courses. In India, IIMs have such programmes which are attended by the senior managers to become effective leaders.

Managerial Grid: Blake and Mouton gave this idea that leadership is a function of concern for people and concern for production. The grid (see Fig. 11.1) is a 9 × 9 matrix, creating 81 different positions in which the leader's style may fall. The managerial grid consists of five main leadership styles – impoverished style (low concern for both people and production), country club style (high concern for people but low concern for production), authoritarian style (low concern for people but a high concern for production), middle of the road style (some concern for both people and production), and team management style (high concern for both people and production).

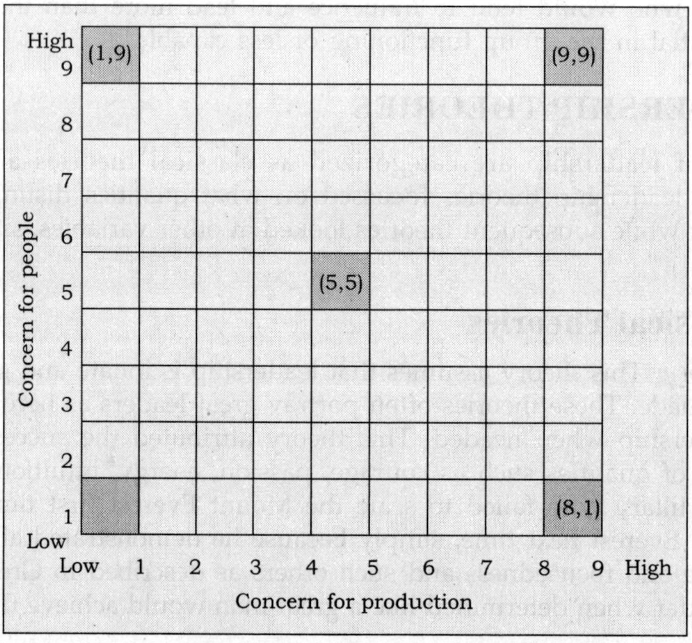

Fig. 11.1 Marogoid god.

11.4.2 Contingency Theories

Fred Fiedler's Contingency Model: It proposes that the key situational factors that determine leadership effectiveness are based on three dimensions: Leader member relations is the degree of confidence, trust, and respect members have in their leaders. Task structure is the extent to which the group's task, goals, and subordinate roles are clearly defined; and position power is the degree of influence a leader has over power variables such as hiring, firing, discipline, promotions, and salary increase. Fiedler stated that better the leader member relations, more highly structured the job, and the stronger the position power, more control the leader has.

Hersey and Blanchard Situational Theory: Successful leadership is achieved by selecting the right leadership style, which is contingent on the level of follower's readiness which refers to the extent to which people have the ability and willingness to accomplish a task. Four types of leadership style are proposed effective with the appropriate situation. Telling style of leadership style is effective when the followers are both unable and unwilling to do a task. Here the leader needs to give clear and specific directions. Selling style is effective when the followers are unable but are willing to do the task. The leader here provides direction and supports the followers. Participative style is effective when the followers are able but unwilling to do the task. The leaders here are supportive but non-directive. Delegating style is effective when the followers are both able and willing to do the task. The leader needs to provide a little support.

As the followers reach higher levels of readiness, the leader would decrease his or her structuring behaviour and increase considerate behaviour. As followers' readiness increases further, both structuring and considerate behaviour diminish, allowing mature subordinates to be self-directed.

House's Path Goal Theory: The effective leaders clarify the path to help their followers get from where they are to the achievement of their work goals and to make their journey along the path easier by reducing roadblocks. House identified four leadership behaviours— directive seadership, supportive leadership, participative leadership and achievement oriented leadership. The directive leaders provide specific guidelines, supportive leaders show concern for interests and well-being of the subordinates, participative leaders invite their subordinates to share their ideas, and suggestions and also allow them to participate in decision making, and achievement oriented leaders set challenging goals for their subordinates and expect the highest level of performance from them. House assumes that the leaders are flexible and the same leader can display any or all of these behaviour styles depending on the situation.

11.5 IMPORTANCE OF DELEGATION

Managers and leaders often delegate their works to the persons working with them. Delegation is a process which enables a person to assign a work to others and entrust them with adequate authority to do it. The art of delegation is that, though a single person in the organization aims for achieving all the objectives for the sense of accomplishment, he couldn't be vested with the entire decision-making authority, so the superior assigns duties or responsibilities to his subordinates and also delegates necessary authority to them (Lois A. Allaen 1958).

According to M. Sakthivel Murugan (2005), "Delegation is the dynamic management process a manager follows, is dividing the work assigned to him." It is about getting someone else to do part of your job, that contributes to completing the work on time.

The principle of delegation is that one should learn to do less and manage more and finding the right persons and giving them the right work to do.

The volume of management responsibilities necessitates delegation. A superior can delegate authority but not responsibility (Culp and Smith 1997). While one should delegate many tasks, one should ensure that he/she does not delegate the control over team.

A subordinate should get instructions from only one superior. This will clear any confusion regarding the delegation and enable effective functioning of concerned persons.

The delegators shouldn't delegate the following responsibilities to the subordinates (Jenks and Kelly 1986):

- Hiring
- Pay issues
- Policy
- Motivation
- Training
- Team-building
- Organization
- Praising
- Performance reviews
- Promotion

Delegation is a vital management skill, but some managers do not delegate effectively. This may be due to fear of insecurity, or the mistaken belief that nobody else can do the job as perfectly as they can. Delegation is a universal process, wherever human beings work in groups, one or the other form of delegation is practised by them.

> **Good to Know**
> The difference between a good and a bad delegator can be understood with the help of dimensions such as ambiguity, assertiveness, perfectionism, and insecurity.

During the delegation process, an area of assertiveness should be given special attention as it helps the managers to:

- Concentrate on planning, organizing, and controlling.
- Accomplish simple and complex tasks.
- Enhance the morale of the subordinates.

11.5.1 Role of Groups in Organizational Settings

Forsyth (2013) emphasized upon research, empirical studies supporting theoretical understanding of groups because the groups (formal or informal from various departments, sections/units/verticals) have significant impact in the business performance in any organizational setting. These groups steer and empower the workforce for aligning their potentials to the goals of an organization.

A group is a number of individuals organized to fulfil a common purpose(s). All groups have purpose, structure, and dynamics. Their complexity lies in the variability and interaction of these aspects (Encyclopaedia of Christianity Online 2014).

Belbin proposed a set of eight significant roles as the core of an effective decision-making group.

Significant Roles of a Group
The group clarifies goals and objectives, helps allocate roles and responsibilities; and articulates conclusions.
Seeks patterns in group decisions, pushes group towards agreement and decision-making.
Advances proposals and offers new ideas, gives new insights on courses of action.
Analyses problems and complex issues, and assesses contribution of others.
Transforms talk and ideas into practical activity.
Gives personal support and help to others.
Introduces external information, negotiates with outsiders.
Emphasizes the need for meeting schedules and targets, and completing the task.

Margersion and McCann (1991) grouped the group roles into four general approaches: explorers, advisers, controllers, and organizers. Within these approaches are eight different roles, which include: reporting and advising on relevant information; promoting the team to outsiders; innovating and creating new ideas; assessing and developing those ideas, organizing the team's activities into coherent stages and objectives; concluding; controlling and inspecting the quality of work produced by the team; and maintaining the social and organizational relationships within the team.

11.6 TYPES OF GROUPS

It is important to differentiate between the work group and work team. A work group interacts primarily to share information and to make decisions to help each member perform within his/her area of responsibility. A work team generates positive synergy through coordinated effort which results in performance that is greater than those individual inputs.

Darrel Ray and Howard Bronstein (1995) described five types of work groups in the organizational settings as mentioned below.

11.6.1 Leader Centred/ Leader Focussed

This work group is highly leader-dependent. It has a manager who is responsible for goal setting, decision making, making job assignments, performance appraisals, and hiring and firing.

The group serves in an advisory capacity only. This group is far from becoming a true team.

11.6.2 Leader Centred/ Function Focussed

This group has an assigned leader who coordinates, assigns work, does performance appraisals, and makes major decisions. He is not a total autocratic, as he can be involving and open. The cohesiveness of the group is dependent upon the manager's skills and style.

11.6.3 Leader Centred/Integrated-task Focussed

In this group, individuals are encouraged by the management to make many of the decisions. Management may set goals, apportion resources, and do performance appraisals. Much more employee involvement is encouraged than in the first two group types. This group is largely skills- and process-centred to support employee empowerment.

11.6.4 Self-led/Time and Task Focussed

This group is mostly project-based with a clearly defined objective and is time-bound. Group members have clearly defined functions. Goal-directedness and time pressure lead the group performance. Participants for this group are volunteers or hand-picked by management.

11.6.5 Self-led/Task Focussed

Self-led work groups operate with determined goals and decisions about how to achieve these goals, and require little formal leadership. These groups stay with the organization for years. The larger organizations encourage and reward these group behaviours.

11.7 STAGES OF GROUP DEVELOPMENT

Theoretically, every new group undergoes certain stages of forming, storming, norming, performing, and adjourning. These are interesting stages or phases in the life of a group. If the group leader and members are aware of these developmental stages, it becomes easier to accommodate the member's behaviour and understand why and how they behave inside the group. According to Tuckman, these stages are discussed below.

11.7.1 Forming

At this stage, members tend to affiliate and accept each other. They interact and gather impressions among them and form preferences for future sub-grouping. Members take interest in the activities of each other and tend to cooperate to achieve the tasks of the group.

11.7.2 Storming

The next stage witnesses competition in the personal relation's dimension and organization in the task-functions dimension. The important attribute in helping the group seems to be an ability to listen to members. Individuals seek clarification on commitment of each other in the group. The group relations tend to become tense as some members don't contribute as much as others.

11.7.3 Norming

Group members acknowledge contributions of each other and solve group issues. They tend to be flexible to accommodate and change their opinions and develop requisite norms, rules and regulations, and code of conduct or behaviours to be followed by members. If some members don't follow the norms, they receive feedback from others to change their behaviours.

11.7.4 Performing

If group members are able to advance to stage four, they understand each other better and each other and perform to their best ability. They tend to experience good relations with members, a sense of achievement and celebrations. The group is more focussed on performance than before.

11.7.5 Adjourning

This phase is for termination, summarizing, and thanksgiving to members. The next plan of action for the group is decided and future meeting time is fixed. The group members depart and hope to meet again.

11.8 FACTORS DETERMINING AND AFFECTING GROUP PERFORMANCE

Group performance effectiveness is determined by a number of factors such as the group size, the willingness and ability of members, the task difficulty, the organizational politics, support and resources available, the group leadership, and so on. The group of people can achieve much more than if the individuals of the team were working on their own. Rubin, Plovnick, and Fry (1977) gave GRPI model for group performance, which stands for goals, roles, processes, and interpersonal relationships. After the goal is defined, the roles and responsibilities become clearer. As individuals work together and go through the processes to achieve the group tasks, they develop the necessary interpersonal relationships needed for best performance.

Some of the factors determining group performance are:

Skills: Group effectiveness depends upon bringing together people who have different skills that somehow complement each other.

Talent– the collective competencies of the team members to get the job done.
Teaming skills– operating effectively to come up and work as a closely-knit team.
Task skills – executing each task efficiently and successfully.

Motivation: Group effectiveness is linked to the interest, energy, and the drive that the group members experience while doing the assignment.

Ability to solve conflicts: Conflict is natural to any groups and should be taken as challenge. Group effectiveness increases through effective conflict management.

Thrust: A common purpose and continuous emphasis about what needs to be accomplished.

Trust: Having faith in each other's ability and willingness to work as team mates.

Group-leader Fit: The degree to which the leader continues to satisfy the needs of his team members.

Group support from the organisation: The extent to which the leadership of the organisation enables the team members to perform and feel supported.

Each of these factors has to be there for groups to be high performing and the necessary organizational and leadership support also are to be made available.

11.8.1 The Group and the Individual in the Organization

A group consists of a number of individual people working together to achieve a common goal. The relevance of the psychological dimensions of the group and the individual has been researched time and again. These psychological processes give reasons why individuals work better in a group. The two processes given by Hayes Nicky (2005) are particularly important.

Social identification is a tendency to belong to social groups, it is a need to be a part of something. We tend to be a part of not only our department or unit but also the entire organization. We wish to know everything of the organization where we work. For example, in an AIESEC organization, the teams have to assign a name to their team and during their inter-team meetings (called GBM or general board meeting) they are asked to give a roll call which could be any song or short jingle the team can come up with. Although this technique is very radical in nature, its main function is to facilitate identification and motivation, the net outcome of which is fun with work. The core of this topic is the identification a person gets through it.

Social representations are the beliefs that we are part of others opinions. The concept of social representation was developed by a French psychologist Serge Moscovici (2001). Most people act or follow the rules and regulations of the company as they want to be represented as an official member of the group or organization. Some people violate these rules and misrepresent themselves as being the not-obeying kind. These are the people who are violating or contradicting the policy of the organization or may want a change in the way a group behaves.

11.9 A RESEARCH CASE STUDY

The group leader impacts the behaviours of his group members. Hence, it becomes vital to ascertain the nature and extent of relationship between the leader and the group. The objective of this research case (H.L. Kaila 2007) is to understand a correlation between the style of the leader and the leader–member exchanges/interactions.

Sixty participants working in teams from different corporate offices were selected for this case study. Data were collected using leadership survey questionnaire, questionnaire on relationship with leader, and team questionnaire (see appendix). There were in all 10 teams with five members each and 10 team leaders from each team. The age of the participants ranged from 24 years to 58 years.

The results of the study indicated that there exists a high negative correlation (r = – 0.90) between the authoritarian score of the team leaders and the degree of leader–member exchanges indicating that authoritarian leadership style would lead to reduced leader–member exchange. It was also found that the team effectiveness is negatively correlated with the authoritarian style of leadership (r = – 0.85). These results indicate that authoritarian style of leadership leads to reduced leader–member exchange and low degree of team effectiveness.

It was also found that the participative score of the team leaders is positively related (+ 0.30) with the degree of leader–member exchange indicating that the participative style of leadership would lead to increased leader–member exchange. In addition, the participative score on the leadership style of the team leaders had a high positive correlation with the team effectiveness. It has been theorized within the context of leader–member exchange theory that because of time restrictions and assorted pressures, leaders generally develop close relationships with only a few key subordinates who are termed the 'in group'. The leader's relationships with members of the 'in group' can result in increased job latitude, influence in decision-making, open communications, support for the member's actions, and confidence in and consideration for the member. The member can reciprocate by providing greater availability and commitment to the success of the entire unit or sub-organization. It has been posited by Dienesch and Linden (1986) that in-group members might eventually serve as assistants or advisors to the leader.

This, in turn, indicates that with more team members in the team results in a more positive outcome of the team's performance as the participative leaders consult with employees about work-related matters and consider their opinions. Therefore, these types of leaders are more likely to have team members within their in-group and develop better relationships with their them. On the other hand, directive or the participative leaders schedule work, maintain performance standards, and let employees know what is expected of them. These types of leaders therefore share a shallow relationship with their team members and result in poor team performance. Leader relationships with out-group members, on the other hand, are characterized by low levels of mutual influence. The primary source of leader influence is legitimate authority in combination with coercive power and a limited degree of reward power. The only requirement for 'out group' members to satisfy the terms of the exchange relationship is their compliance with formally prescribed role expectations (for example, job duties, rules, standard procedures) and with legitimate directions from the leader. As long as such compliance is forthcoming, the subordinate receives the standard benefits such as, compensation for his or her position in the organization. Thus, a leader with more of an authoritarian style is more likely to have team members from the out-group. It is evident that a leader with more of an authoritarian style would result in a less degree of leader-member exchange with his team members and those with a participative style would result in a higher degree of leader-member exchange with his team members.

The democratic/participative leadership style is a very open and collegial style of running a team. Ideas move freely amongst the group and are discussed openly. Everyone is given a seat at the table, and discussion is relatively free-flowing.

The democratic leadership style means facilitating the conversation, encouraging people to share their ideas, and then synthesizing all the available information into the best possible decision. The democratic leader must also be able to communicate that decision back to the group to bring unity the plan is chosen. Democratic leadership style can bring the best out of an experienced and professional team. It capitalizes on their skills and talents by letting them share their views, rather than simply expecting them to conform. Thus, leader with a participative style of leadership will lead a team more effectively than an authoritarian leader. This would contribute to higher team effectiveness.

Employees prefer to work for democratic leaders as they feel that they are being listened to, whereas authoritarian or autocratic style leaders tend to preside, resulting in discontent, hostility and aggression and employees attrition. The results of the study also supported a myth that participative leadership style would lead to greater team effectiveness as compared to an authoritarian leader.

Though the study supported the expected views, there are some limitations of the study. First, while correlational studies can suggest that there is a relationship between two variables, they cannot prove that one variable causes a change in another variable. In other words, correlation does not equal causation. Thus, the study showed that the more a leader has a participative approach towards his team members it will lead to increased team effectiveness as well as increased leader member exchange. However, it does not indicate whether a particular leadership style increases or decreases team effectiveness or leader-member exchange. A comparative study could be conducted between leaders with a participative style and authoritarian style.

SUMMARY

- Researchers observed that the authoritarian dimension of leadership style is negatively related to the degree of leader-member exchange with its team members and team effectiveness.
- The participative dimension of the leadership style is positively related to the degree of leader-member exchange with its team members and team effectiveness.

- This chapter described the meaning and nature of leadership, models and styles of leadership, the importance of leadership skills, the functions of a leader, and the meaning and principles of delegation.
- It also focussed on the role of groups in organizational settings, types of groups, stages of group development, and the factors affecting group performance.

EXERCISE FOR CLASSROOM PRACTICE

For better understanding of the subject matter of this chapter, please read and check each of the following statements whether True (T) or False (F) or Uncertain (U).

1. Leadership means engaging and empowering all organizational members and groups, both formally and informally towards achieving business goals.
2. Leader's leadership style can affect the followers' performance and their beliefs towards the leader and indeed affect the relationship.
3. Leadership skills have no influence on the employee's behaviour.
4. Two most important functions of a team leader are nurturing conflicting milieu and communicating role ambiguity.
5. Role clarity and communication among members of a group by the leader is the primary function without which the individuals feel less motivated to perform.
6. Team members must be reasonably qualified to perform their jobs and have the desire to cooperate.
7. Teams work well when integration of skills and knowledge is done.
8. Leadership style refers to a set of approaches or behaviours that are used by the leader while interacting with his team members or employees in an organization.
9. Successful leadership is achieved by adopting any leadership style.
10. Delegation is a vital management skill, but some managers do not delegate effectively due to the mistaken belief that nobody else can do the job as well as they can.
11. The roles of any group can be clubbed into four general approaches: explorers, advisers, controllers, and organizers.

Answers: All statements are **True** except that statement numbers 3, 4, and 9 are **False.**

REVIEW QUESTIONS FOR DISCUSSIONS/EXAMINATIONS

1. Describe the meaning, nature, and fundamental concepts of leadership.
2. Discuss various models and historical evolution of leadership.
3. Address the relevant functions and leadership skills of a leader.
4. Discuss the need, meaning, and principles of delegation.
5. Explore leadership theories with reference to Indian organizations.
6. Emphasize the role of groups in organizational settings.

7. Discuss the stages of group development.
8. Define certain types of groups and their relevance.
9. Describe the factors determining and affecting group performance.
10. Elaborate relationship between leadership style and team effectiveness.

FIELD RESEARCH REPORT

This is a research assignment section for students for their internal marking by the teacher during the semester. This assignment is for understanding the practical applications of the subject.

An action research project: Identify a group of minimum 15 executives and 15 non-executives across an organization preferably where you are placed for an internship. Conduct interviews with them by using a set of closed/open-ended questionnaire to signify the issues and concerns pertaining to the leadership styles in your organization. Also highlight successful leadership practices. Prepare a report of about 15 pages reflecting an action plan for better management practice.

REFERENCES

Avolio, B.J., B.M. Bass and D.I. Jung (1999). 'Re-examining the Components of Transformational and Transactional Leadership Using the Multifactor Leadership Questionnaire.' *Journal of Occupational and Organizational Psychology*, 72 (4), 441–463.

Barbuto, J.E. (Jr.) (2005). 'Motivation and Transactional, Charismatic, and Transformational Leadership: A Test of Antecedents.' *Journal of Leadership and Organizational Studies*, 11 (4), 26–40.

Barnett, K., J. McCormick and R. Conners (2001). 'Transformational Leadership in Schools – Panacea, Placebo or Problem?' *Journal of Educational Administration*, 39 (1), 24–46.

Bass, B.M. (1990). *Bass & Stodgill's Handbook of Leadership: Theory, Research and Managerial Applications* (3rd edition.) New York: The Free Press.

Brown, F. W., & Moshavi, D. (2005). 'Transformational Leadership and Emotional Intelligence: A Potential Pathway for an Increased Understanding of Interpersonal Influence.' *Journal of Organizational Behavior, 26*, 867-871.

Bryant, S.E. (2003). 'The Role of Transformational and Transactional Leadership in Creating, Sharing and Exploiting Organizational Knowledge.' *Journal of Leadership and Organizational Studies*, 9 (4): 32–44.

Burns, James MacGregor (1978). *Leadership*. New York: Harper and Row.

Carlson, D.S. and P.L. Perrewe (1995). 'Institutionalization of Organizational Ethics Through Transformational Leadership.' *Journal of Business Ethics*, 14 (10), 829–839.

Culp, G. and A. Smith. (1997). Six Steps to Effective Delegation. *Journal of Management in Engineering*.

Dienesch, R.M. and R.C. Liden (1986). 'Leader-Member Exchange Model of Leadership: A Critique and Further Development.' *Academy of Management Review*, 11, 618–634.

Downton, J.V. (1973). *Rebel Leadership: Commitment and Charisma in the Revolutionary Process*. New York. Free Press.

Encyclopaedia of Christianity Online (2014). Group and Group Dynamics. Retrieved on 07 May 2014 <http://referenceworks.brillonline.com/entries/encyclopedia-of-christianity/group-and-group-dynamics-G273>

Feinberg, B.J., C. Ostroff and W.W. Burke (2005). 'The Role of Within-group Agreement in Understanding Transformational Leadership.' *Journal of Occupational and Organizational Psychology*, 78, 471–488.

Forsyth Donelson R. (2013). *Group Dynamics*. CA: Wadsworth Cengage Learning.

Gellis, Z.D. (2001). 'Social Work Perceptions of Transformational and Transactional Leadership in Health Care.' *Social Work Research*, 25 (1): 17–25.

Graen, G.G. and M. Uhl Bien (1995). 'Relationship Based Approach to Leadership: Development of LMX Theory over 25 years; Applying a Multi-domain Perspective,' *Leadership Quarterly*, 6 (2), 219–247.

Hayes Nicky (2005). *Principles of Social Psychology*. New York: Psychology Press.

Jeffrey, F.C. (2009). Analyzing Leadership Styles of Incident Commanders. Dissertation, North Central University, Arizona

Jenks J.M. and J.M. Kelly (1986). *Don't Do, Delegate*! Bridles Ltd. Jones, Patricia.

Judge, T.A. and R.F. Piccolo (2004). 'Transformational and Transactional Leadership: a Meta-analytic Test of Their Relative Validity.' *Journal of Applied Psychology*, 89 (5): 755–768.

Jung, D.I. and Avolio, B.J. (1999). 'Effects of Leadership Style and Followers' Cultural Orientation on Performance in Group and Individual Task Conditions.' *Academy of Management Journal*, 41 (2): 208–219.

Kaila H.L. (2007). *Organizational Behavior & HRM* (2nd edition). Delhi: AITBS Publishers.

Kelly, M.L. (2003). Academic advisers as transformational leaders. The Mentor. http://www.psu.edu/dus/mentor/030101mk.htm (retrieved on 5th January 2015).

Kumpher, K., C. Turner R. Hopkins and J. Librett (1993). 'Leadership and Team Effectiveness in Community Coalitions for the Prevention of Alcohol and Other Drug Abuse.' *Health Education Research*, 8(3), 359-374.

Lois A. Allaen (1958). *Management and Organization*. New York: McGraw-Hill.

Lussier, R.N. and C.F. Achua (2004). *Leadership: Theory, Application, Skill Development*. (2nd edition). Eagan, MN: Thomson-West.

M. Sakthivel Murugan (2005). *Management Principles and Practices*. New Delhi: New Age International.

Margersion C. and McCann D. (1991). *Team Management Practical Approaches*. Mercury Books. England.

Ray, Darrel. and Bronstien, Howard (1995). *Teaming Up* (1st Edition). Singapore: McGraw-Hill International Editions.

Robert N. Lussier and F. Achua Christopher (2010). *Leadership: Theory, Application, & Skill Development*. CA: Wadsworth Cengage Learning.

Rubin, I.M., M.S. Plovnick and R.E. Fry (1977). *Task Oriented Team Development*. New York: McGraw-Hill.

Sanders, J.E. (3rd), W.E. Hopkins and G.D. Geroy (2003). 'From Transactional to Transcendental: Toward an Integrated Theory of Leadership.' *Journal of Leadership and Organizational Studies*, 9 (4): 21–31.

Serge Moscovici (2001). *Social Representations: Explorations in Social Psychology*. NY: New York University Press.

Spreitzer, G. M., K. H. Perttula and K. Xin (2005). 'Traditionality Matters: An Examination of the Effectiveness of Transformational Leadership in the United States and Taiwan.' *Journal of Organizational Behavior*, 26: 205-227.

Toteja, M.M. (1999). *Changing Human Values and Leadership Styles*. New Delhi: Printwell Publishers and Distributors.

Waldman, D.A., Bass, B.M., & Yammarino, F.J. (1990). 'Adding to Contingent-reward Behavior: The Augmenting Effects of Charismatic Leadership.' *Group & Organization Studies*, 15(4), 381-394.

Yukl, G. (1989). 'Managerial Leadership: A Review of Theory and Research.' *Journal of Management*, 15 (2), 251-289.

APPENDIX

Leadership Survey Questionnaire

Instructions: This questionnaire contains statements about leadership style beliefs. Next to each statement, circle the number that represents how strongly you feel about the statement by using the following scoring system:

- Almost Always True – 5
- Frequently True – 4
- Occasionally True – 3
- Seldom True – 2
- Almost Never True – 1

Be honest about your choices as there are no right or wrong answers – it is only for your own self-assessment.

1.	I always retain the final decision-making authority within my department or team.	5	4	3	2	1
2.	I always try to include one or more employees in determining what to do and how to do it. However, I maintain the final decision-making authority.	5	4	3	2	1
3.	I and my employees always vote whenever a major decision has to be made.	5	4	3	2	1
4.	I do not consider suggestions made by my employees, as I do not have the time for them.	5	4	3	2	1
5.	I ask for employee ideas and input on upcoming plans and projects.	5	4	3	2	1

6.	For a major decision to pass in my department, it must have the approval of each individual or the majority.	5	4	3	2	1
7.	I tell my employees what has to be done and how to do it.	5	4	3	2	1
8.	When things go wrong and I need to create a strategy to keep a project or process running on schedule, I call a meeting to get my employees' advice.	5	4	3	2	1
9.	To get information out, I send it by email, memos, or voice mail; very rarely is a meeting called. My employees are then expected to act upon the information.	5	4	3	2	1
10.	When someone makes a mistake, I tell him or her not to ever do that again and make a note of it.	5	4	3	2	1
11.	I want to create an environment where the employees take ownership of the project. I allow them to participate in the decision-making process.	5	4	3	2	1
12.	I allow my employees to determine what needs to be done and how to do it.	5	4	3	2	1
13.	New hires are not allowed to make any decisions unless it is approved by me first.	5	4	3	2	1
14.	I ask employees for their vision of where they see their jobs going and then use their vision where appropriate.	5	4	3	2	1
15.	My workers know more about their jobs than me, so I allow them to carry out the decisions to do their job.	5	4	3	2	1
16.	When something goes wrong, I tell my employees that a procedure is not working correctly and I establish a new one.	5	4	3	2	1
17.	I allow my employees to set priorities with my guidance.	5	4	3	2	1
18.	I delegate tasks in order to implement a new procedure or process.	5	4	3	2	1
19.	I closely monitor my employees to ensure they are performing correctly.	5	4	3	2	1
20.	When there are differences in role expectations, I work with them to resolve the differences.	5	4	3	2	1
21.	Each individual is responsible for defining his or her job.	5	4	3	2	1
22.	I like the power that my leadership position holds over subordinates.	5	4	3	2	1
23.	I like to use my leadership power to help subordinates grow.	5	4	3	2	1
24.	I like to share my leadership power with my subordinates.	5	4	3	2	1
25.	Employees must be directed or threatened with punishment in order to get them to achieve the organizational objectives.	5	4	3	2	1
26.	Employees will exercise self-direction if they are committed to the objectives.	5	4	3	2	1
27.	Employees have the right to determine their own organizational objectives.	5	4	3	2	1
28.	Employees seek mainly security.	5	4	3	2	1
29.	Employees know how to use creativity and ingenuity to solve organizational problems.	5	4	3	2	1
30.	My employees can lead themselves just as well as I can.	5	4	3	2	1

Scoring Key

Item	*Score*	*Item*	*Score*	*Item*	*Score*
1	_____	2	_____	3	_____
4	_____	5	_____	6	_____
7	_____	8	_____	9	_____
10	_____	11	_____	12	_____
13	_____	14	_____	15	_____
16	_____	17	_____	18	_____
19	_____	20	_____	21	_____
22	_____	23	_____	24	_____
25	_____	26	_____	27	_____
28	_____	29	_____	30	_____
Total	_______	Total	_______	Total	_______
	Authoritarian Style (autocratic)		Participative Style (democratic)		Delegative Style (free reign)

Questionnaire on Relationship with Leader

Instructions: This questionnaire contains items that ask you to describe your relationship with your leader.

For each item, indicate the degree to which you think the item is true for you by circling one of the responses that appear below the item. Please make sure to give your true responses. Your responses will be kept confidential.

	Survey Questions	*1*	*2*	*3*	*4*	*5*
1.	Do you know where you stand with your leader and do you usually know how satisfied your leader is with what you do?	Rarely	Occasionally	Sometimes	Fairly often	Very often
2.	How well does your leader understand your job problems and needs?	Not a bit	A little	A fair amount	Quite a bit	A great deal
3.	How well does your leader recognize your potential?	Not at all	A little	Moderate	Mostly	Fully
4.	Regardless of how much formal authority your leader has built into his or her position, what are the chances that your leader would use his or her power to help you solve problems in your work?	None	Small	Moderate	High	Very high

5.	Again, regardless of the amount of formal authority your leader has, what are the chances that he or she would "bail you out" at his or her expense?	None	Small	Moderate	High	**Very high**
6.	I have enough confidence in my leader that I would defend and justify his or her decision if he or she were not present to do so.	Strongly disagree	Disagree	Neutral	Agree	**Strongly agree**
7.	How would you characterize your working relationship with your leader?	Extremely ineffective	Worse than average	Average	Better than average	**Extremely effective**

Team Questionnaire

Instructions: For each statement, put a tick in the column that best describes you. Please answer questions as you actually are (rather than how you think you should be).

	Statement	*Not at all*	*Rarely*	*Sometimes*	*Often*	*Very often*
1.	My team is knowledgeable about the stages of development teams can be expected to go through.					
2.	Team members are provided with a great deal of feedback regarding their performance.					
3.	Team members are encouraged to work for the common good of the organization.					
4.	There are many complaints, and morale is low on my team.					
5.	Team members do not understand the decisions that are made, or do not agree with them.					
6.	People are encouraged to be good team members, and build good relationships.					
7.	Team members are provided with development opportunities.					
8.	Meetings are inefficient and there is a lot of role overlap.					
9.	Team members are encouraged to commit to the team vision, and leaders help them understand how their role fits into the big picture.					
10.	Team members are often given a chance to work on interesting tasks and stretch their knowledge and capabilities.					

11.	The team understands what it needs to accomplish and has the resources needed to be successful.						
12.	Conflict and hostility between members is a pervasive issue that does not seem to get better.						
13.	People feel that good work is not rewarded and they are not sure what is expected of them.						
14.	Team members balance their individual needs for autonomy with the benefits of mutual interdependence.						
15.	Working relationships across units or functions is poor, and there is a lack of coordination.						

12

Performance Management

Learning Objectives

This chapter would help the readers:

- to recognize the concepts of performance management;
- to be familiar with the performance appraisal techniques;
- to acquaint with competency mapping in organizations; and
- to reflect upon the case study about competency mapping.

An Opening Story: Challenges of Performance Management

Performance management has been a major concern of companies, and they have ever revised methods to check the performance of employees and the organization. Of course, various methodologies have cropped up from time to time to improve performance evaluation techniques. However, companies even today keep on trying new innovative ways to maximize excellence in performance that would directly or indirectly boost business results. One of the major business groups in India has faced this challenge to look up to the existing and new approaches of performance management and taken the benefits of utilizing a variety of such ways to deal with low, average and high performers. The company revised the performance measurement techniques right from the employee appraisals, ratings by supervisors to feedback methods such as 360 degree and now adopted effective performance management strategy which involved every procedure and practice in the career cycle of employees right from the scientific selection, placement, induction, technical and soft skill training, knowledge updating, appraisal and evaluation, competence mapping, mentoring, team building, project management, individual development plan, career advancement, work-life balance, welfare measures, personnel policies, communication, adequacy of technology, business etiquette, and so on. This overall comprehensive and integrated approach towards performance management has given a huge headway and leverage to all departments and functions of the company in terms of quality, production, safety, maintenance, and environment. Many other corporates have followed similar integrated performance management methodology which helps both the employees and employer in the individual growth and business development.

12.1 INTRODUCTION

Change in individual performance contributes to change in organizational performance. Hence, an individual considered an asset for any company for meeting the desired results.

The most important concern of organizations is to find out whether the performance of the employees can be objectively measured and improved over a period of time. This would help in knowing the four basic aspects of performance management.

1. Setting performance goals or targets.
2. Measuring whether the performance of the employees is:
   - increasing over the time,
   - decreasing over the time, or,
   - remains same over the time.
3. Providing feedback for performance areas to be improved and enhancing the competencies or strengths of the employees.
4. Rewarding good performance or taking corrective action for low performers.

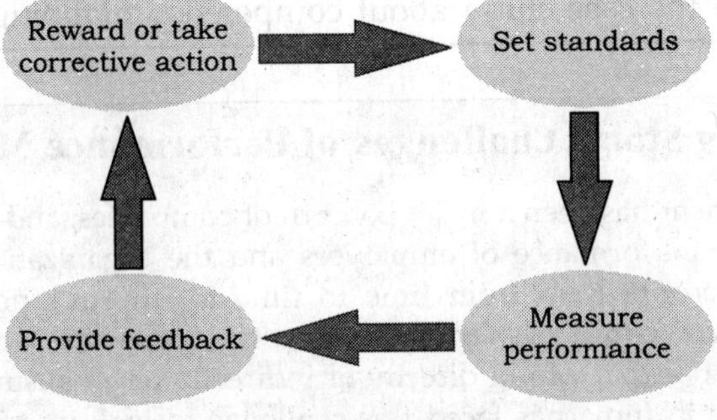

Performance management

Performance management is a collective approach (from top to bottom in an organization) associated with all actions back and forth right from the intake of the person up to the induction, training, development, rewarding, retaining, and other such actions.

Performance management system (PMS) is a tool to enhance productivity and learning, not merely an instrument for rewards. It is a system in which the line or people managers are in the driver's seat and HR department is a navigator. The competencies are in the limelight in PMS implementation. Inclusion of self-development goals and organizational developmental goals is the main objective. PMS feedback is a two-way and continuous process. It is a non-stop improvement of performance at all levels in an organization. The PMS should be based on participative planning, and the individual performer must play a more active role than his senior in seeking feedback explaining his realities, accomplishment, and constraints. If PMS fails, it is because of poor implementation of its process. The existing PMS process in organizations does not drive performance culture rather it simply helps evaluate people for compensation or promotion. We tend to find low or high performer, in fact everybody can become a high performer. There is need to move from appraisals and numbers to a culture of development, quality, and synergy. According to Anil Kaushik (2014), despite having PMS, the organizations in India are not able to develop performance culture because the focus is on performance evaluation with ingredients of command and control. The existing PMS is used as a tool for granting compensation, promotions, pay increases, and other benefits. Fifty-four per cent of employees feel that the PMS is not effective as the shop-floor managers are not competent in people skills, and this system suffers from bias, subjectivity, and fear. It is high time that the performance management system emphasis moves from competitive evaluation to coaching, development, and recognition in order to develop performance culture in organizations.

12.2 IMPORTANCE OF PERFORMANCE EVALUATION

We hire people on skills and qualifications and we review performance on behaviour and attitudes. This gap must be reduced. Either we have more skill-based performance reviews or increase the component of attitude and behavioural measurement during selection.

Three cardinal rules of performance management are: (1) tell me what is expected of me; provide an environment for me to perform; (2) evaluate me on that and provide feedback in feed-forward way and (3) Keep things simple and without biases.

> **Good to Know**
> Performance means both behavior and results. Behavior emanates from the performer and transforms performance into business outcomes/ results.

Performance evaluation and management is a course of action of creating a work environment in which people are empowered to perform the best of their abilities towards fulfilment of the organizational goals and business outcomes. It is a deliberate and systemic approach to delivering continued success to organizations by improving the performance of the people and groups by developing their capabilities.

Performance is all about what and how activities are done. Primary focus is on the competency levels of the performer. On the other hand, PMS is a whole work system that begins when a job is defined as needed (Raju 2004).

Performance management is a broad composition involving human performance in an organization. Performance appraisal, performance improvement, performance development are all related aspects.

Performance management has three stages: goal setting which is done in the beginning before any action plan is executed; encouragement, when the task is being accomplished; and reward when the task is completed.

12.3 TECHNIQUES OF PERFORMANCE EVALUATION

There are multiple criteria for evaluation; broadly divided in two parts. Part 1 looks at results, for example, for sales target versus achievement, margins, repeat business, and the like. The same is for delivery, for example, on-time, defects. These are all measurable. Part 2 is about the attributes of the person, for example, social skills like peer bonding, team player, learning and teaching, and so on. The first part is normally used for determining pay hike, performance band, and a combination of 1 and 2 is used for determining promotions and job profile changes.

A lot of companies fall into the trap of doling out promotions on the basis of Part 1 alone and there are many examples of a total loner being made a team leader. This person is likely to fail as his skills are in individual performance and he may be a misfit as a leader. A superstar sales representative is not necessarily a superstar sales manager material.

Performance appraisal defines and measures the performance of the employees and the organization as a whole.

> **Good to Know**
> The most difficult part of the performance appraisal process is to accurately and objectively measure the employee performance.

Measuring the performance covers the evaluation of the main tasks completed and the accomplishments of the employee in a given time period in comparison with the goals set at the beginning of the period (Fischer 2004).

Therefore, a balanced set of measures (commonly known as balanced scorecard) should be used for measuring the performance of the employee (Landy and Conte 2005).

Locher and Teel (1977) found that the three most common appraisal methods in general used are rating scales (56%), essay methods (25%), and result oriented or MBO methods (13%).

Certain techniques in performance appraisal have been thoroughly investigated to yield better results than others. A survey reveals the percentage of organizations using each method: 65% rating scales, 57% essay methods, 30% checklist, 18% critical incidents, 36% management by objectives, and 8% ranking.

12.3.1 Ranking Technique

Employee ranking methods give emphasis to how employees compare with one another. The three rankings among employees are done by way of simple ranking, paired comparison, alternative ranking, and forced distribution. The rater considers all individuals to be evaluated and lists them in order for performance dimensions.

12.3.2 Management by Objectives (MBO)

In MBO appraisal, subordinates work with their superiors to establish performance objectives for the next six months or one year. This involves self-appraisal for personal development for employees. This approach is considered an excellent method both by the appraiser as well as the appraisee. MBO is appreciated by employees as the targets are set jointly by the manager and subordinates.

12.3.3 Forced Choice

This method can eliminate the personal bias errors. It ensures that those doing the rating have an idea whether they are evaluating a person favourably or not. The appraiser is required to opt for choice or category for employee performance.

12.3.4 Trait Rating

The individuals are appraised on traits such as achievement orientation, initiative, cooperation, leadership, and so on. These characteristics will have a bearing on each other as performance criteria. The traits are measured on a scale.

12.3.5 Critical Incident

Notable contributions or behaviours are listed out with reference to the quality of job performance and handed over to the superior for evaluation and feedback during performance appraisal review/interview session. Certain significant incidents on the job performed by an employee during the year can have special impact on the appraisal.

12.3.6 Behaviourally Anchored Rating Scale (BARS)

Critical behaviours needed on the job are a major concern. The appraisers rate the critical employee behaviours. BARS technique is an evaluation related to specific behaviours for success or failure on the job. This method is considered useful in many organizations.

12.3.7 Checklist

A checklist contains an inventory of descriptors, job behaviour, and personal traits linked to job performance which are check-marked by an appraiser as reflected in the appraisee performance during the period of evaluation.

12.3.8 Behavioural Observation Scale (BOS)

BOS is a practice in which an appraiser rates the occurrence or the number of times a critical incident or job behaviour on a 5-point rating scale as seen in an employee's performance.

12.3.9 Performance Appraisal Interview

An essential part of performance appraisal structure is an appraisal interview which provides an opportunity for the discussions of an employee's performance results by providing feedback regarding promotion, incentive, corrective decisions, and training and development needs and the like. Supervisors or managers conducting an appraisal interview are trained regarding the importance and conduction of the interview.

> **Good to Know**
>
> The performance evaluation techniques are used in combination by organizations for fair assessment and development of each employee who is regarded as human capital.

The ways to improve performance can be:

- Praise/positive feedback from the supervisor.
- Experience
- Mastery in their field of practice due to the time factor
- Observation of a peer doing a good job increases motivation to do much better.

In India, the performance appraisal processes face a lot of obstacles, the most prominent being the lack of quantifiable indicators of the performance (Rao 1999). The problems in the implementation of the performance appraisal processes are anticipated and efforts are made to overcome them. In this regard, Donna and Sharlene (2013) emphasized the credibility of the evidence of evaluations in order to deal effectively with the appraisal issues in organizations.

12.4 COMPETENCY MAPPING

Competency is a relatively enduring characteristic of an individual which statistically predicts effective or superior (one standard deviation above the mean) performance in the job.

Around the world, an increased pressure is being exercised on the organization's capability to get more out of the available resources they have, and this often translates into stress on the individual employees. This is where competency mapping has risen up in the priority list for many organizations.

Competency can be defined as the process of identifying key attributes and skills for each position and process within the company. There are two basic levels of competencies: technical – which is related to the job competencies and behavioural – which is associated with behaviour and personality of an individual.

Competency mapping is of great importance in any organization. It plays a vital role in selecting, recruiting, and retaining the right people. It assesses the inherent strengths and weaknesses of the individual and helps him develop himself.

> **Good to Know**
>
> As a result of competency mapping, the HR processes like talent induction, management development, appraisals, and training yield much better results.

An Individual Development Plan (IDP) is basically a clear statement of an employee's career goals, a device for a supervisor to estimate resources needed for employee training and development, and for an organization to develop its workforce to meet future needs.

Human Resource Management in Practice with 300 Models, Techniques and Tools authored by Srinivas R. Kandula (2003) focusses on the competency development model of a multinational IT firm. This company maintained an edge over its competitors because of its competence advantage. They achieved it through a well crafted and implemented competency development model. They have a specific programme for the development of competencies called Skills Development Programme SKUD. This model has been implemented involving a large number of employees on a global level and the evaluation reports reveal that the programme is successful and contributed in keeping the company in a high competency zone.

Human Resource in an Indian Context authored by H. L. Kaila (2008) has some special concerns as to how a pharmaceutical company, developed Sanofi-Aventis competency framework and how the development need analysis (Individual Development Profile [IDP]) of the employees was made. The objective of this study was to find out the IDP, using competency mapping for the corporate sector of the organization.

12.5 A RESEARCH CASE ON COMPETENCY MAPPING

As a vital part of the performance management, this detailed research case framed its objective as to uncover the IDP using competency mapping at a power company in India (H.L. Kaila 2007).

A total of 128 employees were taken from 17 departments. These employees belonged to the following departments: Administration, Business Development, CSG, Environment, Sustainability, MIS & Budgeting, Taxation, Payroll & Trust, Accounts, Human Resources, Engineering, Treasury & Investors, Transmission Projects, Risk Management & Internal Audit, Regulation, InfoTech, and Corporate Social Responsibility. Employees belonged to three different grades. There were 20 employees from E Grade which is advanced officers, 26 employees from F Grade which were intermediate officers, and 82 employees from G Grade which are beginners.

Tools used for this case study were as follows:

- Competency frameworks was used which defines the competency requirements that cover all the key jobs in an organization. The head of the department (HoD) has to identify the frameworks required by the department on the basis of knowledge and the ability to: (refer appendix for Sample Framework).
- Assessment sheets: On the basis of the frameworks developed, three assessment sheets for each department were made depending on the employee was a beginner, intermediate or advanced. The HoD had to give ratings on the basis of his performance on that particular frame on a 5-point scale and his remarks are put in (refer appendix for Sample Assessment Sheet).
- IDP evaluation sheet: It captures the status of the IDP for every employee. Once the competency gaps are identified the HR suggests suitable training course for that particular employee. After every quarter the HoD has to fill the status of the IDP in terms of percentage (refer appendix for Sample IDP Evaluation Sheet).

First the competency frameworks were developed for three different grades of employees by fixing appointments with the HoDs of each department. Once the frameworks were ready the assessment sheets were made and were given to the HoD who evaluated his employees on a 5-point rating scale and gave his remarks as to where the individuals lack. There was total cooperation from all the HoDs. After collecting all the assessment sheets, IDP of the department was made where the actions were to be taken or the training programmes were suggested for each employee. At the end of every quarter, the IDP status was collected from each HoD.

This power company is India's largest integrated private power company. It has an installed generating capacity of over 2700MW and presence across the entire value chain in generation (thermal, hydro, solar, and wind), transmission, distribution, and trading. The company has emerged as a pioneer in the Indian power sector, with a track record for performance and has been a frontrunner in introducing state-of-the-art power technologies. The company has been associated with the growing legacy of Mumbai as a business city over nine decades and having served Mumbai's consumers for over nine decades has since spread its footprint across the country and abroad.

Table 12.1 Departmental IDP scores for Quarter 1 and Quarter 2

Sr. No.	*Department*	*No. of Employees*	*Quarter 1% IDP*	*Quarter 2% IDP*
1.	Business Development	08	0	70
2.	Corporate Administration	07	18	48
3.	Corporate Social Responsibility	02	63	68
4.	CSG	17	0	23
5.	Human Resources —Corporate	08	0	30
6.	Infotech	20	0	0
7.	Regulation	03	63	70
8.	Risk Management & Internal Audit	02	17	33
9.	Engineering Department	17	28	28
10.	Transmission Projects	12	29	52
11.	Treasury & Investors	10	12	35
12.	Sustainability	01	9.50	39
13.	Environment	03	50	68
14.	Finance-Corporate Taxation	05	0	43
15.	Finance-Corporate Accounts	05	0	16
16.	Finance-MIS	05	4	4
17.	Payroll and Trust Management	03	51	72

Table 12.1 shows the IDP of each department for Quarter 1 and Quarter 2. Here a total of 17 departments have been covered. The total number of employees was 128.

Referring to Business Development Department, it is seen that out of the eight employees whose competency gaps were done, in the first quarter none of the employees were able to attend the training programmes due to constraints of work. The HoD was not able to release his employees. Similar cases were found in departments like CSG where 17 employees were not able to attend, and from the HR department eight employees did not attend. In the finance departments like accounts and taxation, the HoD's were not able to release their employees because the internal audit was taking place during that quarter.

The administration department had seven employees out of which three employees were not able to attend the training, the rest of the employees in the department had their status of developmental actions in progress. Corporate social responsibility had only two employees whose IDP was 63%. The employees in this department were able to go for their training needs. Similar cases were found in regulation department which had three employees, internal audit and risk management departments had two employees and payroll and trust management were able to release most of their employees for training. Thus, it could be seen that in Quarter 1 not many departments were able to attend training due to the constraints of their workload.

Referring to the last column of Table 12.1 it shows the IDP for Quarter 2. It is clearly seen that in a lot of departments IDP scores have gone up. Departments such as business development whose IDP score for Quarter 1 was 0% increased to 70%. This shows that the HoDs were able to release their employees plus a marked difference in their performance was also seen. Similar cases could be seen in departments such as CSG where 17 employees were present, their average department score was 20%, even in the HR department the score went up to 30%. Finance section such as the tax department had 43% for Quarter 2 and accounts department had a score of 16%. Departments such as administration, CSR, regulation, sustainability also showed improvement. Their performance improved after the training session were attended by theses employees.

Other departments such as the Infotech who had 20 employees have 0% of IDP score in both the quarters as the HoD said that due to lack of manpower in the department the employees were loaded with work because of which he was not able to release them for the training. Engineering department had a score of 28% in Quarter 1 and Quarter 2 because the employees had attended training in the first quarter but were not able to attend it in the second quarter. Thus, their scores were carried to the second quarter as their learning which had taken place in the first quarter would remain in the second quarter as well. This was similar for Finance MIS, only one person has attended the training. The rest have not. So looking at the scores in general, marked differences could be seen in most of the departments from Quarter 1 to Quarter 2 showing a sign of improvement in the IDP profile of the employees.

Table 12.2 Overall IDP Score in Corporate

	Quarter 1	*Quarter 2*
Corporate	29%	48%

Table 12.2 shows the overall IDP score in corporate for both the quarters. It is the average of all the departments whose competency mapping has been done.

In Quarter 1, the overall IDP score is 29% whereas the overall IDP score for Quarter 2 is 48%. It is clearly seen that the IDP score for Quarter 2 is more than Quarter 1 showing an increase of development actions of the employees in the corporate office. One could see that a lot more number of people have started going for training and the improvement could be seen in their day-to-day performances by their HoDs.

Whereas in Quarter 1 it was seen that due to other factors such as board meetings, work-load, and so on the employees were not released for the trainings. Thus, it is could be seen that once discussion was held with the HoDs as to how important it is to send their employees for training so that they would be able to see marked changes in their performances, as it assesses the inherent strengths and weaknesses of the individual and helps him develop himself.

The IDP scores for Quarter 2 was 48% whereas for Quarter 1 it was 29%. Clearly showing a gradual and marked improvement in the development actions which were followed in these two quarters. Training was given to the employees so that their competency gaps could be closed by the end of the financial year and thus help them improve their performance in the organization, thus allowing the company to be in a high competency zone.

Competency mapping, when conducted in the organization, may leave no room for an individual to work in a field that would best make use of his or her competencies. If the company does not respond to competency mapping by reorganizing its employees, then it can be of little short-term benefit and may actually result in greater unhappiness on the part of individual employees. If the employer cannot provide a position for an employee that fits him or her better, competency mapping may be of little use. Thus, it is very important for the organization to place the employees in the right position depending upon their competencies.

12.6 USING EVALUATION RESULTS FOR BETTER MANAGEMENT

The intention and aim behind any performance evaluation conducted for employees is to understand whether an organization could manage it for better performance.

In such a study (H.L. Kaila 2007), it was hypothesized that there will be a significant difference in the performance of the employees in the first three months of joining the organization and last three months of completion of one year.

The sample consisted of 25 sales executives whose performance was rated by their supervisors. All these sales executives were between the age of 23 and 27 years.

All were graduates with some experience in the marketing field. All 25 sales executives had just completed one year in the organization and all were male sales executives.

A performance appraisal form (appended) standardized by the organization for the sales executives was used to evaluate performance of the employee on six parameters such as:

- Competence
- Customer/quality focus
- Initiative
- Commitment/self-discipline
- Communication
- Attitude and orientation

The supervisor rated the employee out of 10 marks on each parameter. There are six parameters. So, an overall rating will be taken out of 60 for 3 months and the same for 12 months.

Ratings given for parameters:

10 - Excellent, 8–9 - Good, 6–7 - Above average, 4–5 - Average,
2–3 - Below Average, 1- Poor, and N.O – Behavior Not Observed

The forms in which raw scores were filled in by the supervisors were collected for 25 employees. The supervisor fills in the scores for each of the 6 parameters – competence, customer/quality focus, initiative, commitment, communication, attitude and orientation. Then each employee's strengths and weaknesses are written down and further analysed. The scores for 3 months and 12 months were taken and compared using an appropriate statistical technique.

The overall scores were obtained by:

- totalling all the 6 scores (6 parameters) for 3 months
- totalling all the 6 scores for 12 months.

The mean, range, SD, and T value were then calculated for understanding whether the obtained mean values were significant or not.

The strengths and weaknesses of sales executives mentioned by the supervisor were considered to see which areas specifically showed improvement in performance and which areas required improvement.

Table 12.3 Overall Performance Score of 25 Employees Over a Period of 3 and 12 Months

No. of Employees	*Performance Measured over 3 Months*	*Performance Measured over 12 Months*
25		
Mean	31.92	37.44
SD	5.97	6.36
t (df = 24) =	3.56 $p < 0.002$ (two tailed)	

The entire research was conducted to understand the changes in the overall performance of employees as a function of time, which is 3 months immediately after joining the organization and 12 months (completion of one year in the organization).

The performance scores of the 25 employees for 3 months formed one set of data and the performance scores of 25 employees measured over a period of 12 months was the second set of data.

Table 12.3: The mean of data for performance measured over a period 12 months is 37.44 which is more than the data for performance measured over a period of 3 months, which is 31.92. The means of the data clearly show us that the performance after 12 months.

The mean values demonstrate that there is a difference in the performance of the sales executives over a period of 3 and 12 months of joining the organization.

But to accurately analyse the data and to know whether the difference is really significant, and that the difference in performance is significant, we need to use a statistical test.

Standard deviation (SD) for performance scores measured over 3 months is 5.97 which is less than the SD for performance scores of 12 months (1 year) which is 6.36. SD shows the variability of the performance scores within the group. As can be seen, the variability of the performance scores of 25 employees was higher for 12 months.

The range for performance scores for 3 months is 26 (46–20) and for performance scores measured over 12 months is 30 (55–25).

A repeated measure, *t*-test, was conducted on the data obtained because each of the two sets of performance scores (for 25 employees) was obtained from the same employee.

The t- value obtained: t (df =24) = 3.56, $p < 0.002$, two-tailed), validated the hypothesis, since the difference seen between the performance scores is significant at 0.002 level.

Various factors can contribute to the improvement of performance. However, it should be noted that during the period of one year, no training or hike in incentives or pay was given by the management to the employees.

The employees have shown improvement in performance on all the six parameters: competence, customer/quality focus, initiative, commitment/self-discipline, communication and attitude, and orientation.

According to the supervisors of these employees under study, the sales executives must improve on:

- Customer targeting
- Maintaining good relations with the stockists, doctors, and retailers
- Effective use of promotional inputs, literature available
- Feedback reporting to be improved
- Rapport with the major customers
- Effective use of selling skills
- Effectiveness in detailing
- Improving the product knowledge
- Ability to handle customer queries effectively
- Planned frequency
- Completeness and clarity in reports
- Promptness in communication
- Initiative for better business perspective and personal development.

Strengths of the sales executives over a period of one year were observed as:

- Being honest
- Punctual in giving reports and feedback

- Positive attitude towards the company products, peers, superiors
- Overall better disposition towards the job, profession
- Good listening skills
- Good problem solving skills
- Urge to learn and constantly improve knowledge and skills
- Positive decisions taken in the interest of the company's business.

Performance may have improved due to many factors that might have interfered during the one year of employment in the organization. These factors can be:

- Positive feedback from the supervisors.
- Observing other colleagues doing a good job, and gaining motivation to do better in one's own job.

Further investigations are needed by the management to see what motivates the employees, what they expect from their job, how performance can be improved, and how these employees can be retained. This study will help in gaining insights about the policies of the company and its effects on its employee performance management.

SUMMARY

- The most important concern is the performance. All interventions and strategies revolve around the challenging question – how can an employee's performance be improved? Indian companies have been linking performance to pay wherein the salary package offered as a variable component or bonus which is directly linked to employees' as well as company's performance.
- Practically speaking, performance management in an organization is an all time big challenge for HR as well as functional managers. It poses tremendous difficulties due to its mechanisms and processes involved.
- How to manage better performance and identify and improve under-performers are questions that need to be explored and discussed.
- This chapter has highlighted the concepts of performance management, provided critical evaluation of the performance appraisal techniques, and described the concept of competency mapping in organizations.
- There is a significant difference in the performance in the first three months of joining of the organization and last three months of completion of one year. Thus, performance of the employees improves over a period of time.

EXERCISE FOR CLASSROOM PRACTICE

For better understanding of the subject matter of this chapter, please read and check each of the following statements whether True (T) or False (F) or Uncertain (U).

1. Performance management is a systemic approach to delivering continued success to organizations by improving the performance of the people by developing their capabilities.
2. Performance appraisal defines and measures the performance of employees and the organization as a whole.
3. Employee ranking methods give emphasis to how employees compare with one another across departments.
4. In trait rating method, the individuals are appraised on traits such as achievement orientation, initiative, cooperation, leadership, and so on.
5. BOS is a practice in which an appraiser rates the occurrence or the number of times a critical job behaviour on a 5-point rating scale as seen in an employee performance.
6. Competency can be defined as the process of identifying key attributes and skills for each position within the company.
7. The intention behind any performance evaluation conducted for employees is to understand whether an organization could manage it for better performance.
8. Research suggests that the performance appraisal and competency gaps are negatively correlated.
9. Once the competency gaps are identified, the HR suggests training course for that particular employee.
10. It is very important for the organization to place employees in the right position depending upon their competencies.

Answers: All statements are **True** except statement numbers 3, 8, and 9 are **False.**

REVIEW QUESTIONS FOR DISCUSSIONS/EXAMINATIONS

1. Discuss the concepts of performance management.
2. Critically evaluate the performance appraisal techniques.
3. Describe the concept of competency mapping in organizations.
4. Review and understand the role of a manager in performance appraisal.
5. Discuss how to manage performance through setting objectives.
6. How to conduct a performance appraisal and the purpose of these meetings
7. Reflect upon how to improve/motivate under-performers and identify non-performers.
8. Evaluate the disciplinary process within the employment process.
9. Discuss the skills on how to provide feedback in a constructive manner.
10. Identify and share your skills at improving performance in the class.

FIELD RESEARCH REPORT

This is a research assignment section for students for their internal marking by the teacher during the semester. This assignment is for understanding practical applications of the subject.

An action research project: Identify a group of minimum 15 executives and 15 non-executives across an organization preferably where you are placed for an internship. Conduct interviews with them by using a set of closed/open-ended questionnaire to signify the issues and concerns pertaining to the performance management of your company. Also highlight successful performance management practices. Prepare a report of 15 pages reflecting an action plan for better performance management.

REFERENCES

Donna M. Mertens, and Sharlene Hesse-Biber (2013). Editors' Notes. Special Issue: Mixed Methods and Credibility of Evidence in Evaluation. *New Directions for Evaluation*, Vol. 2013, Issue 138, 1–4.

Fischer, S.G. (2004). *The Manager's Pocket Guide to Performance Management*. Mumbai: Jaico Publishing House, HRD Press, Inc.

Kaila H.L. (2007). *Organizational Behavior & HRM* (2nd edition). Delhi: AITBS Publishers.

Kaila, H.L. (2008) *Human Resource in an Indian Context Some Special Concerns*. Ambala: The Associated Publishers.

Kaushik Anil (2014). Editor's Note: From Past to Future. *Business Manager*, 16 (10), 03.

Landy, F.J. and J.M. Conte (2005). *Work in 21st Century: An Introduction to Industrial and Organizational Psychology*. New Delhi: Tata McGraw-Hill Company Ltd.

Locher, A.H. and K.S. Teel (1977). Performance Appraisal – A Survey of Current Practices, *Personnel Journal*, 56 (5), 245–257.

Raju, P.L. (2004). Performance Management: *Concepts, Metrics and Cases* (1st edition). Hyderabad: ICFAI University Press.

Rao, T.V. (1999). *Appraising and Developing Managerial Performance* (2nd edition). New Delhi: T.V. Rao Learning Systems Pvt. Ltd. Excel Books.

Srinivas R. Kandula (2003). *Human Resource Management in Practice with 300 Models: Techniques and Tools*. New Delhi: Prentice-Hall of India Private Limited.

APPENDIX

Form for Measuring Performance (Appraisal Form)

Name of the employee:__________________

Date of joining:__________________

Designation:__________________

Supervisor:____________________

Head/quarter:________________

Appraisal period: (date): From __________ to ___________ .

Appraisal no.___

Ratings:

Excellent: 10

Good: 8–9

Above average: 6–7

Average: 4–5

Below average: 2–3

Poor: 1

Not observed: 0

Ratings
(Out of 10 for each parameter)

(1) Competence:
(Product knowledge, Technical knowledge) ________

Remarks:

(2) Customer/Quality focus.
(Customer targeting, rapport) ________

Remarks:

(3) Speed/Action/Simplicity/Initiative: ________

Remarks:

(4) Commitment:
(Self-discipline) ________

Remarks:

(5) Communication: ________

Remarks:

(6) Attitude and orientation: ________

Remarks:

Overall rating for this appraisal: ____________________

Areas to improve on:	Strengths:
____________	________________
____________	________________
____________	________________
____________	________________

Sample sheet of Competency Framework

Level	*Community Development Initiatives*	*System Initiatives*
Advanced	Thorough knowledge of: • Business Administration Ability to: • Formulate sustainable CSR policy with respect to Triple Bottom Line/ GRI requirements • Liaison with decision-makers, community leaders for innovative initiatives & conflict resolution • Handle pressure groups & the local press for risk mitigation of negative publicity by generating reciprocal understanding, and creating positive brand image for the organization • Develop long-term relations with various stakeholders (community/ govt/community enablers)	Knowledge of: * TBEM/ Risk Management/SAP/ Sustainability Reporting. * Approval Procedures and Schedule of Authority. Ability to * Review monthly/weekly reports and shares it across SBUs. * Organize Review Meetings/ Brain Storming Sessions/Library at departmental levels to upgrade the skills of the team members. * Prepare Annual Goals and Targets/ARR targets/SDM for departmental activities. * Review and approve Annual Budgets and Utilization plan * Prepare and Document Risk Mitigation plans.
Intermediate	Knowledge of: • Social Science & basic appreciation of Management concepts • Risk Management Ability to: • Strategize various ways in which you can implement the CSR policies in the organization • Mobilize resources for the various initiatives • Encourage employees to contribute for volunteering initiatives • Analyse Risk Indicators • Encourage employees to contribute for volunteering iniatives	Knowledge of * Industry Best Practices Ability to * Prepare and Document TBEM manuals/ EPM processes * Approve Orders and Service Entry Sheets through SAP * Prepare Annual Goals and Targets * Review and approve Annual Budgets and Utilization Plan
Beginner	Knowledge of: • Social Science Ability to: • Undertake need assessment through PRAs	Knowledge of: Budget Utilization * Volunteering Schemes

	• Appreciate & analyse the needs of the local communities • Prepare reports based on detailed analysis & generate viable solutions for the problems identified	Ability to * Update and maintain all records pertaining to systems as well as daily routines (e.g. Reports) * Identify non-conformities and timely reporting

Sample Assessment Sheets

- Beginner Level

COMPETENCY EVALUATION SHEET					
LEVEL: Beginner					
Name:			Grade:		
Area:			Date:		
	No.	*Competency*	*Weightage*	*Scale (0 – 5)*	*Remarks*
Community Dev. Initiaves	1.	Knowledge of Social Science	70%		
	2.	Ability to undertake need assessment through PRAs			
	3.	Ability to analyse need of local communities			
	4.	Ability to prepare reports of the CD Initiatives			
	5.	Ability to identify risk indicators			
System Initiatives	1.	Ability to update and maintain records of CD Initiatives	30%		
	2.	Ability to identify non-conformities and timely reporting			
	3.	Ability to initiate and activate volunteering schemes			
	4.	Ability to record periodic Budget Utilization Report			
		Weighted Average Score			

- Intermediate Level

<table>
<tr><td colspan="6">COMPETENCY EVALUATION SHEET
LEVEL: Intermediate</td></tr>
<tr><td colspan="6"></td></tr>
<tr><td colspan="3">Name:
Area:</td><td colspan="3">Grade:
Date:</td></tr>
<tr><td colspan="6"></td></tr>
<tr><td></td><td>No.</td><td>Competency</td><td>Weightage</td><td>Scale (0 – 5)</td><td>Remarks</td></tr>
<tr><td rowspan="5">Community Dev Initiatives</td><td>1.</td><td>Knowledge of Social Science, Management Concepts, and Risk Management.</td><td rowspan="5">50%</td><td rowspan="5"></td><td rowspan="5"></td></tr>
<tr><td>2.</td><td>Ability to strategies implementation of CSR policies</td></tr>
<tr><td>3.</td><td>Ability to mobilize resources</td></tr>
<tr><td>4.</td><td>Ability to motivate and encourage employees for volunteering activities</td></tr>
<tr><td>5.</td><td>Ability to analyse risk indicators</td></tr>
<tr><td></td><td colspan="5"></td></tr>
<tr><td rowspan="5">System Initiative</td><td>6.</td><td>Knowledge of Industry Best Practices</td><td rowspan="5">50%</td><td rowspan="5"></td><td rowspan="5"></td></tr>
<tr><td>7.</td><td>Ability to develop and document EPM processes</td></tr>
<tr><td>8.</td><td>Approvals and bill verifications, payments through SAP</td></tr>
<tr><td>9.</td><td>Ability to develop goals and targets</td></tr>
<tr><td>10.</td><td>Ability to review and analyse budgets and utilization plan</td></tr>
<tr><td colspan="3">Weighted Average Score</td><td></td><td></td><td></td></tr>
</table>

- Advanced Level

COMPETENCY EVALUATION SHEET

LEVEL: Advanced

Name:			Grade:		
Area:			Date:		
	No.	*Competency*	*Weightage*	*Scale (0 - 5)*	*Remarks*
Community Dev Initiatives	1.	Knowledge of Business Administration	40%		
	2.	Ability to formulate CSR policy w.r.t. Triple Bottom Line Concept and GRI requirements			
	3.	Ability to liaison with decision makers, community leaders for innovative CD initiatives and conflict resolution			
	4.	Ability to handle pressure groups and local press for risk mitigation			
	5.	Ability to develop long-term relations with various stakeholders			
System Initiative	6.	Knowledge of TBEM/ Risk Management/ SAP/Sustainability reporting.	60%		
	7.	Ability to review Monthly/Weekly Reports and share across SBUs			
	8.	Organize review meetings, brain storming sessions			
	9.	Prepare Annual Goals and Targets			
Weighted Average Score					

Sample IDP Evaluation Sheet

Sr No	*Name*	*Level*	*Trainings to be undergone*	*Suitable Training Course/Action*	*Status of identified Training course/ Developmental Actions (To be filled by HOD)*	*% IDP completed (To be filled by HOD)*
1.	ABC	Intermediate	Management concepts	Generic training on project management concepts		
			Risk Management	Generic training on risk management		
			Analysing skills	Generic training on analytical skills		
2.	XYZ	Advanced	Handle pressure groups, local press for risk mitigation	On the job training through mentoring		
			Triple bottomline concept and GRI requirements	Training on GRI requirements and triple bottom-line concept		
			Train the trainer	Training on train the trainer		
3.	LMN	Beginner	Knowledge of Social Science	On the job training through mentoring and relevant material reading		
			Needs exposure in recruitment and selection	On the job training		

13

Employee Counselling

Learning Objectives

This chapter would help the readers:

- to understand the concept of employee counselling at workplace;
- to acquaint with few case studies of employee counselling;
- to be familiar with the problems of employee attrition and retention;
- to reflect upon cases about employee counselling.

An Opening Story: A Case on Employee Counselling

The accounts executive (A) resigned from the company due to the finance director. According to the employee A, the director was creating unnecessary obstacles in his work, was losing his temper on every small issue and did not possess interpersonal skills as well as managerial qualities.

On conducting a detailed analysis it was found that not only people in the accounts department had problems with the finance director, but also across the department, a lot of friction was present due to his behaviour. After seeing the entire scenario, the vice president of HR department suggested of sending the finance director on the training programme for effective leadership, coaching, and mentoring. When he returned from the training, his department people found change in his approach while dealing with others.

Hence, people need to recognize that the individual cognitive and/or behavioural problems, when identified at the right time and corrective actions taken, have solution for correcting the attitudes and behaviours of people in organizations.

13.1 INTRODUCTION

In total, the number of absences for stress, anxiety, and depression increased 30% from 5,643 absences in the 2010–11 financial years to 7,399 in 2011–12. The Employee Assistance Programme (EAP) cost the BBC £130,485 last year (Alice, Philipson 2013). Organizations support the EAP and its role in furthering employee and organizational health. The program exists to serve the needs of all employees (Employee Assistance Programme Committee 2014).

A new trend coming up in the corporate HR across the world is employee counselling at the workplace. In the world of ever increasing stress in the lives, especially the workplaces, employee counselling has emerged as the latest HR tool to attract and retain its employees and also to increase the quality of the work life (QWL).

Employing counselling refers to the services intended to assist individuals of any age and at any point throughout their lives. It helps to build confidence and to empower. Counselling system works to put up features of a healthy organization ensuring that the employee level of stress is low; organizational commitment and job satisfaction are high; sickness, absenteeism and turnover are managed well; industrial relations are good, that is, strikes are infrequent; safety and accident records are good; and the fear of litigation is absent.

Technically, psychological counselling is used by the counselling experts to analyse the work related performance and behaviour of the employees to help them cope with it, resolve the conflicts, and re-enforce the desired results.

Employee counselling can be defined as a process which is initiated by the counsellor or the manager to assist the employee to gain knowledge, understanding, and insights on the performance concerns.

Counselling of staff is becoming an essential function of the managers. The organization can either take the help of experienced employees or a professional counsellor to take up the counselling activities. Increasing complexities in the lives of the employees need to address various aspects like: performance problems, personal, social, family well-being and other such aspects.

13.2 CONCEPT OF EMPLOYEE COUNSELLING

> **Good to Know**
> Employee counselling is a technique for providing emotional and social support to the employees to face and navigate through the difficult times in life and at work.

At many points of time, people come across severe problems either in their work or personal life when it starts influencing and affecting their performance and increasing the stress levels of the individual. Counselling is emotionally guiding, consoling, sharing, and helping to resolve their problems whenever the need arises (Kaila 2002).

Counselling interaction is a helping process between an afflicted employee and an emotionally mature manager/an experienced colleague that involves the use of skills such as intelligent listening, analysing, and communicating feelings of employees back to them in a right perspective which would help them feel better and manage their anxieties under control which, in turn, improves performance.

Counselling of staff is becoming an essential function of the managers, at all levels who motivate and direct people working along with them. The managers need training into the concept and process of counselling to deal with serious issues of their employees that affect their performance on the job (Kaila 2007). Increasing complexities in the lives of the employees need to address various aspects like:

- Performance counselling: The need for employee counselling arises when the employee shows signs of declining or slow performance, being stressed in office-hours, bad decision-making, and the like. In such situations, counselling is one of the best ways to deal with them effectively. It should cover all the aspects related to the employee performance like the targets and deadlines, employee's responsibilities, problems faced, employee aspirations, interpersonal relationships at the workplace.
- Personal and family well-being: Families and friends are an important and inseparable part of the employee's life. Many a times, employees carry the baggage of personal problems to their workplaces, which affects their performance adversely. Therefore, the counsellor needs to strike a comfort level with the employees.

Good to Know

Counselling sessions involving families of employees can help resolve their problems and getting them back to work with all the fresh energy and zeal.

- Other problems: Other problems can range from work-life balance to health problems. Counselling helps to identify the problem and help him/her to deal with the situation in a better way. Sometimes issues such as transfers, promotions, interpersonal conflict, and such others need attention of the functional managers who are close enough to employees to understand their issues.

A research by Upton and Dave (1997) focussed on the counselling services provided by a major national organization. The main aim was identification of managerial mechanisms that might instituted to facilitate the development of workplace counsellors. It comprised three main studies which utilized both quantitative and qualitative methods. Over a period of eight months, corresponding quantitative data were collected after each new counselling session from 694 clients and 46 counsellors. In addition, qualitative data in the form of case notes were obtained from the counsellors, 43 of whom also completed Levenson's locus of control questionnaire which was analysed in order to investigate discrepancies between the two groups that might identify a means of focus for managing the service. As a result of the study, an instrument was developed which provides a tool to facilitate counsellor development within a professional supervisory relationship, inside or outside of the organizational context. The counsellors' own locus of control and their perceptions of their clients were found to play an important role. The study findings showed implications for counsellor development in organizations.

Another study by Peter Tong Hing Tham (1998) examined the need of employee counselling programmes in the Malaysian workplace and the key issues involved in the designing and promoting of such programmes. The research covered the essential elements of employee counselling programmes and the appropriate steps needed to successfully implement the programme. It also addresses the values and culture of the Malaysian workforce that may affect the success of implementation of the programmes. It was conducted on 102 employees from two companies in Malaysia to find out the attitudes towards counselling services and the types of problems commonly being experienced by the employees in the organization. The results indicated that the employees were positive toward the provision of counselling programmes in the company and that the main problems experienced were that of career, financial, and health. The dissertation also included the recorded responses of employees to an existing employee counselling programme in the National Bank of Malaysia.

The study provides the conceptual framework upon which counselling programmes in the Malaysian workplace are based, as well as the types of activities and skills that are involved. The focus is on such programmes that will help employees deal with personal or health problems that might affect their productivity. This shows that an employee counselling programme can succeed only in the context of an organizational commitment to its goals. The successful programmes tend to be that are carefully planned, efficiently implemented, and well received by the people it has been designed to serve (Kaila 2006).

13.3 EMPLOYEE ATTRITION AND RETENTION

Employee attrition and retention are the most important issues of employee counselling in organizations. Understanding the main causes of attrition and to recommend retention policies in order to reduce attrition is a major challenge.

If employees love their jobs, they never leave. But in the real world, employees do leave, either because they desire more money, dislike their working conditions or co-workers, or seek a change.

> **Good to Know**
> New employees quit organization within a year of joining the work as they feel misfit due to gap between their expectations and what the company provides.

Attrition is reduction by means of resignations, retirements, and death. The attrition rate has always been a sensitive issue for organizations. Attrition rates can be calculated using a simple formula:

Attrition = (No. of employees who left in the year/average employees in the year) × 100

Thus, if the company had 1000 employees in April 2004, 2000 in March 2005, and 300 quit in the year, then the d**ifference between turnover and attrition is to be addressed.** The difference being that attrition is a function of a declining workforce, whereas turnover is the function of a stable or expanding workforce (Morten Blekesaune 2012).

The significant question is: how does healthy attrition benefit an organization? Executive Vice President, California Software Company, lists a few advantages (Sudipta Dev 2007):

- Remove bottlenecks in the progress of the company
- Creates space for the entry of new talents, external as well as internal
- Assists in evolving high performance teams

Employee retention is a process in which the employees are encouraged to remain with the organization for the maximum period of time or until the completion of the project (*The Economic Times* 2012).

Dr Perriera, the former HR head at L&T would often say in his speech, 'Our aim is to see that the person who joins our company, retires from us, we take care our employees so much so that they don't leave us.'

Some retention strategies that need to be implemented to control employee attrition are as follows (Suzanne Dibble 2005):

- recognizing a well-done job
- personalized thank-you cards from supervisors
- congratulation cards sent to spouses/families
- messages from top management
- periodic days off for good performance such as
    - Wedding gifts
    - Anniversary gifts
    - Newborn baby gifts
    - Scholarships for employee's children
    - Get well cards/flowers
    - Birthday cards, celebrations, and gifts
    - Home insurance plans

13.4 A RESEARCH CASE ON EMPLOYEE ATTRITION

A comprehensive study (H.L. Kaila 2007) was conducted to understand the major causes of high rates of attrition and the various measures which can be taken by the organization to identify and control the unrest an employee is feeling at the initial stage so that the consequences of attrition an employee would be facing can be solved and early action can be taken.

The sample consisted of 100 employees between the age of 25 to 50 years in various organizations (including private and public sector, and MNCs) from Mumbai and its suburbs ranging from banks to IT, power generation companies to call centres. Data was collected from varied work backgrounds and different levels of management: Upper, middle, and lower working in various departments through in-depth personal interviews and e-mails in a few cases with the help of a structured questionnaire using open-ended questions as well as closed questions with a 5-point rating scale (see appendix).

The results of the study reveal the following:

(a) *Conducive Working Environment (CWE):* On the basis of the data obtained through the rank scale, rating scale, and interview, it was observed that the conducive working environment was not one of the major and crucial factors for an employee to leave the organization. In fact only 5.4% of the participants felt that the conducive working environment was a factor responsible for attrition.

The reason why only 5.4% of the participants felt that CWE was not a major source of attrition is as follows:

> **Good to Know**
> Companies are now becoming extra careful in giving their employees, good working environment.

The companies are setting up a good working environment by giving their employees:

- Comfortable seating arrangement
- Maintaining proper temperature, lighting, and ventilation
- Safety measures to ensure less injuries/accidents
- Having a good office décor
- Cleanliness of the surroundings
- Adequate break timings, and others.

For those who felt that this can be potential reasons for attrition did have the above facilities lacking in their organization. It can also be observed that for some individuals CWE is not restricted only to the physical surrounding but also other factors like

- Interaction with other employees around
- Cooperation from other members of the organization
- Personal differences with other colleagues.

Table 13.1 Percentage of Respondents for each Question on the 5-point Rank Scale

1.	Conducive working environment	5.4%
2.	No further learning on the job/Work not challenging enough/low work responsibility	10%
3.	Lack of growth opportunities	10.4%
4.	No skill enhancement initiatives from the company	5.6%
5.	Lack of job rotation	6.4%
6.	Inadequate compensation	5.6%
7.	Inadequate recognition at work	6.2%
8.	No transparency in terms of appraisal and organization structure	9.6%
9.	Dissatisfaction with superior/lack of cooperation from superior	9.8%
10.	Lack of teamwork/cooperation from colleagues	6%
11.	Company lacks direction/no clear long-term strategy	5.4%
12.	Health	4.4%
13.	Marriage/Family Care/ Maternity	4.2%
14.	Inconvenient daily commuting	5.2%
15.	Further studies	5.8%

(b) No further learning on the job/work not challenging enough/low work responsibility is the 2nd highest crucial reasons for an employee leaving an organization.

This is mainly because after doing the same monotonous work, the employee feels bored. Many a times the employee feels that his/her creative abilities are not utilized in the work, or the work does not give much scope to utilize the employee's creativity. Employers often fail to understand the importance of providing opportunities for development of their employees or their career growth. A conducive working atmosphere, good culture, training, and career growth with adequate salary are some provisions that control attrition. From the survey it was seen that employees wanted to do a variety of work, rather than the same routine work. Many of the participants conveyed that they left the previous organization and joined the new because of greater opportunity to explore their talent, to do challenging work, to demonstrate their capabilities which they couldn't in the previous company. Ten per cent of the participants considered this factor to be one of the top reasons for attrition.

Seeing that this factor is one of the potential reasons of an employee leaving the organization, the organization should therefore keep the following points in consideration to retain or preserve its valuable/quality workforce:

- Provide the employee with a variety of work: People do want to try new things, to feel skilful, and to experience the personal satisfaction of higher levels of achievement.

Good to Know

Work responsibility is to be so well designed that the employee feels recognized in the organization.

- Make the employee feel good with his/her contribution: Recognize outstanding achievements promptly and publicly, but also take time to commend on the many small contributions your staff makes every day to the organization's vision, mission, and growth.
- Understanding and evaluating the employee's abilities and capabilities so that a right job profile can be made.
- Money may always not be an issue. Organization should understand that employees today want more challenging jobs, exposure to newer technologies, and expansion of their domain capability.

(c) *Lack of growth opportunities:* This factor is one of the most crucial reasons for an employee leaving an organization. In fact, this was one of the highest rated reasons for attrition. From the quantitative data it can be seen that 10.4% of the participants rated this as a factor responsible for attrition.

To explain why this is the most frequently rated cause of attrition is as follows:

- Every employee works for better financial growth, better position and better learning/exposure at work. However, when an employee feels that one or all of these factors are becoming stable or the scope of these factors is reducing, the employee feels dissatisfied and at this points s/he feels the need of looking for other better opportunity.

In order to resolve such issues the organization must consider the following points:

- Job rotation: This would help people to utilize their skills and experience growth and satisfaction.
- Better benefits and compensation, (for example, medical insurance, corporate credit cards, and discount coupons). Fair compensation alone does not guarantee employee loyalty, but offering below-market salaries makes it much more likely that employees will look for greener pastures.
- Career planning: Implement a career ladder and make sure employees know what they must do to earn and go in for progression. A clear professional development plan gives employees an incentive to stick around.
- Analysing the person's abilities and making use of them for the organization's benefits.

Apart from this, growth opportunity differs from employee to employee: for instance.

- Among management-level employees, the key attrition drivers are such concerns as 'opportunities for management', 'ability of top management', 'use of skills and abilities' and 'work/family balance'.
- For professional-level employees, the key attrition drivers are concerns about 'coaching and counselling from one's supervisor', 'company having a clear sense of direction' and 'chance to do interesting and challenging work'.
- Among clerical employees, the key attrition drivers are such concerns as 'type of work,' 'use of skills and abilities' and 'opportunity to learn new skills'.

(d) *Inadequate Recognition of Work:* When an employee puts in 100% of his work s/he, in turn, expects that there is proper recognition/appreciation of his/her work. By this the employee feels motivated and wanted in the organization.

This factor was the moderate crucial factor for attrition, as 6.2% of the participants agree that this is a potential source of employees leaving the organization. Some employees stated that this was the sole reason for leaving the previous company.

The companies can therefore take appropriate action before this becomes a highly potential reason of attrition. Some of the ways to do this are:

- Structuring a proper performance appraisal.
- Designing reward policies which appreciate good performance.

Having daily/weekly meetings with the supervisor/HoDs so that performance can be clearly recorded. It seems that now more than ever employee recognition is limited at best in many organizations. Unfortunately, many managers don't understand the importance of recognizing a team member's hard work and a job well done. Many might even ask why they should recognize their employees when they are 'just doing their job'.

The fact is that recognizing employees for their hard work is one of the least expensive and easiest ways to improve the level of employee retention in your organization. The return on investment for a manager's time and limited expenses can be incredible.

Recognizing an employee's performance reinforces positive behaviour and encourages additional positive behaviour. If team members feel that they are appreciated, they will be much more likely to repeat their behaviours in the future and even put out more effort than before. When a business leader understands the power of recognizing his or her employees the culture of an organization reacts to this recognition and moves in a positive direction, helping to retain more employees.

(e) *No transparency in terms of appraisal and organization structure:* On the basis of the data obtained through the rank scale, rating scale, and interview, it can be observed that the above mentioned factor is the fourth highest reason for an employee leaving an organization.

When an employee joins the organization he has the full right to know about the history, growth plan, appraisal system, structure of the organization, policies, and so on.

Every employee comes to his organization with some aspiration. An organization is viewed as a place where employees meet their aspirations of growth and development, values of trust, teamwork and transparency. If a company respects them and their skills, realizes their potential and provides them with a healthy environment to learn and grow with flexible compensation, employees take that as a strong reason to stay on.

If the organization values its employees, recognizes, and appreciates their skills and work, it pays. 'It is important to keep an eye on fast track people who are intelligent and excellent performers'. Performance is a primary requirement; therefore, excellent performers should be valued. They should be identified, nurtured, and provided with growth opportunity.

Most of the participants stated that their previous company lacked proper performance appraisal. Also the organization sometimes did not stay with the commitments that were made at the time of hiring.

The companies should therefore consider the following points:

- Proper and extensive induction programme
- Clear and stable company policies
- Appropriate performance appraisal
- Adequate and required training
- Consider both a person's culture-fit and job-fit
- Understand the expectations at the entry level
- Do not make false promises about benefits.

(f) *Dissatisfaction with superior/lack of cooperation from supervisor:* An inefficient boss creates a poor work culture, which is one of the frequent reasons for quitting.

Good to Know

People don't leave jobs, they leave bosses.

When an employee joins in the organization it is the supervisor's responsibility to make the employees understand the procedure and help the employees resolve his/her problems. If there is lack of cooperation from the supervisor, the employee will feel helpless and will not be able to perform.

It is observed from the survey that the most common and the most potential source is employees being dissatisfied and quitting the organization.

The companies can therefore take the following actions:

- Giving training to supervisors/managers, in order to enhance their skills.
- Management must show an interest in helping people develop to their fullest potential.
- Companies should think of training as career development, and be sure it's relevant to an employee's job and offered early in a worker's career.

Keeping into account all of these factors of attrition and the cost involved in the whole process, some suggestions which can help reduce attrition rates as well as help in retaining the current employees are:

- Hire the right people in the first place
- Empower the employees: Give the employees the authority to get things done
- Make employees realize that they are the most valuable asset of the organization
- Have faith in them, trust them, and respect them
- Provide them information and knowledge
- Keep providing them feedback on their performance
- Recognize and appreciate their achievements
- Keep their morale high
- Create an environment where employees want to work and have fun.

13.5 PROBLEMS ENCOUNTERED IN EMPLOYEE COUNSELLING

Individual employee counselling is all about interaction between the counsellor and the counsellee's context and issues. It is important to develop understanding into the intricacies of problems being encountered by the individual employees.

The 15 cases described below were gathered from diverse workplaces (H.L. Kaila 2006, 2007a) which would provide deep insights into the nature and context of employee problems and issues that require attention in counselling process in organizations. These cases do not explain a procedure of reporting or how the counsellor approached the situation to help the employee but describe only the kinds of problems that employees face at workplaces. Names in cases have been changed for confidentiality reason.

Employee No: 1

Name:	Kuttyamma
Age:	48 years
Gender:	Female

Profession:	Teaching
Qualification:	Degree
Experience:	25 years
Designation:	Senior Teacher
Organization:	St. George High School

She is teaching in a government high school. Her major job is to teach students their concerned subjects. She is also a class teacher, so overall functioning of her class has to be taken care of. She has to specially concerned for her students' psychological well-being. Her family problems that interfere with studies have to be given resolution. She not only has to actively participate in preparations of board questions papers but also has responsibility to maintain the chemistry and physics laboratory. Students should also be taken for extracurricular activities. As part of the teachers association she prepares time table for their schools. She is also in charge of organizing annual school functions, science exhibitions for students, as well as teachers' functions. She has to go for teachers training programmes twice in a year. She is also called for government duties like preparing voters list, making voters ID, patrolling election and other such duties.

She has interpersonal problems in the school. One incident she explained was that during the time of promotion usually there are major incidents of interpersonal conflicts. Some of them persist even after the situation is resolved but others are purposefully solved for the betterment of students.

The second major problem is the lack of good facilities provided to students as well as to teachers. Lack of proper funds, areas to conduct activities, maintenance of school and surroundings and the like are their primary problems. She thinks that the government has to take special care of these children and school as they are the future of our nation. These are all the concerns that bother her and interfere with her performance on the job and well-being.

Employee No: 2

Name:	Jeena
Age:	36 years
Gender:	Female
Profession:	Nursing
Qualification:	Degree
Experience:	16 years
Designation:	Nurse
Organization:	St. John's Hospital

She is now working in a government hospital in Kerala. She is appointed as a nurse in the gynaecology department. Her main job is to assist gynaecologists. She assists them mainly during operations as well as when they go for their patient waiting rounds. During operations she also has to assist the anaesthetist. She has to organize and arrange the operation tables, tools used for operation, and medicines have to be ready at hand. She also has to give medicines as well as help them in dressing wounds after operations. She also shifts patients as well as takes care of patients till they are shifted to post-operation wards. She maintains their reports and records.

She faces lots of trouble as her family stays 5 hours far from her working place. So she stays in a hostel and visits them twice in a month. Because of this she has health problems and lack of enough leave. She had problems with surgeons especially when there is more than one surgeon expecting her to assist them. She says there are many problems because of lack of facilities from the government's part. There is shortage of fans, medicines, proper lighting, and electricity. She seems not having any interpersonal problems with other co-workers. Even then she finds difficulty in dealing with patients who are less understanding of these poor facilities.

Employee No: 3

Name:	Raju
Age:	54 years
Gender:	Male
Profession:	Banking
Qualification:	Degree
Experience:	33 years
Designation:	Assistant General Manager
Organization:	Federal Bank

He is chief in-charge of a branch of a bank in Bengaluru. His main work is to manage this branch and their human resource there. He accepts deposits and grants loans for customers. He has to take care of staff management and customer satisfaction. He has control over cash and ATM management of his branch. He has responsibility to reach the targets set by his organization. Annually he conducts performance appraisals for his co-workers. He has overall authority as well as responsibility for this branch.

His major problem is managing staff. Their needs have to be taken care of and it's not possible to fulfil all their needs which lead to interpersonal problems. The other problem is taking care of customers and maintaining the reputation of the bank as good, and best place to work as well as to trust. He also has responsibility to maintain employees' relations and banks public relations which he finds difficult. He also has problems with work-life balance.

Employee No: 4

Name:	Varsha
Age:	24 years
Gender:	Female
Profession:	Insurance

Qualification:	Degree
Experience:	3 years
Designation:	Front Executive
Organization:	IDBI Fortis Life Insurance

She started working after her marriage and has been working now for nearly three years. Her designation is of front door executive. She has to attend the calls and transfer them to the concerned person in the organization. She also maintains the attendance registers and coupon facilities there. She also fixes appointments of employees and takes care of the security system there. She takes care of all stationery, medical facilities, and other requirements in the organization.

Her major problem is balancing between work and life. She has a small child who needs consistent attention from parents and it becomes difficult during working days. During the time when the child falls sick she finds difficult to work as she keeps on worrying about her and if she is with the kid she worries about her responsibilities in the organization. She does not seem to have much family life, other than work-life balance, and interpersonal problems in the office. She is found to be enjoying her job and is looking forward for new dimensions of her job.

Employee No: 5

Name:	Jescanta
Age:	22 years
Gender:	Female
Profession:	Insurance
Qualification:	Degree
Experience:	1 year
Designation:	HR Executive
Organization:	IDBI Fortis Life Insurance

She has been working in IDBI Fortis Life Insurance for the past one year. Prior to it she was working in a call centre. She is working in recruitment and her main job is to line up people for the concerned positions. She has to follow and look through their selection procedure till that employee joins her organization. Sometimes she has to take or attend their interviews and rate them basing on it. She also has to maintain and track the records of the employees and collect as well as verify their documents.

Her main problem is with their organizations feedback system. She thinks she had a better feedback of her performance when she was working for the call centre. She also has interpersonal problems with her co-workers as well as with her supervisors. Major problem with co-workers is competition and lack of clear communication is with superiors. She is also doing her MBA along with her work schedule and hence faces problems with her studies due to lack of time to attend her classes.

Employee No: 6

Name:	Roy
Age:	32 years
Gender:	Male
Profession:	Engineering
Qualification:	Degree
Experience:	9 years
Designation:	Accountant in charge
Organization:	Kerala Electricity Board

His main function is to maintain the records of the accounts in the regional office. He has to collect the concerned amount from the different people who stay within the particular region. He also maintains their records. He has to find out whose electricity connections have to be disconnected as they haven't paid their bills. And once they make their payment he has to make a list of people whose connection has to be reconnected. He also approves the new connections to be made in that area. He also works as a committee member in their union.

The major problem in his organization is the upcoming controversies of shifting the management to a private company. This organization which has been owned by the government for many years faces new problems with the private company. Employees find it very disturbing and unjustifiable. This has created serious problems to their health as well as to their family life. There are also interpersonal problems, some due to the above-mentioned reasons and others due usual problems of seniority and promotion.

Employee No: 7

Name:	Jain R.
Age:	30 years
Gender:	Female
Profession:	Teaching
Qualification:	Degree
Experience:	9 years
Designation:	Senior Teacher
Organization:	St. Pius Girls School

She started working as a teacher when she was 21 years. She enjoys teaching children, and especially girls. She is the senior-most teacher in chemistry in her school and because of this, she has many other responsibilities. She is in-charge of chemistry lab and deciding the particular books to be used according to their syllabus. She is also responsible for the extracurricular competitions and science exhibitions. She also maintains attendance and record books of students. Once in a year she has to go for State Board examination paper checking as well as for election duties.

She does not have many interpersonal problems and she takes them as a part of everyday job. She has problems because of her health conditions. She also has many problems because of her new house location and travelling from there affects her health. She also thinks that there is lack of many good facilities in her school and many schools especially because these schools are government schools.

Employee No: 8

Name:	Joy M.
Age:	45 years
Gender:	Male
Profession:	Engineering
Qualification:	Degree
Experience:	23 years
Designation:	Manager in charge of running staff
Organization:	Cochin Shipyard

He manages the running staff in the shipyard. He has to take care whether employees are coming to work and are putting in their best performance. He gives training to employees when a new machine is to be introduced. He mostly works on employees who handle the vessels and similar machines. He has to maintain the chart list of the employees under him. He also does maintenance work of the vessels.

Main challenge for him is managing employees of different ages. Elderly employees are always complaining about their health issues and he thinks that managing without making them feel less wanted or without hurting their feelings for their health concerns. These workers in a shipyard need strong physical abilities to perform their duties. It becomes difficult to manage them and get their targets fulfilled. Even when training is given, it's difficult to manage their performance, especially when new machines are employed. During the time of replacement or change of requirement in policies or in salary and the like it takes a very long time to make decisions and more time to implement them.

Employee No: 9

Name:	Vikram
Age:	23 years
Gender:	Male
Profession:	Business
Qualification:	Engineering
Experience:	2 years
Organization:	Antique gold jewellery shop.

He handles his father's business and works with his brothers. He mainly works in the region of Vishakhapatnam and his brothers work in other regions of Andhra

Pradesh. He has to maintain the records, and appoint and maintain workers. He also has a shop where these items are sold in wholesale even though his major business is from selling it to retailers. He also has to travel to different places in Delhi, Mumbai, and Rajasthan to get designs for these ornaments.

His major problem is that he is from the engineering field and his work is completely different from it. Thus, he finds his studies are of no use. He is in a confused state and is unable to decide should he change his profession or not. Another major problem is that he is very young and people who work under him are of different ages and he finds it difficult to communicate with them. He finds it difficult to set targets and give an unbiased performance appraisal to them.

Employee No: 10

Name:	Rinu
Age:	23 years
Gender:	Female
Profession:	Engineering
Qualification:	Degree
Experience:	3 years
Designation:	Asst. Project Manager
Organization:	Sasken Communication

She started working as a hardware engineer from 2006. She was selected from the campus and had three months training period. She then joined Sasken – a communication company as assistant in project works. She was working on different projects but most of them dealt with decoding the computer codes. She also worked in a project where she was asked to check the mistakes of the already existing codes. Now she is working in a new project for which she has to go to a distant place one hour away. There she studies about their working techniques and she helps them in similar kind of works.

Her major problem is with the distance she has to travel now for work. By the time she comes back she is very tried and weak. She finds it difficult to manage her family life because of the same reason. She also had many problems during her marriage because of the ongoing project's targeted date, difficulty in getting permission for leave, and the like. She is also bothered by the travelling she does during weekends for visiting her parents as well as her in-laws. Even then she wants to continue working in Sasken.

Employee No: 11

Name:	Babu
Age:	32 years
Gender:	Male

Profession:	Mechanical Engineering
Qualification:	Degree
Experience:	10 years
Designation:	Asst. in charge of lab
Organization:	Sacred Heart College

He works in the college mechanical laboratory as an assistant. He helps the superior-in-charge, the students as well as teachers in using the machines. He also teaches them the consequences and dangerous parts of these instruments. He maintains records of students' attendance, their performance inside the lab, their ratings, number of experiments conducted by them, and so on. He also collects and records their lab fees paid as well as unpaid. He also has to take care of the penalty for spoiling the equipment.

His major problem is with travelling. He stays with his family five hours away from his workplace. Even though he didn't complain about his health, he finds problems with balancing his family work life. He is not able to give enough time for his child. So he has tried for transfer but hasn't got one. He loves his work but this problem is a stressor for him. He does not seem to have too many interpersonal problems.

Employee No: 12

Name:	Pearl
Age:	24 years
Gender:	Female
Profession:	HR
Qualification:	MBA-HR
Experience in work:	3 years
Designation:	Asst. Manager — Performance Appraisals and Employee Engagement.
Organization:	IDBI Fortis Life Insurance

She assists the manager in-charge of performance appraisals and looks after employee engagement programmes. She works on newsletters which are published every quarter in a year. She also works on other employee engagement programmes like town halls and library and such others. She works on performance appraisal programmes for agency employees and is working on a project to launch a special performance appraisal system for them.

She finds it difficult to stay in Mumbai as her home town is in Karnataka but she is satisfied with the type of work she has to do here. She also finds difficulty in conducting employee engagement programmes as people may prefer something less that others would like. Managing employees of different ages with different interests is challenging and difficult. She also experiences interpersonal problems in the office but takes it as part of corporate business.

Employee No: 13

Name:	Yamuna
Age:	22 years
Gender:	Female
Profession:	Counselling
Qualification:	Degree
Experience:	1 year
Designation:	Counsellor
Organization:	St. John School

She is working as a counsellor in the school. She has to figure out the problems of the students who comes to her voluntarily or through referral of teachers. She also does career counselling for them. She has to keep track of the concerned students' performance and their emotional well-being. She is also responsible for organizing the school functions. She has to also take care of the anti-ragging cell in the school and is also responsible for parent-teachers' organization and welfare committee.

Her major problem is adjusting with her family and work life. She got married this year and this sudden change has caused many problems for her. She finds it difficult to cook and do rest of the household chores and then go for her job. From the emotional perspective also she has to handle her students' emotions as well as her family's emotions. So it's difficult and it acts as a major stressor in her life. Even then she likes her job and wants to continue with it. Next major problem for her is confronting parents with the information about their children's problems. It is very difficult to make them understand and realize their mistakes the consequences.

Employee No: 14

Name:	Sijo
Age:	26 years
Gender:	Male
Profession:	Engineering
Qualification:	Degree
Experience:	5 years
Designation:	Team Manager
Organization:	IBM

He started working as a software engineer from 2003. He was selected from the campus and had six months training period. He then joined Infosys. After two years he shifted to IBM. He was working on different projects there. He got promoted a few months ago as team manager. Now he is working on a new project for which he has got a team management. He has to manage his co-workers' performance and their evaluations. He also leads the project and sets the target and its time limit.

His problem is that his time shift is between 11 am–9 pm because of which he comes home late and has difficulty in balancing family and work life. By the time he reaches home his wife who works from 7 am–6 pm is stressed out. He finds it difficult to manage his family life. He also had problems while adjusting to IBM while he was shifting. He is also bothered by the travelling he has to do during the weekends for visiting her parents. He does not seem to have any interpersonal problems.

Employee No: 15

Name:	Anu
Age:	22 years
Gender:	Female
Profession:	Medical
Qualification:	Degree
Experience:	1 year
Designation:	Nursing
Organization:	Amala Hospital

She is now working in Amala Hospital. She is appointed in paediatric department. Her main job is to assist the paediatricians. She assists them mainly during examinations. Rarely does she assist them in operations; she also has to assist the anaesthetist, if needed. She also has to do all that a surgical nurse does, i.e., arranging operation table, keeping track of operation timings, doctors' schedules, patients, convenience, and so on. She also has to give medicines to patients as well as help them in dressing and other basic functions.

She finds difficulty as her family stays away from her working place. So she stays in a hostel. Because of this she has emotional and health problems and problems due to lack of leave. She has problems with patients especially during the time for medicines as she has to deal with kids and it's difficult to make them have medicines. She says that many problems are because of lack of facilities in the hospital. She does not have any interpersonal problems with other co-workers.

13.6 CONCLUSION ON EMPLOYEE COUNSELLING

The description of problems of employees indicates that these workplace concerns are real and personal. The issues and concerns of employees, if not heard or redressed for a long time, become serious and start affecting their performance, health and so on. They try to cope-up with these issues and sometimes opt to move away and quit. In order to retain employees, it becomes absolutely important that the managers or supervisors understand their problems with sensitivity.

Companies in Mumbai such as Larsen & Toubro and Mahindra & Mahindra have well established professional counselling systems to support their employees.

Employees always prefer workplaces which are close to their houses. This reduces their travelling difficulties especially weakness and health problems due to this. In such cases they also get enough time for their families, enhancing better work-life balance. This indicates that distance or travelling aids are strong indicators of emotional well-being and job satisfaction. Therefore, organizations must give high importance to travelling difficulties faced by employees.

The other major problem is interpersonal relationships. Some employees readily agreed that they have difficulties in their organization with interpersonal relations, others didn't. Every organization has its own interpersonal problems, though it can never be resolved; HR can always try to reduce its impact on their employees. Finally, major problem identified is that employees find the difficult to adjust when there is lack of facilities; the major difficulty is found to be in government workers. This has to be taken care of specifically either by the government itself or by the concerned organizations.

Other problems include time-schedule problems which can be rectified to an extent by arranging flexible time limits; lack of proper timing in decision-making can be resolved by making a proper channel of communication; problems due to age difference in employees can be rectified by educating and arranging good communication channels; motivating employees and inculcating a team spirit in them can be done by engaging them in team work exercises; adjusting to and so on new environment can be solved by providing good welcome facilities and better induction programmes and so on.

This chapter clearly indicates that employees have different as well as similar problems. These problems can be resolved if handled with rational cognitive analysis. In such situations employee counselling comes into play. In order to identify such problems, people should be given opportunities to open up.

In the current economic transitional scenario where competition and targets are hitting organizations, they should give importance to employees' personal as well as work related well-being, and employee counselling can play a major role in attrition rate (Kaila 2006).

SUMMARY

- Employee counselling approach can play a remarkable role in empowering employees, reduction of attrition rate, and retaining them in an organization.
- Employee counselling is a system to facilitate and support the employees to face the difficult times in personal as well as professional life.
- This chapter has provided the concepts of employee counselling, the problems employees face at workplace, and gives a clear idea about employee attrition and retention. It has also covered a research case on employee attrition.
- It was found that many factors lead to attrition including the immediate bosses of the employees, job dissatisfaction, lack of growth opportunities, hike in salary in another company and other such factors.

EXERCISE FOR CLASSROOM PRACTICE

For better understanding of the subject matter of this chapter, please read and check each of the following statements whether True (T) or False (F) or Uncertain (U).

1. Counselling of staff is an essential function of the managers at all levels who motivate and direct people working with them.
2. The need for employee counselling arises when the employee shows signs of declining or slow performance, being stressed in office-hours resulting in bad decision-making.
3. Issues such as transfers, promotions, interpersonal conflicts need attention of the top management who are close enough to employees to understand their issues.
4. The significant question is: How does healthy attrition benefit an organization?
5. One of the retention strategies that needs to be implemented is recognizing a job well done.
6. Conducive working environment is one of the major factors for an employee to join and leave the organization.
7. Work not challenging enough is the second highest crucial reasons for an employee leaving an organization.
8. The work responsibility is to be so properly designed that the employee feels wanted in the organization.
9. Growth opportunities are one of the most crucial reasons for an employee to join or quit an organization.
10. An inefficient boss creates poor work culture, which is one of the frequent reasons for quitting.

Answers: All statements are **True** except that statement numbers 3, 6, and 9 are **False.**

REVIEW QUESTIONS FOR DISCUSSIONS/EXAMINATIONS

1. How would you define employee counselling at workplace?
2. Discuss a few case studies of employee counselling.
3. Discuss the fundamental concepts of attrition and retention.
4. What factors lead to employee attrition?
5. How employee counselling can reduce employee attrition?
6. Discuss how employee retention can lead to improving performance?
7. Address how employee stress can affect attrition?
8. Reflect upon the role of counselling in Indian organizations.
9. Explore the managerial perspective of employee counselling.
10. Discuss whether attrition is always bad for an organization.

FIELD RESEARCH REPORT

This is a research assignment section for students for their internal marking by the teacher during the semester. This assignment is for understanding practical applications of the subject.

An action research project: Identify a group of minimum 15 executives and 15 non-executives across an organization preferably where you are placed for an internship. Conduct interviews with them by using a set of closed/open-ended questionnaire to signify the issues and concerns pertaining to the employee counselling system in your company. Also include successful employee counselling practices and experiences. Prepare a report of about 15 pages reflecting an action plan for better management practice.

REFERENCES

Dev, Sudipta (2007). Is Attrition Always Bad for an Organization? financialexpress.com 29 October 2007.

Dibble, Suzanne (2005). *Keeping Your Valuable Employees: Retention Strategies for Your Organization's Most Important Resource.* London: Oxford University Press.

Kaila, H.L. (2002). 'Stress is a Way of Life for Mumbai Workers.' *Psychology International*, 13 (3), 1–4.

Kaila, H.L. (2006). *Counselling in Indian Organizations: Dialogue with Managers.* Ambala: Associated Publishing Company.

Kaila, H.L. (2007). *Organizational Behavior & HRM* (2nd edition). Delhi: AITBS Publishers.

Kaila, H.L. (2007a). Managerial Perspective of Employee Counselling in Indian Organizations: A Qualitative Analysis' for an edited book '*Positive Health Psychology*'. New Delhi: Global Publishing House.

Morten, Blekesaune (2012). *Job Insecurity and Sickness Absence: Correlations between Attrition and Absence in 36 Occupational Groups.* Norway: University of Agder, Kristiansand.

Philipson, Alice (2013). BBC spent £1, 30,000 on counselling for stressed staff last year. http://www.telegraph.co.uk/culture/tvandradio/bbc/9926372/BBC-spent-130000-on-counselling-for-stressed-staff-last-year.html Retrieved on June 12, 2013.

Tham, Peter Tong Hing (1998). *Employee Counselling Programs in the Malaysian Workplace.* Malaysia: St. Clement University.

The Economic Times (2012). Employee Retention, Mumbai: 31 January.

Upton Dave (1997). *Developing Employee Counselling.* Cranfield University Dissertation. USA.

APPENDIX

Interview Schedule for Employee Attrition

Name of the Employee:
Designation and Grade:
Age:
Location:
Date of Joining:
Date of Resignation:
Total work experience (in years):
Summary of career in your previous company:

Reasons for Separation (Please rank the top 5 reasons for leaving the company in order of priority and rate these on a 5-point scale):

		Rank	*Strongly Disagree → Strongly Agree*				
		1/2/3/4/5	*1*	*2*	*3*	*4*	*5*
1.	Conducive working environment						
2.	No further learning on the job/work not challenging enough/low work responsibility						
3.	Lack of growth opportunities						
4.	No skill enhancement initiatives from the Co.						
5.	Lack of job rotation						
6.	Inadequate compensation						
7.	Inadequate recognition at work						
8.	No transparency in terms of appraisal & organization structure						
9.	Dissatisfaction with superior/lack of cooperation from superior						
10.	Lack of teamwork/cooperation from colleagues						
11.	Company lacks direction/no clear long-term strategy						
	Personal reasons						
12.	Health		Any other reason (Please specify)				
13.	Marriage/Family Care/ Maternity						
14.	Inconvenient daily commuting						
15.	Further studies						

What in your opinion are the strong and the weak points of the departments in which you have worked?

Were there any company policies or procedures that made your task more difficult?

Any suggestions on the following aspects of your company:

- Training:
- Performance appraisal:
- Superior-subordinate relationship:
- Benefits:

Any significant reasons, circumstances, or any flashpoint that prompted you to look for a change:

Would you be willing to rejoin your previous company at a later date?

Would you recommend your company to your family/friends?

Information regarding the new assignment :

Name of the New Organization :

Competitor/Different Industry/ Related Industry :

Designation :

Percentage hike in salary offered (cost to company) :

Is your present job more satisfactory than your previous company?

What factors made you join this company?

Any further comments/suggestions or experience you would like to share about the company (previous or present).............

14

Statistical Techniques

Learning Objectives

This chapter would help the readers:

- to understand various measurement techniques;
- to be familiar with the scale construction techniques;
- to recognize the fundamentals of sampling; and
- to acquaint with techniques of data analysis.

An Opening Story: A Case of Organizational Statistics

Normally the organizational statistical data about absenteeism, accidents, alcoholism, performance, safety, production, occupational health and so on are available for a variety of uses in order to improve the relevant indices for improvement in these areas. However, the validity of such statistics is always doubted by the functional managers in the company as some data are reported and some remain unreported. Hence, the real scenario is not presented in these available data. Therefore, companies would always review the present situation along with these data.

There is always a tendency to improve the bad data such as accidents or alcoholism rate in the company. In one company, the alcohol rate, once upon a time, was as high as 7%. The company launched an alcoholic rehabilitation programme (ARP) to improve this rate so that the affected employees could be useful to their families as well as perform better on their job. Under this ARP, the company developed many initiatives: maintained contact with the family members of the alcoholic employee, invited a psychiatrist to treat these employees, trained counsellors within the company for regular counselling, created a group of alcoholic anonymous (AA) for regular meeting with all these affected employees. With all these ARP activities, the alcoholic employees recovered, and these recovered alcoholics proved very effective to sober other employees affected with alcohol abuse. This programme was very successful and finally the company improved its bad data to useful data. Similarly, other companies have launched their successful programmes to deal effectively with other bad data such as high rate of absenteeism or accidents or occupational health problems, low performance or production, and other such problems.

14.1 INTRODUCTION

According to Prof. Horace Secrist (1999), statistics basically means 'aggregate of facts numerically expressed or estimated according to reasonable standards of accuracy, collected in a systematic manner for a predetermined purpose'.

Statistical techniques have a special place in organizational psychology perspectives. The knowledge and insight into statistical methods is essential for a student of Organizational Psychology; it does not mean that he/she becomes a statistician instead he/she is better placed to interpret the behaviour at workplace. The application of statistical methods helps in measuring and understanding organizational behaviours.

> **Good to Know**
> The organizational behaviours get measured and understood as scientific facts with applications of statistical methods.

Statistical techniques include all those gadgets of analysis by means of which statistical data are systematically collected and used to describe a given phenomenon.

Abramovich and Ritoy (2013) introduced statistical theory as the underlying ideas and principles of major statistical concepts, including parameter estimation, confidence intervals, hypothesis testing, and asymptotic analysis.

The study of statistics techniques in Organizational Psychology begins with a review of univariate statistics before addressing multivariate statistical techniques, focussing on the understanding of the issues underlying the choice the of appropriate statistical technique, and the interpretation of findings (Monash University, 2014).

In order to choose the right statistical techniques for research, one should know the various techniques available. This chapter highlights a variety of techniques available in the statistical literature and used in psychological researches and interventions such as descriptive, correlational, and inferential.

14.2 MEASUREMENT AND SCALING TECHNIQUES

C.R. Kothari (2004) states that the most widely used measurement scales are nominal scale, ordinal scale, interval scale, and ratio scale.

Nominal Scale: It is simply a system of assigning number symbols to events in order to label them. This is the least powerful level of measurement. It indicates no order or distance relationship and has no arithmetic origin.

Ordinal Scale: This scale places events in order, but there is no attempt to make the intervals of the scale equal. Ordinal scales only permit the ranking of items from the highest to the lowest. Ordinal measures have no absolute values.

Interval Scale: Here the intervals are adjusted in terms of some rule that has been established as a basis for making the units equal. It can have an arbitrary zero.

They provide more powerful measurement than ordinal scales for they also incorporate the concept of equality of interval.

Ratio Scale: Ratio scales have an absolute or true zero of measurement. They represent the actual amount of variables. Researchers in physical sciences generally describe variables in the form of ratio scales, but in behavioral sciences they are generally described in interval scales.

14.3 IMPORTANT SCALING TECHNIQUES

Rating Scale: It involves quantitative description of a limited number of aspects of a thing or of traits of a person. Here we judge an object in absolute terms against some specified criteria, for example, like/dislike or average/above average/below average. Generally 3–7 point scales are used. These scales can be either graphic/itemized.

Advantages of rating scales are that they require less time, they are interesting to use, and have a wide range of applications. The disadvantages are: (a) Error of leniency – when respondents are easy raters/hard raters. (b) Error of central tendency – when respondent is reluctant to make extreme judgements. (c) Error of hallo effect – when respondent carries over a generalized impression of the subject from one rating to another.

Ranking scale: These are used when we make relative judgements against other similar objects. Comparison can be against two or more objects. There are two approaches for this: (a) method of paired comparisons (used for two objects) and (b) method of rank order.

14.4 SCALE CONSTRUCTION TECHNIQUES

Various scales used for measuring the attitudes of people are given below.

> **Good to Know**
>
> While measuring attitudes of people we generally follow the technique of an attitude scale. There are various approaches one can take to develop an appropriate scale suitable for a specific study.

Arbitrary scales: These are developed on an adhoc basis through researcher's own subjective selection of items. Researcher collects a few statements that he/she feels are unambiguous and appropriate and includes them in the measuring instrument. The advantages of such scales are that they are easy to develop, quick and less expensive, and highly specific. The disadvantage is that there is no objective evidence that such scales measure the concepts for which they have been developed.

Differential scales (or Thurstone-type Scale): This uses consensus scale approach. Here selection of items is made by a panel of judges who evaluate the items in terms of whether they are relevant to the topic and unambiguous in implication. Usually, this method is used to measure attitudes towards issues like war, religion, and the like. The main advantage of this method is that it is appropriate and reliable to measure a single attitude but the cost and effort required to make this scale is huge and the method is not completely objective.

Summated scales (or Likert-type scales): These scales are developed by utilizing the item analysis approach wherein a particular item is evaluated on the basis of how well it discriminates between those persons whose total score is high and those whose score is low. Thus, summated scales consist of a number of statements which express either a favourable or unfavourable attitude towards the given object to which the respondent is asked to react. Numerical score indicates its favourableness or unfavourableness, and the scores are totalled to measure the respondent's attitude. Therefore, the overall score represents the respondent's position on the continuum of favourable–unfavourableness towards an issue.

The advantage of this scale is that it is easy to construct and no panel of judges is required, it is more reliable, it provides more information and takes less time to construct. The disadvantage is that it does not measure how much more or less favourable are the respondents to a position. The position on the scale may not be equally spaced.

T.L. Holmes and Rajesh Srivastava (2002) in their study on 'Effects of Job Perceptions on Job Behaviors: Implications for Sales Performance' have used seven-point Likert-type scales for measurement of variables. Here the reliability has been assessed using Cronbach's coefficient Alpha. The analysis has been done by finding mean, SD, correlation, and regression.

14.4.1 Cumulative Scales (Guttman's Analysis)

This consists of a series of statements to which a respondent expresses his agreement or disagreement. The special feature of this type of scale is that the statements in it form a cumulative series, which means statements are related to one another in such a way that an individual who replies favourably to say item 3 will also reply favourably to item 1 and item 2. And if he replies favourably to item 4 he will reply favourably to 3, 2, and 1 also. If one knows the total score, one can estimate as to how a respondent has answered individual statements constituting cumulative scales. The advantage of this analysis is that it assures that single dimension of attitude is being measured. The researcher's subjective judegments do not affect the result. The disadvantage is that the development procedure is tedious and complex. This analysis is difficult compared to other methods.

14.4.2 Osgood's Semantic Differential Scale

This scale is an attempt to measure the psychological meanings of an object to an individual. It is based on the presumption that an object can have different dimensions of connotative meanings which can be located in a multidimensional property space. This scaling consists of a set of bipolar rating scales. It is an efficient and easy way to secure attitudes from a large sample. These attitudes may be measured in direction and intensity both. The total set of responses provides a comprehensive picture of the meaning of an object as well as a measure of the subject doing the rating (Osgood et al., 1957).

14.4.3 Data Analysis

Data analysis is the heart and backbone of organizational behaviour management (OBM) studies which refer to the computation of certain measures along with searching for patterns of relationship that exist among the groups. Survey analysis involves estimating the values of parameters of the population and testing of hypotheses for drawing inferences.

> **Good to Know**
> Broadly, data analysis is categorized as descriptive analysis and inferential analysis.

Descriptive Analysis: This is largely the study of distribution of one variable. If analysis is in respect of one variable it is unidimensional analysis, if two variables are there then bivariate analysis, and if more than two variables it is multivariate analysis.

Canonical Analysis: It can be used in case of both measurable and non-measurable variables for the purpose of simultaneously predicting a set of dependent variables from their joint covariance with a set of independent variables.

Inferential Analysis: This is concerned with the various tests of significance for testing hypotheses in order to determine with what validity data can be said to indicate some conclusions.

14.4.4 Data Presentation

R. Panneerselvam (2007) mentions that after the data is collected, it must be classified and presented in meaningful form to have better insight of a research problem.

Different tools of classification and presentation of research data are frequency distribution and charts.

Frequency Distribution: When data is of repetitive nature, then it is presented in the form of number of occurrences of each value of the data of a particular type. Frequency distribution can be classified as discrete frequency distribution, continuous frequency distribution, cumulative frequency distribution, and relative frequency distribution.

Charts: Data can be presented in graphical form or charts. They are classified as pie/bar/stacked bar charts, histograms, frequency polygons, and ogive curves.

14.4.5 Statistics in Research

As per C.R. Kothari (2004) statistics in research function as a tool in designing research, analysing its data, and drawing conclusions and directions. There are two major areas of statistics:

> **Good to Know**
> Describing data decides the roadmap and directions for further analysis.

Descriptive Statistics: It concerns the development of certain indices from the raw data.

Inferential Statistics: It is concerned with the process of generalization. It is usually concerned with two major types of problems. One is the estimation of population parameters and second is the testing of statistical hypotheses. It is also known as sampling statistics.

Some of the statistical measures that are used to summarize the research are given below.

(a) Measures of Central Tendency: This tells us the point about which items have a tendency to cluster. Such a measure is considered the most representative figure for the entire mass of data. It is also known as the statistical average. The most popular averages are mean, median, and mode.

Mean: It is also known as arithmetic average and is the most widely used measure of central tendency. R. Panneerselvam (2007) defines mean as 'the ratio between the sum of the observations and the number of observations'. Mean can be worked out in different ways.

Median: It is the value of middle item of series when arranged in ascending/descending order of magnitude. It divides the series into two halves; in one half all items are less than median, whereas in the other half all items have values higher than median. Median is a positional average and is used only in the context of qualitative phenomenon.

Mode: It is the most commonly or frequently occurring value in a series. The mode in a distribution is that item around which there is maximum concentration. It is useful in situations where we want to eliminate the effect of extreme variations, for example, the shoe most in demand in the market.

(b) Measures of Dispersion/Variation: Averages can represent a series, but cannot reveal the entire story of any phenomenon under study. It fails to give any idea about the scatter of the values of items of a variable in the series around the true value of average. Statistical devices called measures of dispersion are used to measure this scatter. Some of the measures of dispersion are given below.

Range: It is the difference between the values of the extreme items of series.

Mean deviation: It is the mean of the absolute deviations of the individual observations from either arithmetic mean or median of the given set of observations.

Standard deviation: R. Panneerselvam (2007) states that standard deviation is also called root mean square deviation and its notation is A*.

The standard deviation (along with several related measures like variance, coefficient of variation and so on are used mostly in research studies and is regarded as a very satisfactory measure of dispersion in a series.

Coefficient of variation: It is also a measure of variation, and is an improved measure over standard deviation. It is the ratio between the standard deviation and mean and is usually represented by percentage. This measure indicates the consistency of the observations within a sample and discriminates a given set of samples sharply in terms of consistency.

(c) Measures of Asymmetry (Skewness): The shape of a distribution explains the nature of the distribution of frequencies of observations, which is defined as the coefficient of skewness and its range is from - 1 to +1. If coefficient of skewness is 0, then the distribution is symmetrical. If it is positive, the distribution is positively skewed.

Skewness is, thus a measure of asymmetry and shows the manner in which the items are clustered around the average. In a symmetrical distribution, the items show a perfect balance on either side of the mode, but in skew distribution the balance is thrown to one side.

(d) Measures of Relationships or Associations: C.R. Kothari (2004) states that the above-mentioned statistical measures are used in context of univariate population, that is, population consisting of measurement of only one variable. But if we have data on two or more variables then it is called bivariate/multivariate population. In such cases for every measurement of a variable X, we have corresponding value of a second variable Y or another corresponding variable Z. In such populations we wish to know the relation of these variables with one another. For this we use correlation/regression techniques. In case of bivariate population we can use techniques like Charles Spearman's coefficient of correlation and Karl Pearson's coefficient of correlation.

Charles Spearman's Coefficient of Correlation/Rank Correlation: It is the technique of determining the degree of correlation between two variables in case of ordinal data where ranks are given to the different values of the variables. The main objective of this coefficient is to determine the extent to which the two sets of ranking are similar or dissimilar.

> **Good to Know**
>
> If data is available in the form of ranks of variables X and Y, Spearman's Rank Correlation technique is used.

Karl Pearson's Coefficient of Correlation (Simple Correlation): This method is widely used for measuring the degree of relationship between two variables. This coefficient assumes the following:

- That there is linear relationship between the two variables.
- That the two variables are casually related which means that one of the variables is independent and the other one is dependent.

Simple Regression Analysis: Regression is the determination of a statistical relationship between two or more variables. In simple regression, we have only two variables, one variable (defined as independent) is the cause of the behaviour of another one (defined as dependent variable).

Multiple Correlation and Regression: When there are two or more than two independent variables, the analysis concerning relationship is known as multiple correlation and the equation describing such a relationship is the multiple regression equation.

14.5 SAMPLING FUNDAMENTALS

Many researchers get confused as to how to do the sampling for their study and how much should be the sample size. This section would answer all sampling related issues as below.

Universe/Population: Universe refers to the total of the items or units in any field of inquiry and population refers to the total of items about which information is desired.

Sampling Frame: Sampling frame consists of a list of items from which the sample is to be drawn.

Sampling Design: It refers to the technique or the procedure the researcher would adopt in selecting some sampling units from which inferences about the population are drawn. Sampling design is determined before any data are collected.

Statistics and Parameters: A statistic is a characteristic of a sample, whereas a parameter is a characteristic of a population. Thus mean, median, or mode derived from samples is called statistic(s) and measures which describe the characteristic of a population are called the parameters. Population mean (μ) implies parameter and sample mean (is a statistic). To obtain the estimate of a parameter from a statistic constitutes the prime objective of sampling analysis.

Precision: It is the range with which the population average will lie in accordance with the reliability specified in the confidence level as a percentage of the estimate.

Sampling Distribution: If we take a certain number of samples and for each sample compute various statistical measures such as mean, standard deviation and the like, then each sample gives its own value for the statistic under consideration. All such values of a particular statistic together with their relative frequencies will constitute the sampling distribution of the particular statistic. We may have sampling distribution of mean or standard deviation or any other statistical measure.

14.6 TESTING OF HYPOTHESES

Hypotheses are generally based on the research objectives and may be defined as a set of propositions or statements set forth as an explanation for the occurrence of some specified group of phenomena to guide research investigation or query. Thus, hypothesis testing enables us to make probability statements about population parameter(s). The hypothesis may not be proved absolutely, but in practice it is accepted if it has withstood a critical testing.

Null Hypothesis and Alternate Hypothesis: It is an assumption about a population. If our study results do not support this null hypothesis, we should conclude that something else is true. What we conclude rejecting the null hypothesis is known as alternative hypothesis. The null hypothesis and alternate hypothesis are chosen before the sample is drawn. Alternate hypothesis is usually the one which one wishes to prove, and the null hypothesis is the one which one wishes to disprove.

Level of Significance: It is the maximum value of the probability of rejecting H_0 (even when it is true), due to sampling error, and it is usually determined in advance before testing the hypothesis.

> **Good to Know**
> Sample surveys are the study of a small portion of the population; hence the inaccuracy or mismatch in the information/data collected between sample and population characteristics is called sampling error.

Type I and Type II Errors: While testing of hypothesis, there are two types of errors we can make.

Type I Error: It is rejection of hypothesis which should have been accepted.

Type II Error: It is accepting the hypothesis which should have been rejected.

There is a trade-off between the two types of errors which means that the probability of making one type of error can only be reduced if we are willing to increase the probability of making the other type of error. Hence, in the testing of hypothesis, one must make all possible efforts to strike an adequate balance between type I and type II errors. Both types of errors can be handled by increasing the sample size.

Two-tailed and One-tailed tests: A two-tailed test rejects the null hypothesis, if for example, the sample mean is significantly higher or lower than the hypothesized value of the mean of the population. Such a test is appropriate when the null hypothesis is some specified value and the alternative hypothesis is a value not equal to the specified value of the null hypothesis.

Sharon K. Parker (2007) in their study on 'How Employee's Role Orientation Affects their Job Performance', have used one-tailed test of significance (since the hypothesis was directional) to evaluate the effect of role orientation on performance.

14.7 TESTS OF HYPOTHESES

Statisticians have developed several tests of hypothesis (also known as tests of significance) for the purpose of testing of hypothesis. These can be classified as parametric tests or standard tests of hypotheses and non-parametric tests or distribution-free tests of hypotheses.

> **Good to Know**
> Hypothesis testing helps to decide on the basis of a sample data, whether a hypothesis about the population is likely to be true or false.

Parametric tests usually assume certain properties of the parent population from which we draw samples but non-parametric tests do not depend on any assumption about the parameters of the parent population. Also non-parametric tests assume only nominal or ordinal data, whereas parametric tests require measurement equivalent to at least an interval scale. Therefore non-parametric tests need more observations than parametric tests to achieve the same results.

14.8 PARAMETRIC TESTS OF HYPOTHESIS

Hypothesis Testing of Means: Mean of the population can be tested presuming different situations such as the population may be normal or other than normal, it may be finite or infinite, sample size may be large or small, variance of the population may be known or unknown. The alternative hypothesis may be two-sided or one-sided.

Analysis of Variance and Covariance (ANOVA and ANCOVA): ANOVA technique is used when we want to compare more than two populations. The basic principle of ANOVA is to test for differences among the means of the populations by examining the amount of variation within each of these samples, relative to the amount of variation between the samples.

One-way (or Single Factor) ANOVA: Here we consider only one factor and observe the reason for the said factor to be important.

This ratio is used to judge whether the difference among several sample means is significant or is just a matter of sampling fluctuations. If the calculated value of 'F' is less than the table value of 'F' then difference is insignificant. If it is equal to or greater than table value then it is significant.

Analysis of Co-variance (ANCOVA): While studying one independent variable 'X', we wish to control the influence of some uncontrolled variable (sometimes called the covariate or the concomitant variable), Z which is known to be correlated with the dependent variable, Y, then we use the technique of analysis of co-variance for a valid evaluation of the outcome of the experiment. While applying ANCOVA technique, the influence of uncontrolled variable is usually removed by simple linear regression method and the residual sums of squares are used to provide variance estimates which in turn are used to make tests of significance.

J.R. Hackman and E.E. Lawler III (1971), in their study on 'Employee Reactions to Job Characteristics', have used analysis of variance to compare the mean scores of employees on the dependent variables. For this means and 'F' ratios were calculated.

In another study on 'Effects of Changes in Job Characteristics on Work Attitudes and Behaviors: A Naturally Occurring Quasi Experiment', J.R. Hackman et al. (1978), have used ANOVA technique and 'F' ratios to find out correlations between the variables.

Williams Steve and Luthans Fred (1992), in their study on 'The Impact of Choice of Rewards and Feedback on Task Performance', have used ANOVA, multiple regression and repeated measures.

14.9 MANOVA TECHNIQUES

14.9.1 Multivariate Analysis Techniques

Lately multivariate techniques have emerged as a powerful tool to analyse data represented in terms of many variables. Univariate analysis does not consider the correlation or inter-dependence among the variables which is covered in multivariate analysis. Multivariate techniques are largely empirical and deal with the reality, they possess the ability to analyse complex data. Hence, in most of the applied and behavioural researches, we generally resort to multivariate analysis techniques for realistic results. Also these techniques help in various types of decision-making.

14.9.2 Correlation Analysis

Correlation is the degree of association between two variables and it is represented in terms of a coefficient known as correlation coefficient. In a bivariate data when both the variables are quantitative, the method used to discover statistical relationship between the two variables is correlation analysis. Correlation co-efficient is the ratio which expresses the degree to which changes in one variable are accompanied by the changes in the other variable. Its range is between –1 and +1.

14.9.3 Regression Analysis

L.N. Aggarwal and Parag Diwan (1998) defined regression as a mathematical measure of average relationship between two or more variables. It is defined as the estimation or prediction of unknown values of one variable from known values of other variable. The variable to be estimated is called dependent variable, while the variable that acts as a basis of estimation is known as independent variable.

If there are multiple independent variables then the corresponding equation is called multiple linear regression equation.

Correlation is merely a tool of ascertaining the degree of relationship between two variables and therefore we cannot say that one variable is cause and the other effect. However, in regression analysis one variable is taken as dependent while the other independent, thus making it possible to study the cause and effect relationship.

Greg R. Oldham and J. R. Hackman (1981) in their study on 'Relationships between Organizational Structure and Employee Reactions: Comparing Alternative Frameworks', have used multiple regression analysis to test directly whether the structure–reaction relationship is better mediated by job characteristics or by personal attributes. The correlational and multiple regression analysis described in this study treated each employee reaction measure independently, as if it were not correlated with the other. This analytic strategy made it possible to compare relationships that involved variables that differed conceptually, for example, internal motivation versus pay satisfaction.

In another study by Sharon K. Parker (2007), regression analysis was carried out to test the hypothesis that flexible role orientation positively predicts higher job performance after controlling for the effects of job satisfaction, generalized self-efficacy, and locus of control. At the initial stage since age, gender, and tenure, all had significant correlations with at least one of the key variables; their effects were controlled for in the regression analysis. In the second stage age, gender, job performance, plus job satisfaction and individual difference variables were controlled and flexible role orientation was entered. It was observed that flexible role orientation contributed a significant amount of variance in job performance and its beta weight in the final equation was significant.

Advanced Multivariate Analysis: This analysis aims at studying the effect of two or more variables on certain evaluation criterion. The evaluation criterion may be good or bad, like or dislike, successful or unsuccessful and so on, for example, while grouping employees after a training programme in terms of their enhanced skills, and the criticism will be above expected level or below expected level. Some examples of advanced multivariate analysis are: discriminant function analysis, path analysis, and so on.

14.10 USE OF STATISTICAL METHODS IN ORGANIZATIONAL PSYCHOLOGY

The application of statistical techniques in the field of organizational psychology is manifold. The applications of statistics have been made with regards to:

- Personnel selection: for using psychological tests and correlating test performance later with job performance of employees
- Performance appraisal: for comparing and forecasting group performances
- Measuring the effects of training and development across the organization
- Competency mapping across departments and verticals
- To measure the influence of organizational development (OD) interventions
- To ascertain the pre- and post-measures of employee counselling
- To use and analyse the effects of assessment centre in the company
- To conduct analysis of organizational surveys such as job satisfaction survey, safety awareness survey, leadership survey, and such others.

Finally, we could say that though we had a glance through many statistical methods, this is not the end of all; there are yet many other methods such as cluster analysis, path analysis, factor analysis, discriminant function analysis, and so on.

A researcher should understand the data and imagine how he/she intends to analyse it, there are many ways one could analyse and understand the same set of data in different perspectives. There are several ways one can deal or play with the data, not really restricting it to a set of research objectives or hypotheses.

There are many computer packages available such as statistical package for social sciences (SPSS) which makes data analysis much easier for the researchers.

For researchers and scholars, the Indian Council of Social Science Research (ICSSR), offers scholarship for their data analysis at the doctoral level.

Hence, the use of statistical methods is tremendous in Organizational Psychology for measuring and understanding organizational behaviours and achieving excellence.

SUMMARY

- What gets measured is understood well. Statistical techniques help in the process of measuring and predicting behaviours in the organization.

- Organizational Psychology students, professionals and managers often look for the knowledge and use of statistical techniques for proper collection of data and analysis for drawing best inferences for making rational application of the research findings in order to improve work situations.
- This chapter gives an overview of the various statistical techniques that can be used for collecting, classifying, analyzing, and interpreting the data for making wise decisions.

EXERCISE FOR CLASSROOM PRACTICE

For better understanding of the subject matter of this chapter, please read and check each of the following statements whether True (T) or False (F) or Uncertain (U).

1. The knowledge and insight into statistical methods is irrelevant for a student of Organizational Psychology.
2. Statistical methods include all those gadgets of analysis by means of which statistical data are systematically collected and used to describe a given phenomenon.
3. Nominal scale is a system of assigning number symbols to events in order to label them.
4. Ranking scales are used when we make relative judgements against other similar objects.
5. In Thurstone-type scale, selection of items is made by a panel of judges who evaluate the items in terms of lack of relevance to the topic.
6. Likert-type scale is developed by utilizing the item analysis approach.
7. Semantic differential scale is an attempt to measure the physical properties of an object.
8. Canonical analysis can be used in case of both measurable and non-measurable variables.
9. Frequency distribution means when data is of repeating nature, then it is presented in the form of number of occurrences of each value of the data of a particular type.
10. Sampling design refers to the procedure, the researcher adopts in selecting some sampling units from which inferences about the population is drawn.

Answers: All statements are **True** except that statement numbers 1, 5, and 7 are **False.**

REVIEW QUESTIONS FOR DISCUSSIONS/EXAMINATIONS

1. Discuss various measurement and scaling techniques.
2. Evaluate a few of the scale construction techniques.
3. Describe the fundamentals of sampling.

4. Critically evaluate the measures of dispersion/variation.
5. Explain different techniques of data analysis.
6. Describe various measures of relationships.
7. Examine the concepts of testing of hypotheses.
8. Describe the analysis of variance and multivariate analysis techniques.
9. Discuss the correlational and regression analysis with examples.
10. Reflect upon the use of statistical methods in Organizational Psychology.

FIELD RESEARCH REPORT

This is a research assignment section for students for their internal marking by the teacher during the semester. This assignment is for understanding practical applications of the subject.

An action research project: Identify a group of minimum 15 executives and 15 non-executives across an organization, preferably where you are placed for an internship. Conduct interviews with them by using a set of closed/open-ended questionnaire to signify the issues and problems pertaining to application of proper statistical methods in organizational practices of your company. Also highlight on the validity of organizational statistical reports. Prepare a report of about 15 pages reflecting an action plan for better statistical practice.

REFERENCES

Abramovich, **Felix, Ritoy Ya'acov (2013).** *Statistical Theory: A Concise Introduction.* London: Chapman & Hall.

Aggarwal and Diwan Parag (1998). *Quantitative Analysis for Management Applications* (1st edition). New Delhi: Global Business Press, Abhinav Publishing Industries Pvt. Ltd.

Hackman, J.R. and E.E. Lawler III (1971). 'Employee Reactions to Job Characteristics.' *Journal of Applied Psychology*, 55 (3), 259–286.

Hackman, J.R. et al. (1978). Effects of Changes in Job Characteristics on work Attitudes and Behaviours; A Naturally Occurring Quasi Experiment, Organizational Effectiveness Research Program, Psychological Sciences Division, Office of Naval Research, Human Systems Department, Arlington, VA.

Holmes, T.L. and Srivastava Rajesh (2002). 'Effects of Job Perceptions on Job Behaviors: Implications for Sales Performance.' *Industrial Marketing Management*, 31, 421-428.

Horace, Secrist (1999). *An Introduction to Statistical Methods: A Textbook for College Students.* New York: The Macmillan Company.

Kothari, C.R. (2004). *Research Methodology, Methods and Techniques* (2nd edition). New Delhi: New Age International (P) Ltd Publishers.

Monash University (2014). Statistics and research design for professional psychology. Retrieved on May 8, 2014. http://www.monash.edu.au/pubs/2014handbooks/units/PSY4210.html

Oldham, Greg R. and J. R. Hackman (1981). Relationships between Organizational Structure and Employee Reactions: Comparing Alternative Frameworks, *Administrative Science Quarterly*, Vol. 26, p. 66.

Osgood, Charles E. G. Suci and P. Tannenbaum (1957). *The Measurement of Meaning*, Urbana, IL: University of Illinois Press.

Panneerselvam, R. (2007). *Research Methodology* (1st edition). New Delhi: Prentice-Hall of India Pvt. Ltd.

Parker, Sharon K. (2007). 'That is My Job: How Employee's Role Orientation Affects their Job Performance,' *Human Relations*, 60 (3), 403–434.

Williams, Steve and Luthans Fred (1992). 'The Impact of Choice of Rewards and Feedback on Task Performance,' *Journal of Organizational Behavior*, 13 (7), 653–666.

Index